the Craft of Revision

Fifth Anniversary Edition

Donald M. Murray

Professor Emeritus

The University of New Hampshire

Australia • Brazil • Japan • Korea • Mexico • Singapore • Spain • United Kingdom • United States

The Craft of Revision, Fifth Anniversary Edition, Donald M. Murray

Senior Publisher: Lyn Uhl

Publisher: Monica Eckman

Acquisitions Editor: Margaret Leslie

Assistant Editor: Amy Haines

Editorial Assistant: Danielle Warchol

Associate Media Editor: Janine Tangney

Executive Marketing Manager: Stacey Purviance

Marketing Coordinator: Brittany Blais

Senior Marketing Communications Manager: Linda Yip

Design Direction, Production Management, and Composition: PreMediaGlobal

Manufacturing Planner: Betsy Donaghey

Rights Acquisitions Specialist: Alexandra Ricciardi

ISBN-13: 978-0-8400-2885-3

ISBN-10: 0-8400-2885-7

Wadsworth
20 Channel Center Street
Boston, MA 02210
USA

Cengage Learning is a leading provider of customized learning solutions with office locations around the globe, including Singapore, the United Kingdom, Australia, Mexico, Brazil, and Japan. Locate your local office at **international.cengage.com/region**

Cengage Learning products are represented in Canada by Nelson Education, Ltd.

For your course and learning solutions, visit **www.cengage.com.**

Purchase any of our products at your local college store or at our preferred online store **www.cengagebrain.com.**

Instructors: Please visit **login.cengage.com** and log in to access instructor-specific resources.

Printed in the United States of America
1 2 3 4 5 6 7 15 14 13 12 11

For Minnie Mae

Who made soup of old bones and mailed out manuscripts in which I had no faith

Other Books by Donald M. Murray

The Lively Shadow: Living with the Death of a Child (Ballantine, 2003)

A Writer Teaches Writing, (Revised Second Edition, Heinle/Thomson, 2004)

Write to Learn, Seventh Edition (Heinle/Thomson, 2001)

My Twice Lived Life: A Memoir (Ballantine, 2001)

Writing to Deadline: The Journalist at Work (Heinemann, 2000)

Crafting a Life in Essay, Story, Poem (Boynton/Cook, 1996)

Writer in the Newsroom (Poynter Institute for Media Studies, 1996)

Read to Write, Third Edition (Heinle/Thomson, 1993)

Shoptalk: Learning to Write with Writers (Boynton/Cook, 1990)

Expecting the Unexpected (Heinemann, 1989)

CONTENTS

FOREWORD

Donald M. Murray, Master Craftsman

Brock Dethier, Utah State University

In 1983, I was a composition adjunct teaching at the University of New Hampshire. Five years after getting my PhD, I found it difficult to maintain my fantasy of publishing my way out of obscurity and easy to get depressed about the future. When I needed a professional boost, I turned to the leader of the UNH composition program, Donald M. Murray. But Don was spending much of the year as a visiting professor in Laramie, Wyoming. So rather than walk down the hall to whine to Don about my plight, I had to write Don the kind of letter that any mentor hates to get: Why doesn't the world love my stuff? What do I have to do to get published?

Don's reply was short. He didn't indulge my self-pity. He mentioned his own moments of despair. He reminded me that acceptance is as capricious as rejection. He told me that I wrote good stuff, and it would find its audience. He filled the bottom half of the page with a self-portrait, single ink lines drawn with remarkable assurance—a big "M" cowboy hat with fried-egg eyes, holster, chaps, a beard, and a grin.

I've had that drawing in my office ever since. I see in it Picasso and Pogo, as well as the man who told me to "find the one who looks like Santa Claus" when we were to meet for the first time. Responding to my whine with a pat on the back and a drawing was one more way Don expressed faith in me as a writer and person, faith that helped keep me writing. Remarkably, Don Murray made almost everyone he came in contact with feel like an interesting, valuable person capable of writing a story that others will want to read. He could create confidence where there was none, turn the surly enthusiastic, persuade staff and management to meet over brainstorming. Hailed as America's greatest writing teacher, he was certainly one of the most influential voices in the teaching of writing of the last half century.

You should read this book because it's the most direct, practical, and succinct exposition of the ideas of this extraordinary writer and teacher. And because it will make you feel like a valuable writer with something to say. Applying Murray's methods to your own writing may be the fastest way to improve your writing ... and your attitude towards it.

The Craft of Revision will help you actually DO the writing, not just talk about it, and the proof of its value will be increased productivity, quality, and enjoyment of your writing experience. Once you've tried some of Murray's suggestions, and see that they make sense and work, you may not care about his prizes and national acclaim. But if you're interested in the man behind this book and why such audacious claims are made about him and his work, read on. I hope with this foreword to introduce you to the man who was, for 28 years up until his death in 2006, my friend, mentor, guru, and benefactor.

Murray had already been a truck driver, sausage-maker, and grocery clerk when he dropped/flunked/was pushed out of high school to work at the *Boston Record* and *Boston American*. A football scholarship (he'd never played) took him to Tilton Junior College; his letter to the school had intrigued them. Despite his poor grades, he was always "a secret scholar" (*My Twice-Lived Life*, 134) with dreams of being a writer, and when his teacher at Tilton sent one of his student newspaper editorials off to be published in *The Christian Science Monitor*, he got an early break. He was a paratrooper and military policeman in World War II, experiences that haunted him for the rest of his life. After the war, he finished his bachelor's degree at the University of New Hampshire and started writing for the *Boston Herald*, achieving national fame when, in 1954, his *Herald* editorials won a Pulitzer Prize for editorial writing. At 29, Murray was the youngest ever to win that category, and his 100 editorials were the most ever entered in one year. The prize helped Murray land a job as assistant editor at *Time*, where he published more than 300 articles. In 1963, he gave up a blossoming freelance career to return to the University of New Hampshire to teach, largely, he said, for the health benefits.

With the publication of *A Writer Teaches Writing* in 1968 and a string of high-profile articles on writing in the 1970s and '80s, Murray established himself as a leader among a growing group of people thinking in new ways about teaching writing. Their work created the foundation for the field of composition, which now boasts PhDs, departments, and journals of its own. Murray was perhaps the first and best-known advocate of the writing process movement, which emphasized studying how good writing was made; over his career he developed hundreds of ways to get the writing done, helping others to achieve their writing goals. He was also a great believer in the one-on-one writing conference; new writing teachers today still learn the ground rules for such conferences by reading Murray's articles such as 1979's "The Listening Eye: Reflections on the Writing Conference." And in the 1980s, he became one of the nation's first writing coaches for newspapers, influencing newswriting and newspaper culture across the country to this day.

As impressive as it is, a fact sheet of Don's life does not capture what made that life extraordinary and does not account for the wide-ranging influence of his ideas. Don inspired almost every writer and teacher he came in contact with. There are teachers around the country today whose love for teaching and creative approach to writing began decades ago, when they read Don's books, heard Don speak, or were lucky enough to take a workshop from him. (Don traveled to 65 colleges and universities and an equal number of school districts.) He was such an influence because of the person you'll see in this book, because of the traits I've sketched below.

Voice

Only those who slog through writing-about-writing in esteemed academic journals can appreciate what Don brought to the composition world: a new, different, more readable voice, "serious without being solemn" as Newkirk and Miller put it (xvi). A voice that breathed, chuckled frequently, used the skills of poetry and journalism to tell his stories with verve and brevity. Don wrote about writing in a way that anyone who writes can understand. And he charmed his readers. He opened up space in the academic world for the rest of us who wanted to be ourselves in our writing, to be personal and informal when appropriate, to have a strong and individual voice.

Don spoke for several constituencies over the years. His landmark book, *A Writer Teaches Writing*, ensured that the voice of a professional writer would help define the emerging field of composition. He insisted that *writers*—not just academics, critical theorists, rhetoricians, semioticians, linguists, grammarians, philosophers, and fourth grade teachers with rulers—could help other writers. To some he appeared a-theoretical, but that was in part because his most basic theory was so simple and practical—study what works and do it again. "When the ball goes in the hoop," he liked to say, "you study the tapes and see what you can learn."

Don studied himself and was even, famously, the guinea pig for an investigation by Carol Berkenkotter, for whom he talked into a tape for 120 hours, noting when he was actually typing and when he was getting coffee. Conclusion: about half of Don's "writing" time consisted of planning and other prewriting activities, and "revising and planning [...] activities were virtually inseparable" (162). By participating in such studies and in the dialogue that ensued, Don became a voice of the teacher-researcher, someone whose teaching and scholarship were inextricably intertwined. He drew on his experiences in the classroom and the newsroom for his publications, and in particular he *listened* to the teachers and writers who shared with him their own insights born of experience.

The 1972 publication of Don's "Teach Writing as Process, Not Product" marked the unofficial birth of the writing process movement, making Don the voice of the movement. But it was just one tributary in a river of ideas started 50 years before and swelling during the late '60s and early '70s with contributions from people like Peter Elbow, Ken Macrorie, and Janet Emig. Teaching writing before "process" was unnerving. During my first semester teaching first-year composition, before I had begun listening to Don, I had the disquieting feeling that nothing I was telling students would change their writing. I didn't have any particular justification for doing something today rather than next week, or last. I found Don's ideas tremendously reassuring: his observation that most problems with writing *products* could be traced to writing *process*, the idea that we could tinker with the *how* of writing in order to improve the *what*, the concept of creating a writing semester as though it were one long writing process. I could teach students the tools in the writer's toolbox, the clubs in the golf bag, show them what they could use at various stages of a paper's progress. I could introduce them to, and help them practice, writing moves that they could use for the rest of their lives. I have taught and written on the basis of that insight for over 30 years, and the fundamental wisdom of it still inspires me.

Some who confused means and ends labeled Don and other writing-process advocates "expressionists," a term Don disliked because it cheapened both the expressive impulse and the scope of the writing he was trying to encourage. Writers use a writing process that can be analyzed and improved whether they're researching an article for *Nature*, writing an op-ed for *Business Week*, or starting a memoir. Don DID believe that writers often write best when expressing themselves, and he urged writers to look for subjects both out in the world and in their memories and experiences. But navel-gazing quickly made him impatient, and in his own writing, even when it dwelled on such painfully personal subjects as his loss of a daughter or his wife's struggle with Parkinson's, he never just vented or wallowed.

Don's ability to write about painfully personal subjects in ways that readers could relate to animated the column he wrote for *The Boston Globe* for 20 years, first called "Over 60," later changed to "Now and Then." Don became the voice of people who spend too much time in doctors' offices or trying to urinate, people who can't understand most of what comes through the telephone and who increasingly find old friends on the obituary page.

It was chiefly as a columnist—and in his memoirs, *My Twice-Lived Life* and *The Lively Shadow*—that Don became the voice of that rarest of commodities, wisdom. He was, wrote Max Frankel in the *New York Times Magazine*, the only "correspondent truly covering the terror-filled front of old age, ... a poet in prose." You can be a professor or a journalist or an MP without being wise, but anyone who knew Don treasured his wisdom on anything from dealing with the neighbor's barking dog to solving a temporary unemployment problem. (See it as a sabbatical and do the writing that calls you.) We miss him most because we've lost that touchstone, that sure voice.

As you study what Don has to say about voice in Chapter 9 of *The Craft of Revision*, think about how Don himself created the voice that generations of writing students have found welcoming, accepting, relaxing. He's on your side, in your corner, ready to murmur advice or just get out of your way and let you show what you can do. His enthusiasm for the subject is hard to resist.

Generosity

Don loved sharing. He gave out mimeographed copies of his favorite writers' quotes, a habit that eventually turned into the book *Shoptalk: Learning to Write with Writers*. He spread word of others' successes and played matchmaker between the many editors and administrators who offered him writing or teaching jobs and the friends, writers, and students he knew who could benefit from such opportunities. And he gave friends copies of everything he wrote. I have one huge file drawer jammed with *some* of the paper that Don sent me over the years before we turned to email. I'm not talking about his books—they have a shelf of their own—but the handouts for classes he was visiting, the notes for speeches he was giving, the oddball piece that he wrote for a little writing journal, or the notes on a new way he visualized revision. I know scores of other people around the country have similar files, some with the same handouts. They guide our teaching and writing to this day.

I'd like to think that Don's generosity helped encourage the atmosphere of selfless sharing and trading that still permeates much of the composition world. I don't think it's normal in academia for people to share as much and as readily as they do in the writing programs I know and on the

WPA listserv. I'm not sure Don lived to appreciate the flowering of one particularly impressive gift to the composition world, the composition search engine CompPile created by Rich Haswell and Glenn Blalock and used for free by thousands of composition researchers. The spirit lives on.

Support of Writing Communities

That kind of cooperation among writers—such a contrast to the cutthroat competition in film versions of creative writing programs—leads naturally to the development of writing communities. Don welcomed anyone serious about writing into a writing and teaching community dedicated to improving and publicizing *everyone's* writing. There was no hierarchy; everyone was a potential star in his community, everyone an "apprentice to the writer's craft," as Don says of himself in the Preface. I never saw him use specific community-building activities; the community developed through writing, sharing, and responding. Critics who label writing process "a-political" ignore the revolutionary cooperative impulse that Peter Elbow articulated best in *Writing Without Teachers.* By giving students unprecedented power in the classroom, Murray and Elbow created a much more liberating political atmosphere than would a professor in any traditional classroom instructing students on Marxism or social construction.

As you read the chapter-end interviews, consider the goals Don accomplished by giving voice to a number of writers who wouldn't normally have a chance to speak to writing students. By explaining a little about their backgrounds, he helps us see that many different paths lead to writing expertise and success. The additional writers' voices, discussing their unique writing processes, act as a chorus to Don's ideas, reinforcing the sense of a community of diverse writers, all trying to help others.

Enjoyment and Encouragement

Despite his support of other writers and general acceptance of writers' problems, Don had little patience for writers whining about how difficult and painful their job was. "If you don't like writing, drive a truck." He enjoyed writing enough that his enthusiasm rubbed off on others, and as he writes in the Preface, "attitude motivates the learning of skills" (xiv). He encouraged other writers to believe in themselves enough to try. And the approaches he advocated had the cumulative effect of making writing easier and more enjoyable. Some writing professors see themselves as gatekeepers to the realm of Serious Writers, giving low grades to the untalented. Don reveled in helping people who thought they couldn't write discover that they were wrong. As Tom Newkirk has said, Don "had the ability to seek people out when they needed support or guidance" (Graves, 48). Two of Don's students, Bruce Ballenger and Barry Lane, expanded on this belief in writing potential in their book *Discovering the Writer Within*. Don insisted that everyone had stories to tell.

Don wasn't uncritically accepting, and he certainly didn't want such acceptance from his readers. He had one criterion by which he judged the value of feedback: it was good if it made you want to return to the writing desk. He was able both to lavish praise on your efforts and to let you know what didn't work for him. The third-grader's haiku or freshman essay would honestly excite him, and that excitement would let you know that you, too, could do something wonderful.

Enthusiasm for Exploration and Surpise

Don argued that people found their stories and how to tell them by exploring with writing and looking for surprises. If the exploratory writing resulted in an insight for writer or reader, so much the better. His first question to students in conference was often, "What surprised you? What didn't you expect?" He had a great faith in words leading the writer to find meaning. "Read what you've written, see where it's headed, where it seems to want to go. And if it's interesting, follow it."

Don usually wrote with his audience, either on the board or on cards, letting students observe him writing badly in order to write well. Seeing how effective it was for him to model the process, I determined to emulate him, though at first I found it terrifying to do so. But I hadn't foreseen that when you're writing on the board in front of a class, every word is a surprise, for you and for those watching you, so it can be a tremendously productive time.

Mixing Genres

Such surprises in the hands of a versatile writer could lead to a poem, a novel, a proposal, a handout. As you'll see in Chapter 5, Rewrite with Genre, Don had respect for genre traditions as one of the elements that can help writers explore, but he tried to free himself and other writers from the constrictions of genre. He could turn an idea into genres as diverse as a faculty motion or an op-ed for *Foster's Daily Democrat*, and he liked the freedom to use whatever genre fit the idea. When he was a professional freelance writer, Don wrote whatever the client wanted, a message to stockholders or paean to Calvin Coolidge, so he could draw from many different kinds of writing experience. He borrowed from journalism a love of honed-down, direct writing and from business writing a desire to use all available highlighting techniques—such as the headings I'm using in this foreword—to get his meaning across clearly and quickly. He was thus able to talk with people in business and journalism as well as English and education, bridge the gap between "town and gown," as it was called in Durham, pull people together around a shared desire, draw from poet William Stafford, coach Red Auerbach, and Boston street language all in the same talk or paper. It was no accident that one of Don's students, Tom Romano, went on to champion the wildly popular multigenre research paper.

Inspiration

Romano is among hundreds, perhaps thousands, of current writing teachers and professors who were inspired by Murray and have gone on to inspire others. The writer who needed Don's piggy bank strategy to stop worrying each page to death (see page 254) was Donald Graves, whose work with younger writers made thousands of elementary school classrooms into fun, productive writing workshops. Don Murray's neighbor and former student Tom Newkirk has written prolifically on composition subjects, from boys' writing to a defense of proven writing approaches threatened by budget cuts. With help from Newkirk, Bruce Ballenger took a Murray-inspired look at the standard research paper and wrote *The Curious Researcher*, the first of his successful "curious" series. Murray worked with both Elizabeth Chiseri-Strater and Bonnie Sunstein, who opened up a whole realm of ethnographic writing with their *FieldWorking*, now in its fourth edition. Through his influence on people like Nancie Atwell and Ruth Shagoury Hubbard, Don and his message have reached thousands of students in middle school and high school, as well as the teacher-researchers who study them. Many of Don's students teach other teachers, so a third and maybe a fourth generation of Murray acolytes now spread the word.

You'll get the most out of *The Craft of Revision* if you write along with Don, experimenting with "writing against expectation" (p. 89), for - instance, or "outline after writing" (p. 125). Don doesn't say it every page because it would get boring, but after every example, you should hear Don egging you on: "Now you try." You'll find it's easier to get excited about your own writing than about somebody else's, and that kind of excitement builds on itself.

Endless Suggestions, Few Rules

"Try this" is the attitude of this book and of Don's approach to writing in general. He believed in "Writing Badly to Write Well," as he titled one of his essays, and he loved quotations like that from poet and novelist James Dickey: "I work on the process of refining low-grade ore. I get maybe a couple of nuggets of gold out of 50 tons of dirt." Writers need to get something down on the page so they can revise until it's good. What will help you get something on the page? "Try this."

Don decried the rigidity with which "THE writing process" has appeared in some textbooks and classrooms. His own view of the best ways to think about process evolved over time. He was always redrawing his charts and diagrams, and renaming steps. When in the process should you work on focusing your thinking? Should you do all your reading first? He explored, experimented, and reported on his explorations, not afraid to change or refine what he'd reported the last time.

Don wrote regularly, in the morning, in his study, but he also scribbled lists in five-minute bursts waiting in doctors' offices and restaurants. If he didn't have his ubiquitous daybook with him, he had cards in his breast pocket and an assortment of his latest favorite pens. He didn't insist that others follow his routines, and was on the lookout for writers who had different habits and patterns. Whatever gets the writing done.

Looking Forward

Don wanted to talk about the writing he was going to do, the narrative puzzle he would challenge the next morning, rather than his most recent publication. He said he threw away his notes at the end of a semester so he could start the next semester fresh. He was the first to adopt any new technology that would benefit the writer, so he taught the rest of us about breakthroughs like Amazon.com and WYSIWYG (What You See Is What You Get—the word processing breakthrough that included formatting). And he adapted his methods to new realities. His focus on revision developed in part because when students switched from typewriters to personal computers, it became impossible to restrain them from just sitting at the keyboard and banging out a draft. So the prewriting activities they neglected became important rewriting activities.

Approach: Master Craftsman/Coach

Starting each semester fresh makes sense because each new group of students is different, and Don saw himself as a craftsman or coach, reacting to and exercising the skills that students brought to his class, looking over the novice's shoulder as the novice swung the racket or guided the chisel. Don wasn't comfortable with the term "professor" because he had learned not to profess. He came to believe that student writing, not the professor's ideas, should have center stage in the writing classroom. Unlike a professor, a craftsman or coach can be wholly positive, bonded with the novice to attain the jointly desired goal of improved writing. He knew what was best about a writer's work, often better than the writer did. In 1980, *The Boston Globe* and *The Providence Journal* gave him the title of writing coach, but I think Don played that role unofficially in the lives of most of the people whose writing he read, giving the crucial word of encouragement, seeing the strength they didn't know was there.

Although the focus of current composition scholarship has largely passed by Don Murray and the writing process, his ideas are as alive, as widely taught and as useful as ever. All of his books reflect the qualities I've sketched above. But if you're going to read just one of Murray's books, *The Craft of Revision* is your best choice. Don conceived of it relatively late in his career (the first edition came out in 1991), after he began to see that "prewriting" would have to become "rewriting" for many writers. He published the fifth edition just two years before his death. Although we may look at writing differently than we did when Don began publishing, understanding, for instance, the social constructedness of every utterance, the act of writing still comes down to one person sitting down with a writing tool and getting the words on paper. And to help with that process, Don Murray has no equal.

Works Cited

Ballenger, Bruce P. *The Curious Researcher*. Boston: Allyn & Bacon, 1994.

Ballenger, Bruce P., and Barry Lane. *Discovering the Writer Within*. Cincinnati, Ohio: Writer's Digest Books, 1989.

Berkenkotter, Carol, and Donald M. Murray. "Decisions and Revisions: The Planning Strategies of a Publishing Writer." *College Composition and Communication*, 34.2 (May 1983): 156–172.

Elbow, Peter. *Writing Without Teachers*. Oxford: Oxford UP, 1973.

Frankel, Max. "Word and Image; The Oldest Bias." *New York Times Magazine*. May 24, 1998, Section 6, 16.

Graves, Seth Robert. "A Life of Process and Progress: The Influence of Writer Donald M. Murray." MA thesis. University of Missouri-Columbia. 2010. MOspace. Web. 24 June 2011.

Murray, Donald M. *A Writer Teaches Writing*. Boston: Houghton Mifflin Company, 1968.

__. "The Listening Eye: Reflections on the Writing Conference." *College English*, 41.1 (September 1979): 13–18. *Jstor*. Web. 24 June 2011. http://www.jstor.org/stable/376356.

__. *The Lively Shadow: Living with the Death of a Child*. New York: Ballantine Books, 2003.

__. *My Twice-Lived Life: A Memoir*. New York: Ballantine Publishing Group, 2001.

__. *Shoptalk: Learning to Write with Writers*. Portsmouth, NH: Boynton/Cook, 1990.

__. "Teach Writing as Process, Not Product." *The Leaflet*: New England Association of Teachers of English, 1972. Reprinted in *Cross-Talk in Composition Theory*, 2nd ed. Victor Villaneuva, ed. Urbana, IL: National Council of Teachers of English, 2003, 3–6.

__. "Writing Badly to Write Well." In *Sentence Combining: A Rhetorical Perspective*. Donald A. Daiker, Andrew Kerek, and Max Morenberg, eds. Carbondale, IL: Southern Illinois University Press, 1985, 187–201. Reprinted in Newkirk and Miller, 101–119.

Newkirk, Thomas, and Lisa Miller, eds. *The Essential Don Murray: Lessons from America's Greatest Writing Teacher*. Portsmouth, NH: Heinemann, 2009.

PREFACE

"Isn't disloyalty as much the writer's virtue as loyalty is the soldier's?" asked novelist Graham Greene. I am still an apprentice to the writer's craft and continue to learn from my daily writing, from my colleagues and editors, and from a lifelong study of the testimony of other writers, living and dead. As a result of my continuing education, I have been gloriously disloyal to my own past ideas about how effective writing is made and how it can be taught.

Some of my colleagues have grown almost theological about their ideas and defend their faith in articles, monographs, books, and talks. I have felt guilty, at times, hearing or reading them. Their ideas are important and deserve respect, but I think I have more fun. Happily irresponsible, I do not reread what I have written in previous editions until I have scratched down the topics I want to explore in the latest edition—recording the answers, questions, doubts, contradictions, insights, and instructive failures that have made my mind itch.

As I begin this fifth edition, I admit surprise that while moving toward 80 years of age, I feel the same seductive fascination with the writing process that I felt when I was a boy scratching letters in the dirt with a stick, unable to read or write, but determined to decode the mystery of written language. I do not take the stairs two—or three—steps at a time as I once did, but I am still young at the writing desk, amazed at the joy—yes, that's the right word—of taking out, putting in, and moving words around so they instruct and surprise me and, I hope, the reader.

New to This Edition

The chapters in the fifth edition move through the writing process as the student finds a focus, chooses a genre, erects a structure, documents each point, develops the draft, tunes its voice, and clarifies the final draft. In each case, my purpose is to give students the practical skills they can, through practice, make their own. In this edition I have again rearranged the process chapters to better serve the student writer and to adapt to my own recent explorations with the rewriting process.

Chapter 1, "Rewrite Before Writing," comes directly from my own experience as a daily writer. I became aware of the vast amount of rewriting I do before I write and share this process with my readers.

Of course we cannot revise what isn't written and so Chapter 2 focuses on "How to Get the Writing Done: Tricks of the Writer's Trade." I still have to go back and reorganize my life to find the time to lose myself in writing. What we write may, if we are lucky, appear to be magic, but each page, like the magician's tricks, are produced by a series of logical acts. I try to eliminate the mystery of a writer's productivity.

Reviewers have convinced me that a chapter on reading for revision should come early in the book so that students have instruction in the active reading that is essential when they are making meaning rather than decoding someone else's. It is now Chapter 3, "Reading for Revision."

Since the fourth edition was published I have become increasingly aware of how much rewriting I do in my mind and in my notebook *before* I attempt the first page. Chapter 4, "Rewrite with Focus," introduces that new concept and shows how students can rewrite before writing.

In Chapter 5, "Rewrite with Genre," I have written a new section called "The Essential Narrative" that I believe will help both reader and writer. I show how all writing—grant application, history essay, book review, occupational therapy case history, physics lab report, business plan—all have an embedded narrative.

Students frequently ask how long the assignment should be. This irritated me in the classroom, seeming to emphasize a trivial issue, and I would usually bark, "Long enough!" Now I ask my editors how long the assignment should be and have come to believe that length is a significant element in effective writing. In Chapter 8, "Rewrite to Develop," I share the process of development I went through to produce a column that had to be lengthened by one-third, then I show how it could be cut by two-thirds.

Years ago one of my students was shocked during an employment interview to see a copy of one of my books on the administrator's desk with his name, in large letters, pasted over mine. She challenged him and he said I had told my readers that they should make my books their own. So I had. This book is no longer mine but yours.

Case Histories and Interviews

We have retained two professional case histories and two student case histories, including one that demonstrates how the research paper can encompass personal experience.

We have also retained interviews with two professional writers and two students that each focus on the rewriting task identified in a particular chapter. These practicing writers describe the attitudes and techniques they use to solve their revision and editing problems.

Exercises

Students are invited to perform specific writing tasks within the book. These exercises (identified by the icon in the margin) are woven into the book so that students may use them in the context of a specific rewriting problem, either on their own or at their instructor's suggestion. More than classroom activities, the exercises are techniques any writer—student or professional—may find helpful when facing a writing problem.

Who Can Use This Text

We have been astonished and delighted at how *The Craft of Revision* has been used in diverse learning environments. It has been adopted for first-year English courses in universities and community colleges, and has also been popular in advanced composition programs.

The Craft of Revision has been used in middle and high school classrooms, in college remedial and honors programs, in graduate seminars, and in teacher training courses and workshops. It has been adopted by corporate and governmental training programs. It has been studied by the writing staffs of newspapers and used as a supplemental text in creative writing courses. And it has been used by individuals who are teaching themselves to write.

How Can Students Learn the Craft of Revision?

In too many classes students have only revised to meet the standards of the teacher that often seem arbitrary to the student since different teachers make different demands. Students will only be invested in revision when it gives them something. They must have an opportunity to revise to discover new meanings, to explore subjects of importance to them in greater depth, to experience the surprise writers feel when the draft reveals how much they didn't know they knew.

Here are some ways this positive attitude can be reinforced in the composition class:

- First readings by the student writer, the instructor, and classmates should focus on potential, not error.
- There should be time for revision, which usually means fewer papers, revised more extensively.
- The best, as well as the worst, papers should have the benefits of revision.
- Students should observe the discoveries of meaning made clear by revision on classmates' papers, as well as on their own.
- The process of revision should be sequential, moving from a concern with meaning, to audience, form, information, structure, and then to language.

Above all, attitude motivates the learning of skills. The instructor should reinforce a constructive attitude toward revision. Some of the ways this can be done are:

- Share evolving drafts that document the positive results of revision. Reveal the instructor's own revision case histories, have students who have revised effectively share their own case histories, share the case histories of successful revision from interviews and biographies of writers.

- Ask class members and possibly faculty members from other disciplines to report on activities in their disciplines that are similar to revision: play and musical rehearsal, practice in a sport, the process of painting, experiments in science.
- Have the class perform quick revisions. For example, write a five-line description of a familiar place or person in five minutes, then do five-minute rewrites from a different point of view, for a different purpose, for a different audience, in a different form, in a different voice, and share the results so the class appreciates the different, diverse products of revision.

Ways to Use *The Craft of Revision* in Your Classroom

This textbook has been designed to support the student and instructor in many different courses. It can be used alone or as a supplement to other rhetorics and readers. Teachers will and should find their own different ways to adapt *The Craft of Revision* to their particular teaching style, the needs of their students, or to the curriculum in which they function. These suggestions are designed to spark the diversity that should be central to teaching writing.

The Craft of Revision can be used as the principal writing text because it helps students create a first draft. The students can use it to help them write weekly papers or to support a sequence of three-week units in which they write a draft and perform two major revisions supported by conferences, peer workshops, and class instruction sessions. I have had good results with students working on one paper all semester, taking several weeks to find the subject, and then moving week by week through the revision process. No, they didn't get bored since they found subjects they wanted to explore. In fact, alumni response has been unusually strong, with former students testifying that they really learned to write when they had time to learn the craft of revision.

The Craft of Revision can supplement a rhetoric that has limited material on revision, or it can supplement a reader, allowing students to understand the craft that created the models and to practice the same craft on their own drafts.

The Craft of Revision can be introduced to the class the first week or two and then used as a desk book by the students as they revise their papers. The best way to do this is to have the students write a paragraph in class, then revise it a number of times, sharing each revision with a small group that will select the most interesting leap toward meaning to share with the whole class. The students may need to be told, in the beginning, what to do since they have only been told to edit in the past. I usually say, "Develop the potential in your draft, exploring the subject in writing any way you want, but if you're stuck you may want to change the point of view from which the subject is seen." Some other suggestions I may make are to try to make the information more specific, revise it for a different publication or audience, write with more emotion or less, try to write in a different voice.

The writing periods should be short, no more than five minutes, and the peer sharing sessions should be no longer than fifteen minutes. It always helps if the instructor performs the same exercise and shares those drafts. Once students experience the discovery that is possible with revision, they can be introduced to the text.

The Craft of Revision may be used in the latter half of a composition semester or term when the students have drafts worthy of careful revision and when they see the need for revision.

The Craft of Revision may be used in a content course in English or any other discipline to help students improve their writing assignments. The text may be assigned to all students in the course or suggested as an aid to those students who are having difficulty revising effectively.

The Craft of Revision can be used as a self-teaching text with the student creating a draft and moving through the sequential steps to practice the skills of revision. In every case the students should use the textbook in connection with their own writing.

The Craft of Revision cannot be learned in the abstract; theory must be illuminated by practice that will, in turn, illuminate theory.

However the textbook is used, it will help the individual student, the instructor, and the whole class—especially if those students who do an effective job of revision testify to the class on what they did and how it was done. I have done this with oral reports, but more recently with quickly written but complete commentaries that the students write, reporting on their writing and revision process, their writing problems, and their proposed solutions. These commentaries encourage students to examine their craft and teach them how they can identify and solve their own writing problems. Those solutions instruct us all.

My students have always instructed me, and I have told worried beginning writing teachers to get their students writing. In every class, some students write better than others. Get them to tell you and the class how they write, and the curriculum will evolve.

Acknowledgments

My developmental editor, Laurie Runion, has once again improved this draft by her kind but insightful demands. It is her book as well as mine. Michael Rosenberg, my publisher, rescued the first draft of this book that I thought was a final draft. It was not and he re-aimed the manuscript to the craft of revision. Without him there would have been no second, third, fourth, or fifth editions. My thanks also to Dickson Musslewhite, my acquisitions editor at Heinle, who now oversees my books.

Minnie Mae, my wife and constant companion, understands only too well the emotional roller coaster of the writer and balances both the highs and lows with support and humor. Chip Scanlan from The Poynter Institute for Media Studies in St. Petersburg, Florida, is at my side as I write each column, essay, poem, or book. We share all the highs and lows of the writing life and his support is a constant source of strength and wisdom.

Brock Dethier, Thomas Newkirk, Donald Graves, and many other colleagues in the writing community at the University of New Hampshire have contributed to my continuing education. Others who have stimulated my thinking and influenced this book include Bonnie Sunstein of the University of Iowa, Thomas Romano of Miami University in Ohio, Lad Tobin of Boston College, and the writer Ralph Fletcher. I am indebted to the significant contribution of Mary Hallet of University of Massachusetts Dartmouth.

Mary Clark of the English Department at the University of New Hampshire is an expert linguist and a fine teacher. She made important contributions to the first edition and her mark remains on this edition.

The reviewers who helped me with their candid and insightful comments on this edition are John Baffa, *Morton College*; Bill Broz, *University of Northern Iowa*; Louise Rodriguez Connal, *Arizona State University*; Elizabeth Hodges, *Virginia Commonwealth University*; Elizabeth Chiseri-Strater, *University of North Carolina at Greensboro*; and Bonnie Sunstein, *University of Iowa.*

I was also instructed by the honest, detailed responses of those who reviewed earlier editions: Kay Baker, *Ricks College*; Kathleen Bell, *Old Dominion University*; Mary Comstock, *University of Puget Sound*; Marie Czarnecki, *Mohawk Valley Community College*; Francine DeFrance, *Cerritos College*; Sandra Maresh Doe, *Metropolitan State College of Denver*; Connie Hale, *University of Puget Sound*; Dick Harrington, *Piedmont Virginia Community College*; Sally Harvey, *Yuba College*; Pat Huyett, *University of Missouri at Kansas City*; Ingrid Jordak, *Broome Community College at Binghamton*; Ernest Lee, *Carson-Newman College*; Joan Tyler Mead, *Marshall University*; Leslie Prast, *Delta College*; Donna Qualley, *Western Washington University*; David Roberts, *Samford University*; Susan Roberts, *Boston College*; Bernard Selzler, *University of Minnesota at Crookston*; David Sudol, *Arizona State University*; Nancy Walker, *Southwest Missouri State University*; and Driek Zirinsky, *Boise State University.*

Chapter 1

REWRITE BEFORE WRITING

Fail. Fail again. Fail better.

—SAMUEL BECKETT

I have missed over five thousand shots in my career. I've lost almost three hundred games. Twenty-six times I've been trusted to take the game winning shot—and missed. I've failed over and over and over again in my life. . . . And that is why I succeed.

—MICHAEL JORDAN

I love the flowers of afterthought.

—BERNARD MALAMUD

Do you ever write badly?

Good. All writers write badly—at first. Nobel Prize winners, Pulitzer Prize winners, writers of blockbuster movies, writers with distinguished academic reputations, writers who influence and persuade, instruct and inspire, comfort and anger and amuse and inform, all write badly. Writers who write novels, speeches, news stories, screenplays, corporate memos, textbooks, plays, poems, history books, scientific reports, legal briefs, grant applications, TV scripts, songs—all write badly—at first.

Then they rewrite. Revision is not the end of the writing process but the beginning. First emptiness, then terror, at last one word, then a few words, a paragraph, a page, finally a draft that can be revised.

Why Do We Resist Rewriting?

Most beginning writers refuse to rewrite. I certainly ignored, fought, resisted, resented any suggestion for revision. When a teacher or an editor suggested a revision I took it as a personal attack. Looking back, I confess that the more the writing needed another version, the more I resisted. It is the same way with an argument. The more I realize my friend, colleague, wife may be right, the more I resist, maintaining an aggressive loyalty to my stupidities.

There is a logic to this. Writing is always an act of self-exposure. When we finish a draft all writers feel vulnerable. Writing strips away our intellectual clothes and shows the world what we know and what we don't know; it reveals what we think and feel; it documents how well we write—from our ability to use language, following or not following the traditions of usage, mechanics, spelling, to our ability to write with clarity and grace.

And what makes it worse is the fact that the only reason most of us write is to be tested, our grade or test, our intelligence (or perhaps lack of it) documented.

Writers begin their careers feeling the same way. Any suggestion for a change in a draft is a personal insult. I have written this chapter as well as I can. It is fresh, original, never said before in this way. It is me. But writers become better writers when they learn the secret of our craft. Writing is rewriting.

Playwright Neil Simon put it best: "Rewriting is when playwriting really gets to be fun. In baseball you only get three swings and you're out. In rewriting, you get almost as many swings as you want and you know, sooner or later, you'll hit the ball."

Of course, writing in school is an effective way of testing what we know and how we think about what we know. Writing is the most disciplined and revealing form of thought.

The writing we most admire, the writing that takes us into other worlds, the writing that allows us to live the experience of others, the writing that influences our thoughts and emotions has evolved through a process of exploration and discovery.

That process is both frightening and thrilling for the writer since progress is made, as it is in science and sports, by *instructive failure*. We attempt what we cannot yet do but in examining the attempt we discover the next step—and then, failing again, the next step.

At the University of New Hampshire I heard the writer Grace Paley say, "We write about what we don't know about what we know," and I wanted to stand up and shout, "Listen to that. She said it. That's what writing is." Instead, of course, I sat quietly writing it down in the journal I call a daybook so I would not forget it.

Novelist Donald Barthelme said, "Writing is a process of dealing with not-knowing, a forcing of what and how. We have all heard novelists testify to the fact that, beginning a new book, they are utterly baffled as to how to proceed, what should be written and how it might be written, even though they've done a dozen . . . At best there is a slender intuition, not much greater than an itch." Syndicated newspaper columnist Ellen Goodman explains, "What makes me happy is rewriting. In the first draft you get your ideas and your theme clear, if you are using some kind of metaphor you get that established, and certainly you have to know where you're coming out. But the next time through it's like cleaning house, getting rid of all the junk, getting things in the right order, tightening things up. I like the process of making writing neat."

The wannabe writer who hasn't written—and there are many—and the writer who has written but not published—and there are many of those—believe in spontaneity, but the published writer knows it takes a great deal of practice to be spontaneous. The singer who "spontaneously" surprises the audience with an unexpected personal style, the basketball star who "spontaneously" fakes right and spins left, the presidential candidate who puts her notes aside and speaks "spontaneously" have all practiced their craft again and again.

I was afraid that if I rewrote I would lose the gift of spontaneity when I received the gifts from my muse. And then I read an article by John Kenneth Galbraith, former journalist and best-selling writer, who I greatly admire for the discipline, the grace, and the spontaneity of his writing on such difficult subjects such as international diplomacy and economics. Speaking to others, he spoke to me, "All writers know that on some golden mornings they are touched by the wand—are on intimate terms with poetry and cosmic truth. I have experienced those moments myself. Their lesson is simple: It's a total illusion. And the danger in the illusion is that you will wait for those moments. Such is the horror of having to face the typewriter that you will spend all your time waiting. I am persuaded that most writers, like most shoemakers, are about as good one day as the next . . . In my own case there are days when the result is so bad that no fewer than five revisions are required. However, when I'm greatly inspired, only four revisions are needed before, as I've often said, I put in that note of spontaneity which even my meanest critics concede."

As writers we are saved from the stupidities of our first drafts by revision, the process of using language to see the subject again and again until we—and eventually the reader—see it clearly. But revision becomes far more than correcting error for the working writer. Revision—re-seeing—is how the writer sees the world and understands its meaning.

I start by writing about my father and how he liked to dress up.

> My father wanted to see his face in his shoes. Beside the glare from his shoes, he wanted his shoes shined, his socks held up by garters, his pants with a knife edge crease, his shirt collar stiff, his tie knotted to the latest style. When I was a boy, wearing my own costume of sloppiness, I felt my father was a phony who dressed so the world would not see him as he really was, a well-meaning failure.
>
> Then as I revised the description of my father I began to understand he dressed this way to hide the fact that his father and mother had worked in the factory, that he had not been allowed to go to high school. He dressed as if he came from a "better" background than he did.

> His formal dress was designed to fool people and I began to see it was heroic in a way. He was trying to make something of himself, to look at least like a boss instead of a worker—and he pulled it off. He achieved it into the middle class, just barely, but his son went to high school and college, he owned a car and a single-family home with a lawn and backyard. By writing I had revised my revision of my father and understood anew what he had done for me.

This is NOT the father I had known all my life, before these two paragraphs. It is a father I understand better than before. Rewriting what I knew about my father, I discover what I did not know I knew. Rewriting is thinking: a process of combining memory, ideas, questions, answers that don't yet have questions, facts, observations, research, theories, ideas in ways that produce a meaning. Writing may, of course, reveal our ignorance, but more often writing and rewriting reveal how much we know. Each draft recovers information from memory of which we were not aware. And that process of rewriting begins before we put a word on paper.

An Invitation: Write with Me

This book is an invitation. It is not a typical textbook in which the author, an expert on the subject, lectures and instructs, presenting the writer's ideas on history, absolute principles on economics, theories of psychology or law, the laws of physics.

This book is different because the author is still learning to write. Each page reflects what I am learning as I write and rewrite this textbook. Write along with me. Try your own experiments in meaning, use your language to explore your world as I use my language to explore my world.

It is all a matter of trial and instructive error. I try to say what I cannot yet say and fail but find the failure instructive. It shows me another way to attempt to say what I have not before said. Fail with me. Remember that when we were infants and took our first steps, our parents held out their hands, just far enough so that we had to attempt a bit more than we had before and we attempted that step and perhaps another. Most of the time we tumbled back down on the rug and our parents laughed with us and held out their hands again, offering another invitation.

I hold out my hands to you. Try what you can't yet write and as you draft a topic that you think you do not know, you may find that you know more than you thought you did. And as you continue to rewrite, you will find that the subject comes clear.

Try what I try. It may work for you. Fine. And it may not work for you as it doesn't work for me sometimes. There are no absolute rights and wrongs in writing. Remember that each day as we come to our writing desks the beginner and the old hand are still learning to write, still exploring their worlds for meaning using the tools of language.

How Do You Find Something to Write About?

Each week for the past 15 years I have had to find a topic for the weekly column "Now and Then" that I write for the *Boston Globe*. It has not been a burden because it increases my awareness of life. I am more alive than I ever was because I observe each experience and record—in the notebook of the mind or in my journal—my personal response to it.

Most weeks I know the territory I intend to explore but there are mornings when I face the weekly deadline and have nothing to say. I have developed the following techniques to help me find a column. Perhaps they will help you.

Brainstorming

To brainstorm, put aside all your notes, take a piece of paper, and put down whatever occurs to you in a fragmentary list. Surprise yourself. Be silly, dumb, an enemy to your own preconceived ideas. You can work by yourself or with a team. Brainstorming is ideal when a committee is planning a party, a marketing campaign, a new research project.

I begin brainstorming by putting down anything that comes to mind even if it seems stupid, embarrassing, or not related to the territory I hope to explore in writing. My wife, Minnie Mae, has Parkinson's, a disease that affects balance, causes tremors, and makes the victim—and whoever lives with a person with Parkinson's—to live in slow motion.

I start with the obvious and see what follows as I write quickly and without censoring myself to see what happens:

limits
now using a cane, what next
we've hired Dot to come in weekday mornings
mornings are worst
this week Minnie Mae has decided she doesn't want to wait in the car when I do the shopping
87 % of conversations are in the car
she has the tv on almost all the time these days
all our important conversations take place in the car
easier for both of us if I hire Dot for an afternoon and go shopping alone
but we lose time together
are we moving slowly toward institutionalization???
MM will lack stimulus
Important?
lichen on fence post
da Vinci quotation

When I finish making the list in five minutes or so, I look up the quotation by the great Renaissance artist Leonardo da Vinci:

> *You should look at certain walls stained with damp or at stones of uneven colour. If you have to invent some backgrounds you will be able to see in these the likeness of divine landscapes, adorned with mountains, ruins, rocks, woods, great plains, hills and valleys in great variety; and then again you will see there battles and strange figures in violent action, expressions of faces and clothes and an*

infinity of things which you will be able to reduce to their complete and proper forms.

Then I read the brainstormed list over looking for two things:

What surprises me?

I am surprised by the importance of our automobile conversations and by the way lichen shows me how a large world can be created within limits.

What connects?

Da Vinci quotation I half remember, lichen, limits, not waiting in car while I'm shopping, limits, conversation, institutionalization

The importance of car conservations may well grow into a column but "lichen" itches. I need to explore that. I start making a list about lichen that grows into an unexpected poem.

What Lichen Knows

I am apprenticed
to lichen, learning
how to live small
within Parkinson's
near horizons, time
slowed, floors
that rise and fall
in unseen storms.
Lichen treasures
what is discarded,
worn out, overlooked,
tossed aside, dying.
The granite stone wall
growing back into earth,
bark of the dying oak,
a stump. Here
continents grow

as seen by a space
ship whirling past,
all life contained
in a geography
of limits.

Interview Yourself

I interview myself to discover what I know that others may need to know, what I know that I need to understand more fully, what I don't know I know until it is explored by writing.

The interview always makes my world expand. My life that seemed dull and ordinary becomes more interesting as I listen to the answers to my own questions. The same thing may happen to you if you answer my questions.

- What am I thinking about while waiting in line?
- What irritated me today?
- What made me laugh?
- What made me angry?
- What did I learn today?
- What contradicted what I know—or thought I knew?
- What made me feel good?
- What made me feel bad?
- What confuses me?
- What does somebody else need to know that I know?
- What questions do I need answered?
- What surprised me today?

Try this. Write down your answers in fragments. Don't worry about spelling or grammar or neatness or fully developed paragraphs or sentences. You are trying to catch an idea, a half of an idea, a quarter of an idea, just the quick glint of where an idea was a moment ago. Play with words, images, facts. See if any of them connect. Pay close attention to anything that surprises you, that is different from what you expected. Follow the surprise or connection in your mind or on paper to see where your thinking may take you.

Circle the Subject

I don't just plunge in and write the obvious response to an assignment or writing task even when I am on deadline. I stand back and study the assignment or my writing idea from different points of view—distant, close up, from inside the subject looking out, from outside the subject looking in, going behind the subject, taking the point of view of those affected by the subject, seeing the subject in the context of the past or the future—the way a candid photographer circles around a rock star to snap pictures from every possible angle. The photo editor then selects the focus. I am my own photo editor and choose the point of view that best serves the reader.

Circling the assignment is important to make sure I am not just taking the easy, obvious approach but finding the one that will best serve the reader. I do the same thing when I don't have a clear assignment or topic that has been given to me by an editor. I write a weekly newspaper column, memoir, textbooks, poems, novels, essays and in each case I rewrite before I write by imagining different stories I could tell and the different ways I might tell them.

The closer I am to deadline, the more important it is that I delay. As the essayist E. B. White said, "Delay is natural to a writer. He is like a surfer—he bides his time, waits for the perfect wave on which to ride in. Delay is instinctive with him." But it isn't instinctive to the inexperienced writer who rushes the writing process. I stand back and try to circle the subject, seeing what is backstage, what connects, what doors might open, what is implied, where might it lead.

The other morning two deer dashed in front of my car as I was on the way to buy my morning coffee. I don't live in the woods but in town, but the deer reminded me that I have seen a fox on my morning walk, watched an otter catch a fish through a hole in the ice on a pond near my house, had raccoons, a fisher, and woodchucks observe me writing through the patio doors that open on the backyard, almost stepped on a skunk and a porcupine. And the other morning a neighbor nodded to a moose as they went their mutual ways.

If I were to write about this subject, I could focus on how one animal has adjusted to an urban environment and how others haven't; how our pattern of backyards are hospitable to some animals and not others; speculate on their danger to domestic pets; I could write about the birds, snakes, and bugs that share my land; imagine how so many animals live a secret life near me but are rarely seen; consider how we can protect them—or get rid of them since deer, for example, can destroy gardens and orchards; debate who really owns my land; and so on. I decide to describe our secret neighbors and will allow the writing to reveal its significance to me and the reader. Each quick, passing thought, however, was a version of the draft I might write. I was rewriting before I wrote.

This rewriting before writing is a form of play that exercises my mind and extends my world and I have developed some techniques that make my casual pre-revisions helpful to me as a writer.

Try Out Lines

For me the play of rewriting usually begins with what I call "instigating lines," fragments of language that contain an interesting conflict, tension, contradiction, irony, unexpected idea.

Each stands for an idea that could be developed. They are rarely sentences, sometimes just a word that has a special meaning for me. "Hero" is such a word. I was in combat in World War II as a paratrooper and I hate the casual use of the word "hero" for veterans of my generation. Few of us were heroes. In fact, many soldiers I served with who wanted to be heroes did stupid things that were both ineffective and betrayed our position, like standing up with a machine gun and firing at the enemy. I don't want to go into combat with heroes. I have written essays, columns, poems, and fiction exploring this topic—and will write more. That well will never run dry.

The line is an individual matter. It reflects your personal experience and private response to the world. Reye's Syndrome is a rare disease that killed my 20-year-old daughter. Those two words are packed with enough meaning that I wrote a book *The Lively Shadow* about losing her and surviving that loss.

I am amused that lawyers have "practices." I want no lawyer to practice on me. The term "mild heart attack" irritates me. MY heart attack was not mild to me; no one's heart attack is mild to the patient.

Lines often float by in my head and I grab one to see what it means. I heard myself say "I had a long two-year marriage to my first wife" and that made me write a piece about the "short" 51-year-long marriage I have had with my second wife. I hear a coach say a player isn't *fast* but he is *quick* and I have an apparent contradiction to explore.

I hear the term "the guilt of silence" and it reminds me of the times I have done harm by what I haven't said. "Unlearning to Write" is a line that became an article on all the lessons that my students had to be untaught—that you have to know what you want to say before you say it, that big words are better than short words, that you have to write formal introductions and endings.

Play with Images

In looking for a subject to write about or a way to respond to an assignment, I often play with images. Writing is a visual art. We see the world through language. When I recall the memories of watching my first grandchild learning to walk, his stumbles, his getting up and trying again, I remember the strong image of watching his mother—my daughter—take her first steps. And then I remember all the difficult first steps I have taken in my life. Images such as these often appear before my mind's eye. Other times they appear in a draft. I may use them or not, but they stimulate my thinking and my writing.

My head is filled with such powerful images but each day brings new ones. The other day I passed a classroom in which a professor lectured at a podium on his desk and his three—yes, three—students sat in the back row as far away from him as possible. I knew he was a bad teacher and that made me think of the geography of the classroom and those teachers of mine who were close to me yet kept a professional distance.

I watch the salesperson who stops talking and steps back when he realizes that I am selling the new bed to my wife and his job is not to interfere. I see moonlight reflected on the snow in my woods and remember how we feared the moonlight that exposed us to the enemy during the war. I notice the distance between the presidential candidate and his daughters and speculate a reason.

I do not think these scenes, I see them, relive them, experience them again in memory. It is as if I were watching a movie in which I was one of the actors. If I decide to use the image in a draft, then I study it with my mind's eye and write it down, usually seeing it even more clearly as I write.

Make Connections

The British novelist E. M. Forster said, "Only connect." It is good advice in the human community but it is essential in writing. The writer is a master weaver, rewriting before writing by making connections between pieces of information, observations, ideas, theories, memories, fears, hopes that when connected create a new meaning.

This chapter is the result of such play.

As I was preparing to revise this chapter, I connected rewriting with prewriting, all that happens during the writing process before the first draft. I didn't think the connection would hold but it has and I have used this idea, new to me, and offer it to you.

Connections reveal our world in greater depth. We listen to what coaches say and realize that football is a militaristic game. We observe and listen to fans and see how this sport is a symbol of our society. I connect the fears I had at summer camp with the fears I had in combat and realize how I was trained for war during summer camp. I see how people waste natural resources to oppose wasting natural resources; how they want to visit a wilderness area, not seeming to realize that their visit stops it from being wilderness.

What If

The writer wonders how our society would change if the speed limit were enforced, if everyone over 70 had their license to drive taken away—or if no one could drive until they were 26 years old. What if you had to take a test to get married or to have a baby? What would be on the test? Would it really hurt education if we eliminated homework? Our world is filled with what ifs that may produce new visions, new ideas.

The writer begins to write by rewriting, playing with what may be in the writer's mind or on the daybook page. This essential play occurs at the writing desk but also when waking at night, eating with friends or family, doing chores, shopping, watching television, driving, taking a shower, jogging, reading. Novelist Robert Cormier described it best:

> *What if? What if? My mind raced, and my emotions kept pace at the sidelines, the way it always happens when a story idea arrives, like a small explosion of thought and feeling. What if? What if an incident like that in the park had been crucial to a relationship between father and daughter? What would make it crucial? Well, what if the father, say, was divorced from the child's mother and the incident happened during one of his visiting days? And what if . . .*

Some of the What Ifs I find most productive:

- What if the roles were reversed—mother was son, son the mother?
- What if he were a woman, she a man?
- What if I stepped back and saw this from a distance, what if I moved close?
- What if the good guy was bad, the bad guy good?

- What if they were younger, older?
- What if their dreams came true?
- What if their problems were solved?
- What if this happened a hundred years ago?
- What if this happened a hundred years from now?

Imagine your own what ifs on a paper you are working on. Writing is so important that it must contain the element of play. No limits. What if your mother had a secret past you knew nothing about? What if you had been a twin? What if a brother or sister you didn't know showed up? What if your father was not your father? What if your parachute didn't open? What if you jumped out of the plane and went up instead of down? What if your bicycle was a motorcycle? What if it was your fault? What if you ate so many beans you exploded?

To imagine you have to disconnect your mind from all that is expected, responsible, logical, proper. Most of the what ifs will not be followed but then one will make the ordinary strange and your draft will lead you where you never expected to go. This is the adventure of writing.

Be Specific

Inexperienced writers believe that writing begins with an inflated idea of a vague, general topic such as "truth," "beauty," or "patriotism" because they have been given such assignments in school. What they don't know is that experienced writers would do as badly as they do with such assignments unless they could come up with an instigating line or an image that is specific and, above all, interesting to them.

As I mentioned previously, the instigating line is a fragment of language, a sentence or less, that I hear in my mind or find myself scribbling in my notebook. It's the line that contains a tension, contradiction, question, feeling, or thought that surprises me and would be productive to think more about in writing.

Let's take those vague topics I just mentioned and see what would happen if we had an instigating line to start us writing:

"Truth"

"Mother—never lie—God burn me in Hell. Mother tells 'stories' to the landlord when we don't have the rent. Dad sick. Not true."

The conflict between religious teaching and home practice interests me. If I describe—in writing—what I was taught and what I observed I may begin to understand how I feel today about telling the truth, church, or paying bills.

"Beauty"

"Told mother I was fat, guys made jokes about me. She had same thing happen at same school—she was too thin, no 'sweater' girl. She weighed same as I weigh."

This observation presents a conflict that needs exploration. Women are shaped by nature and so are men. Fat and thin are relative terms. So is beauty. Look at the pictures of film stars years ago. How dangerous it is to allow society to define you? How many are hurt who are not considered beautiful? How many are hurt by being considered beautiful or handsome and not taken seriously as a student? What does it say about our society that there are Web sites extolling the virtues of being anorexic (and tips on how to be a good one!)? What does it mean that people are having Botox parties and having the botulism virus injected into their faces to make them look younger? Those are a few of the topics that might grow from one line.

"Patriotism"

"Spies are traitorous patriots."

A fascinating and thoughtful essay for a course in history, ethics, or political science could grow out of this fragmentary idea. Graham Greene once asked, "Isn't disloyalty as much the writer's virtue as loyalty is the soldier's?" Good question. Is the role of artists to stand apart from society and take stock? What about priests who criticize the Vatican's policy on sexual abuse? And senators who vote against their party, soldiers who oppose a particular war? And what is a patriot anyway? All these are good pieces that could be researched and written.

Writers also find writing can begin with an image, a mind picture that itches the imagination, that makes you look at it again and again to see what it means. All of us have images that haunt us. I remember seeing my face when I was a baby reflected in the glass of a china cabinet, and that became a poem. I remember the long, empty corridors of high school between classes, so different from the way I usually saw them crowded with students. When I found why I remembered them—why I was so often alone in the corridor—I found an essay.

When I am given an assignment to write an academic paper, I do the same thing I do when searching for a poem. I sit with pen in hand and notebook open, in front of my computer screen, or without anything but my own thoughts. Sometimes I think about what I think about when I am not thinking: when I'm waiting for class to begin, sitting in a car waiting for someone, when my mind drifts away from the people to whom I should be listening, during the commercials on television, when I'm walking alone, just before I drop off to sleep. At these times, an image, a word, a fragment of language will pass through the black emptiness like a shooting star. I capture it in a scribbled note.

Other times I listen to what I'm saying when I talk to myself, or I remember what has surprised me recently. What did I see, think, feel, hear, watch, read that was not expected—in fact that ran against expectations, shocking or confusing me—contradicting what I thought I had known or believed?

Many people believe writing comes to the writer like a computer printout, flowing along, finished, complete. Writing usually comes in fragments—details, hints, clues, collisions of information, half ideas and quarter ideas, bits of pieces of information, scraps that have fallen out of books, from TV or radio, from conversations at the next table or in another room. The writer plays with these scraps to see what they may mean.

End-of-Chapter Interviews

Years ago I was invited to work with pupils in elementary school, but I wondered what a professional writer had to offer children, what would we say to each other. I am 6′ 3″ and 240 pounds. I had an awful time trying to squeeze my belly into desks designed for small people. The lined paper had a lot of space between the lines and the student's printing was labored. When we wrote together, however, I had a surprise. They were writers. I might be writing a book and they a paragraph but we were all writers, trying to solve the same problems.

At the end of many of the chapters in this book we have included interviews with published writers because they have found some of the solutions to the problems you face. Read them realizing that Elizabeth Cooke, Christopher Scanlan, Kathryn S. Evans, and Jennifer Bradley-Swift may be more experienced than you are, but are also students, still learning to solve the problems you discover on your page.

Interview with a Published Writer

Elizabeth Cooke

Elizabeth Cooke, who has published two novels, *Complicity* and *Zeena*, articles, essays, poetry, and short stories, teaches writing at the University of Maine at Farmington. She and her husband live in a nineteenth-century farmhouse surrounded by woods, mountains, sky, and a myriad of wildlife, all of which allow her the room to dream and write.

How do you find something to write about?

It's not so much a question of "finding" it, as it is listening to it call to me. In fact, I don't think I have ever "tried" to find something to write about. The things I write about come at me—while I am walking in the woods, driving the car, reading my mail, any time at all. Since I don't start with an idea, but with a visual image or a voice, I need to be "listening" all the time. Connected to the image or the voice is a feeling I can't let go of—I may not even know what the feeling is, but something is tugging at me that requires my attention, that says: Put this into words and see what it is.

How do you get over the resistance to write?

In part, I don't. I can always find an excuse—the laundry, my students' essays, a letter to write, a phone call—and often I let those things get in the way of writing. I don't fight it too much because I know that when the thing I am listening for gets loud enough, I won't be able to do those other things anyway. The thing I am listening for will take center stage, and there's nothing I can do then but write. Until I am done with the work, I have no resistance to write.

But how do you get over your resistance to write when you have an assignment as students do?

I try to find my way into the assignment. I try to make it mine. When I was a student, I imagined I was not writing for my professor, but for myself. I asked: What interests me in this question? What do I believe is important here? I got tangled up when I thought about the grade, about whether I was doing the assignment correctly, about whether it was what the professor wanted. If I could let that kind of thinking go (the thinking that censors creativity and exploration) and write because I cared about the subject, I could overcome the resistance to the work.

As a teacher of writing, I tell students, "Follow your interest in the subject. Let the assignment take you somewhere. Let it let you discover what you think."

How do you develop a draft that may be rewritten?

Every draft I write will need to be rewritten—that's what a draft is. It's a start. Then comes the next draft. And the next, and the next. Each draft is *What I Have So Far*. Rewriting is implicit in the word "draft." If writing can be compared to a tree, then revision is its process of leafing out. The first draft might be the wintry tree, branches like lace in the sky, but leafless. Revision fills out the tree, gives the writer the depth and breadth she needs. Revision never stops. Even after something is published, the revising goes on, even if only in the writer's head as she reads the printed words.

The early part of the process is then like this: After I get a possible first line, I write some more, then read what I have written, making changes along the way. Every new word and line requires changes in the lines around it, and maybe even adjusts what I have done in the previous paragraphs. Then I write some more, then read, make changes. Reading over what I have written keeps me on track and helps me go deeper. I have to keep reading the words to tell me what I have said so I can decide if that is what I mean and so I know what to say next.

Once I have a draft, revision begins. I read it so I can know what it is I have, so I can get ready to start again with the first line and go through, line by line, revising, adding new sections, moving lines and sections around, reshaping the development and expanding, always expanding, cutting, always cutting, adjusting, always adjusting as I go along.

Revision not huge, mainly details

How do you know when you need to rewrite?

Ernest Hemingway said it best when he stated that revision is "getting the words right." This is it. So I revise when the words don't sound right in my head; when I read the words and cringe; when I feel gaps open before my eyes; when, as I read the words, I keep wanting to change them, to make them sound better. When I keep thinking, "I'd better show this to so-and-so for another opinion." When I don't know if it's good enough or says what I mean to say.

I don't know what it feels like to not need to rewrite, since rewriting is what writing is.

What attitudes do you find helpful as you begin to revise?

In all areas of my life, I am an impatient person. Except in writing, and in the revision that implies. When it comes to writing, I am eternally patient. I forget about time, about responsibilities, about the bread in the oven, about my friend next door who is not feeling well, about my dog who needs a walk. Some might call it selfish, but I call it being patient with the writing.

Some might call it discipline, but I still call it being patient with the writing. Patience is what allows me to linger over a paragraph, to reconsider a line 25 times, to search for a word or the meaning I am trying to find. Patience is returning to the first line over and over again until I am ready to go on. In writing one novel, I spent three months revising the first twelve pages; then I went on to write the rest of the story—over four hundred pages—in six months. That's patience.

I love my subjects and want to get the writing as close to "right" as I can. If I don't feel strongly about a subject, if I don't really care, I will let it go. But when I am invested in it, when I believe that what I have to say matters (if only to me), and when I want to find out what it is I am trying to say, then I revise because it's the only way to go. If I want to see spring come to the wintry tree, I have to draw in the leaves.

What specific process(es) do you try when rewriting?

I rely on line-by-line reading as the basis for all revision. In the single line are the words that tell me what I need to know: Do I need more? Do I need less? Have I gotten it right? What do the words say? Is that exactly what I mean? The word "exactly" is the key—this is the heart of revision for me.

When I change a line, then I go back to the start of the paragraph again and read it through, making more changes. This will often take me back to the previous paragraph, which may take me back to the start of the section or chapter. Over and over, reading, adjusting, reading, adjusting. This is the only revision I know.

Leaving the work for short periods is also helpful to me. This allows the unconscious to get to work, to tell me what I need to know. If I turn my attention to something else—cooking, walking, grading papers, writing a letter—at some point the writing will budge its way into my thoughts. A word, a phrase, a line will come. A piece of information, retrieved from some deep place inside my brain, will nudge me. If I can't go directly to the writing, I jot down the idea. "Leah will write a letter to Will before she leaves home." Or, "Don't forget to include what Lewis said." Or, "More on the motorcycle." If I don't write these thoughts down as they come, I lose them.

Once I have a draft, it is helpful to find a reader I can trust, someone who will act as a mirror to me and tell me what I have done. I don't need a lot of response at this point. I need to know what works, first; what doesn't work, second. Once I learn these things, it's time to go back to the first line of the first page and start in reading and revising against the backdrop of the reader's response.

Revision is, again, a process of being patient so the material can tell me what I need to know.

What tools do you use?

My tools might also be the atmosphere in which I write, the cup of tea I hold against my cheek when I am thinking so the steam rises before my eyes, the books on the shelves beside the place where I write, the photographs on the wall, and the window which opens to a small grassy area, then to woods and sky.

It took me a long time to give up paper and pencil as I composed. The texture of paper, the feel of the pencil in my hand, the beauty of the letters as they were shaped, these were once important tools for me. Now I use paper and pencil only for note taking. Now the computer, a laptop, is the main concrete tool of writing.

What three things do you wish you'd known as a college student about writing?

Before college I had written poetry, and bits and pieces of essays, on my own; my school experience with writing had been discouraging and disheartening, nearly squashing the wish I had first felt at age nine to be a writer when it was a fascination with words, a delight in imagination, and a recognition that stories conveyed the human experience that drew me.

Amazingly, in college I learned that academic writing is not the only way to express oneself. In my freshman composition class I wrote personal narrative essays—it was my first school experience with writing about what mattered to me. I learned what it felt like to be immersed in a writing project. I learned the thrill of the private world of writing, that discovery and learning take place for me by writing to find out what I think and know. I learned the importance of shape and form through the discovery of the subject—a revelation! Form follows content, I discovered. There is hope, I thought.

My college writing instructor opened the door to what writing is all about. Though I was given specific assignments, within those assignments was great latitude. I was asked to write a compare/contrast essay, and was given two possible forms for this assignment, but I was allowed to choose my own subject. I was asked to write about a person who had influenced me, but the shape and development of the essay was of my own choosing. I thrived and was successful for the first time in an academic setting.

The rest of my college experience was purely academic; all of it was valuable, but not always for the reasons my instructors intended.

Mainly learned other styles in college

Chapter 2 HOW TO GET THE WRITING DONE:

TRICKS OF THE WRITER'S TRADE

If one wants to write, one simply has to organize one's life in a mass of little habits.

—GRAHAM GREENE

This is the first important lesson that the writer must learn. Writing a novel is gathering smoke. It's an excursion into the ether of ideas. There's no time to waste. You must work with that idea as well as you can, jotting down notes and dialogue. . . . It doesn't matter what time of day you work, but you have to work every day because creation, like life, is always slipping away from you.

—WALTER MOSLEY

If writing a book is impossible, write a chapter.
If writing a chapter is impossible, write a page.
If writing a page is impossible, write a paragraph.
If writing a paragraph is impossible, write a sentence.
If writing a sentence is impossible, write a word and teach yourself everything there is to know about that word and then write another, connected word and see where the connection leads.

—RICHARD RHODES

Writing is a not a mystery. It is a craft, a habit, a discipline that can be understood and practiced. It is rooted in a daily habit. The writer who writes for revision does not wait for a final draft but works through a series of discovery, development, and clarification drafts until a significant meaning is found and made clear to a reader.

There is something wonderfully ordinary about writing. The result may be magical, it may even be called art, but the work of great writers and ordinary writers is the same: it is the product of ass-in-writing-chair, day after day, week after week, month after month, year after year.

After writing for more than 60 years, I still take instruction from Camilo José Cela, the Spanish Nobel laureate:

> *Picasso once said, "I don't know if inspiration exists, but when it comes, it usually finds me working." One time a woman asked Baudelaire what inspiration was, and he responded by saying, "Inspiration is something that commands me to work every single day." And Dostoyevsky said, "Genius is nothing more than a long, sustained patience." What a person has to do is sit himself down before a stack of blank papers, which is in itself terrifying. There is nothing as frightening as a stack of blank pieces of paper and the thought that I have to fill them from top to bottom, placing letters one after the other—and I begin to write. If nothing occurs to me, I remain seated at the writing table until something finally does come to mind.*

Flannery O'Connor, short story and novel writer, explained:

> *Every morning between 9:00 and 12:00 I go to my room and sit before a piece of paper. Many times I just sit for three hours with no ideas coming to me. But I know one thing: If an idea does come between 9:00 and 12:00, I am there ready for it.*

Writers write. It is that simple. And writers suffer the same problems in getting started as nonwriters. In fact, the more you are published, the higher the expectations placed on you by editors, readers, and yourself and, therefore, the more likely you are to suffer paralysis. We never are prepared enough; never feel we have the authority to be an authority; never believe we write well enough; never have the time, the place, the tools; always have other responsibilities that have to be faced first; and on and on. All the excuses may be legitimate, but writers write despite all the good reasons not to write.

Here are some tricks of the writer's trade that will help get the writing done.

Nulla Dies Sine Linea

"Never a day without a line" was probably what the ancient cave artists told their young before written history. It was the counsel of Horace, who lived from 65 B.C. to 8 B.C., and it has been the counsel of writers in every century since. Put rear end in chair every day and keep it there until the writing is done.

Writing becomes relatively easy if writing becomes a daily habit. I write in the morning in my office where I have my computer, my files, my music. I have my own writing ritual: pick out the CDs I will play while working, check my e-mail, then attend to the writing task I assigned myself at the end of yesterday's writing. I know the task and my brain has been working on what I may say. Most mornings, the writing flows.

The writing becomes expected in the way you are expected to wait on tables, show up for your job in the emergency room, deliver papers early every morning. Roger Simon of the *Baltimore Sun* explained, "There is no such thing as writer's block. My father drove a truck for 40 years. And never once did he wake up in the morning and say: 'I have truck driver's block today. I am not going to work.'"

Most writers, myself included, were late-at-night writers in college. This was true for me also when I first worked on a newspaper. It is a romantic time to write, and I still remember the special feeling of loneliness, of being awake when others slept, that seemed to encourage great thoughts. But most writers, by the time they are 30, follow the advice of the great German author Goethe who said, "Use the day before the day. Early morning hours have gold in their mouth." John McPhee, the master nonfiction writer, used to loop his bathrobe belt through a chair and tie himself in until the writing was done. Novelist Jessamyn West stayed in her nightclothes until she reached her daily quota. John Hersey, journalist and novelist, said, "To be a writer is to sit down at one's desk in the chill portion of every day, and to write."

Amos Oz testifies, "I . . . have my coffee and come down to this room, sit at my desk and wait. Without reading, listening to music or answering the phone. Then I write, sometimes a sentence, sometimes a paragraph, in a good day half a page. But I am here at least seven or eight hours every day. I used to feel guilty about an unproductive morning, especially when I lived on the kibbutz, and everyone else was ploughing fields, milking cows, planting trees. Now I think of my work as that of a shopkeeper: it is my job to open up in the morning, sit and wait for customers. If I get some, it is a blessed morning, if not, well, I'm still doing my job. So the guilt has gone, and I try to stick to my shopkeeper's routine."

Productivity is the result of regularity. I count words, trying to write every day, but failing. On my bulletin board wall are the word counts for the past five years and five months. In that time I have written 1,472,199 words. I had 1,976 possible writing days but only used 1,640 of them, or 83%. I did, however, average 898 words per writing day. In that same period I experienced all the distractions of ordinary life, but day by day some work got done.

Establish Achievable Deadlines

Most students see deadlines as an enemy. The deadline is my friend. If I do not have a deadline I never finish a piece of writing. I welcome, in fact, insist that editors give me deadlines. Then I set my own deadline a bit earlier to give myself room for life's interruptions. My Tuesday column for the *Boston Globe* is due by Friday. I deliver it on Monday, nine days ahead of publication. If for some reason the unexpected occurs—a doctor's appointment, a long weekend, a sick computer—I do not worry. I have plenty of time to write—and rewrite in response to the editor's reading.

Break a Writing Assignment into Small Daily Tasks

Once the deadline is established, I work backward, breaking the project down into a series of small daily tasks. Years ago, a nephew of mine, a psychology professor at the University of New York at Stony Brook, told me that 90 minutes is the maximum learning time for most people. That made me keep track of my writing time for months, and, indeed, 90 minutes was the maximum time I was efficient. In fact, I usually produced drafts in much smaller chunks of time—4 minutes, 7, 12, 20, 30, 45, 60. A computer program called "Time Tool" makes it possible to keep track of exactly how long it takes to complete a writing task. It is usually far less than we imagine.

I am also most productive when I have a single writing task each day. Sometimes I have to work on two projects—as I am doing right now to meet deadlines on this edition and a new book, due the same week—but I do not like to divide my concentration. I break long projects into brief daily tasks: "draft beginning for Chapter 1," "develop middle of Chapter 1," "get new character on stage in second chapter of novel," "develop hospital scene," "sketch in antipollution argument," "write essay ending." I know the task I am going to be working on the next morning when I leave my writing desk.

I do the same thing with research: "get list of sources from library," "call first three sources," "schedule victim interview," "read brain scan article," "watch operation tape, take notes," "e-mail secondary sources." As a rock climber explained as she completed a record several-day climb in California, "You eat an elephant a bite at a time."

Know Tomorrow's Task Today

One of the most important tricks of the writer's trade is, at the end of the writing session, to know the writing task you face when you return to your desk. You don't know what you are going to write—the writing comes in the writing—but you should know the territory and the task. *I'm going to write a*

Thanksgiving Day column for the Boston Globe. I don't know what I'm going to say, but I do know I'm going to deal with the giving of thanks and that it will be done in about 800 words. Or the task may be drafting a sketch outline for Chapter 4, developing the middle of Chapter 4, finishing Chapter 4.

The writer A. Manette Ansay states that, "At the end of each day of writing, I leave myself with a technical question I can come back to the next day. By technical question, I mean maybe there's a passage of dialogue I want to look at because it sounds stilted or it doesn't sound realistic. Maybe I notice that the voice isn't strong—there are some bobbles—and I want to look at diction. I want to look at the consistency of my word choice and begin there, by trying to work with particular words to see what isn't quite authentic to the character. Maybe I've noticed four or five or six really heavily connected words that are suggesting a theme that I wasn't aware of in the work, and so I'm going to begin with that problem. Maybe I'm going to look at the way in which I'm motivating flashback, because if I'm using the same device [over and over] there's a problem. Maybe some of those flashbacks don't need to be there."

Keep a Daybook

I have just started my 113th daybook, National 33-008, 80 narrow-ruled Eye-Ease green pages, eight by ten inches, spiral bound. It is my mobile office, carried in the outside pocket of the case that is always near me, upstairs, downstairs, at the meeting, the hockey game, the concert, in the car, on the plane.

I call it a daybook because it is not a journal. When I called it a journal, I become pompous and laughed at what I had written with self-conscious self-importance. It is not a diary. I am far too well married. It is a writer's log, a field book, a lab book, a business account book. I chose "daybook" for its very ordinariness. It is not a literary book but a working notebook in which I keep account of my daily writing, record problems and solutions, new ideas, observation notes, quotes from writers, and these days sketches. It is also a place where I can paste things I want to reread, a place to make notes, draft titles, lists, lines, what I am talking to myself about.

Rehearse

My writing day really begins when I finish the morning's writing. Each morning I discover that the well has filled in the last 24 hours, and I can draw from it because I assigned my conscious, unconscious, and subconscious to play with what I may write tomorrow. Writing is thinking, and thought does not begin with a conclusion but an itch, a hint, a clue, a question, a doubt, a wonder, a problem, an answer without a question, an image that refuses to be forgotten. I rehearse what I may write, trying out lines, hooking fragments of information together, seeing patterns of meaning in my head, on the three-by-five-inch cards I always carry in my shirt pocket, in my daybook, and, sometimes, on the computer. I silently—and sometimes out loud to my wife's surprise—talk to myself about what I may write.

When I return to my writing desk the next morning I often feel empty, barren of any ideas, but when I start to write I find writing comes to the screen. And if I haven't rehearsed or rehearsal has not worked, I don't wait for an idea; I start writing. Writing produces writing.

A Writer's Place

A writing room reinforces the writing habit, and I am fortunate these days to have my own writing room under the back porch (with a glass wall that looks out on my woods), with my computer, fax, copier, scanner, printer, all my tools as well as my music and my books. But I am not always here and I have learned to create a writing space in an airport or on a plane, in a hotel room or on my daughter's dining room table, on a roadside picnic table or in a doctor's waiting room.

If you can't have a room, use a desk in a corner of a room, or a table in the library or cafeteria, or an empty classroom you can make into your writing room.

I have a shoulder bag that holds my daybook, calendar/address book, a "to read and edit" file, pens, glue, scissors, and, often, my laptop computer. When I am not traveling the laptop sits beside my chair in the room where we read, watch TV, listen to music. I open up the laptop and have a writing space away from my office. Learn how to make a space where writing will happen.

Each writer has to develop a writing habit, and that pattern will change according to the writer's experience with a writing task, the writer's thinking and working style, as well as the external demands on the writer's time. Develop your own writing habit. Mine keeps changing with experience, new writing tasks, changes in my life, but discipline is essential to the writing and rewriting process. Study the conditions when the writing has gone well and try to reproduce them. And be realistic. Don't try to schedule what will take two hours in fifteen minutes before class or plan your writing time to coincide with the kids coming home from school or with the nightly hall hockey game in the dorm.

All these habits are aimed at producing a draft that is worthy of revision—and as many following drafts as is necessary to discover and clarify a meaning.

As novelist Richard Bausch explains, "I go into the workroom and shake the black ball and wait for something to surface. If I don't recall it, then it probably wasn't worth remembering. I have faith that the good things will resurface, will rise, if given the chance. I merely have to be faithful enough to the task to provide it with that chance. And that means showing up for work in the mornings: Doing, each day, this day's work. That's what I keep saying to my students: to recite that mantra and live by it. No other questions asked, no other thoughts, no worries about outcomes or the future or what the next writer is doing. Just: This day's work. 'Did I work today?' That is the only question you allow yourself, and you aim to be able to answer 'Yes' on most days, and then leave it there."

Chapter 3 READING FOR REVISION

Be careful what you read. Willa Cather used to read from the Bible every morning before she started writing. There's some possibility, of course, that it was an act of piety, but it was also, I'm sure, a way of getting those rhythms, that music, that poetry.

—David McCullough

I read stories I love over and over again. I just finished reading a Lorrie Moore story—you know, the one about the baby with cancer ["People Like That Are the Only People Here," The New Yorker, *1/27/97]—that I must have read twenty times. And it isn't, obviously, that I'm reading it to find out what happens. I just want to be there with her. Any story that I really love can make me feel like that.*

—Alice Munro

One has to have a good ear, but you also have to read what you're working on aloud. Even if you have a good inner ear there are certain awkwardnesses that only become apparent when you speak out loud. At some stage, you have to at least mutter to yourself. When I'm writing it out, I do a lot of muttering.

—Denise Levertov

When writers finish the final draft, the job of writing isn't finished. They use test readers the way actors and directors use a dress rehearsal to see how those who have not seen the rehearsals react. Writers need readers who have not seen early drafts, do not know what the writer hopes is on the pages. Their response helps the writer produce a final draft that is final.

Test Readers

To make sure we have read what is on the page, we turn to test readers who will read our writing in progress, when change is not only possible but inevitable. We have developed, clarified, documented, shaped, and polished the draft until we need to have it read by stranger eyes. The process of discovery goes on. They do not agree. They bring their own autobiography to the reading and their seeing makes us see in our own drafts what we have not seen before.

Where Do We Find Test Readers?

We are surrounded by potential test readers:

- *Writing colleagues.* The friends and associates who also write and with whom we share writing problems, attitudes, solutions, complaints. They are engaged in the writing process and they can help us understand where we are in the writing process.
- *Topic authorities.* We can try our drafts on those who are expert in the field in which we are writing. They can help us understand the topic, the context, the nuance, the structure of our writing.
- *General reader.* We need to try a draft on readers who do not know—or care—about our topic to see what we need to add, cut, or change.
- *Members of the class or work group with whom we are writing.* They face the same tasks as we do and can be very helpful in responding to our drafts.
- *The teachers, editors, and employers for whom we are writing.* Everyone around us is a potential test reader.

What Test Readers Do

Test readers first ask two key response questions.

What Works?

I often know what is wrong with a draft; in fact, I often feel that everything is wrong with the draft, that I have failed as a writer, that the project is hopeless, that I cannot write and will never learn to write well.

Readers can tell me what does work for them, what meanings and feelings are found in the draft—or sparked in the reader. Effective revision begins, as we have discussed, by building on what is effective in the draft, and readers-in-process help us discover our strengths.

What Needs Work?

Once we know what works we can attend to what needs work, what needs development, explanation, attribution, documentation, clarity, grace.

I have never learned to like criticism but I know I must not blame the reader, but find a way to make that reader understand. If a test reader doesn't get my meaning, other readers won't. My job is to find a way to make my writing clear to the most reluctant, disinterested, critical reader.

The Danger of Test Readers

Not everyone, however, is a good reader for us on this draft at this stage of the process. My scissors and glue stand in a wooden holder in which is carved a quotation from the writer H. G. Wells: "No passion in the world is equal to the passion to alter someone else's draft."

It is easy to get readers, hard to find good readers who can help us improve what we have written. Every edition of this text is reviewed by test readers who are careful, professional, and detailed in their criticisms, but some are less helpful than others. Those who are not a great help respond in terms of the book they want to write or the book they imagine I should write, not the book I am writing or can write. They may be right—but they are not helpful. I need readers who can make my writing better.

We must pay attention to test readers—but not too much attention. I have drafts of poems, stories, articles, and even books I have written that will never be published because I paid too much attention to irrelevant or destructive criticism. And sometimes that criticism comes in praise that is destructive, congratulating me for meanings in which I do not believe.

I pay attention to those test readers who nail me for trying to get away with shortchanging the reader. I had tried, for example, to skimp on doing a complete job of research, on providing objective evidence to support each point in my argument. I knew I needed more research—or more development, a stronger structure, a surer voice, more polish—and the reader sent me back to the writing desk where I knew I should have gone on my own.

I pay equal attention to those readers who shock me with their response, saying what I never expected. If I have a prejudice—and we all do—I am pro-Semitic. I was most comfortable as a teenager the year I lived in an Orthodox Jewish neighborhood, many of my best friends are indeed Jews, one of my son-in-laws is Jewish, and my grandsons are, therefore, half-Jewish. Yet a test reader charged that a novel of mine was anti-Semitic. Believe me, I paid attention, reading it line by line to make sure I wasn't and submitting it to other Jewish readers to make sure that was not possible.

And I have a rule that I could not always invoke when I was a student and can't always follow when I write for a publication or a particular publishing house, but always follow in choosing my personal test readers. I never return to a reader who doesn't make me eager to get back to my writing desk. The criticism I received may be extensive, hard-to-take, but the good reader makes me see new possibilities, new challenges in the draft. I seek and treasure such readers. They are the readers on whom I depend during my lifelong apprenticeship to the writer's craft.

Setting the Reader's Agenda

Chip Scanlan, friend and writer, is usually my first test reader and I am his but it took us a long time to realize how often we were giving the writer more than he wanted at that stage of the writing process. We found there were many kinds of readings and that the reading changed as we moved through the writing process.

Reading before Writing. It is often helpful to talk before writing, to hear how we describe the project to another person. We often hear ourselves saying what we do not expect and what we say may reveal unexpected possibilities or reveal predictable problems that will have to be solved in the research or writing. The reader's response to the idea can help us focus our attention and we can also hear the questions that must be answered. William Maxwell, novelist and editor, said, "I feel that the novelist has a moral obligation not to leave the reader with unanswered questions." That is just as true for nonfiction as fiction.

Reading a Rough Draft. After we complete a first draft or even a later draft that is still rough and unfinished, we often need a reader to ignore the undeveloped sections, the lack of documentation, an uneven pace, poor sentence structure, incorrect spelling, typos and concentrate on a key question the writer needs answered: will this topic interest a reader, do I have a working skeleton or structure that can be filled in, do I have an approach that will serve the reader, is this genre the best one, what research must I do, what questions will the reader have that I must answer.

Making a Movie. When the draft is close to being finished, do what many of my writing friends call making a movie of our reading. The reader gives the writer a live, running commentary on how the reader is responding to the draft. The reader can point out where the writer gives too much or too little, what stimulates the mind or emotions or does neither, where the draft needs to be sped up or slowed down, where more documentation is needed.

Line-by-Line Reading. When we have completed the final draft, then we invite a test reader or two to go through it line by line, not ignoring the larger questions if they come to mind, but focusing on each word, each sentence, each comma or dash, each paragraph. Every nit must be picked and each sentence examined in context. Chip often reads his final draft aloud to his wife, Kathy Fair, and I have my wife read my drafts, red pen in hand.

George Orwell's rules are good ones to follow in a line reading, especially:

(i) Never use a metaphor, simile, or other figure of speech which you are used to seeing in print.

(ii) Never use a long word where a short one will do.

(iii) If it is possible to cut a word out, always cut it out.

(iv) Never use the passive where you can use the active.

(v) Never use a foreign phrase, a scientific word, or jargon word if you can think of an everyday English equivalent.

(vi) Break any of these rules sooner than say anything barbarous.

Reading Writing in Process

When I share a draft without telling the reader what kind of help I need, I get into trouble. If I reveal a tentative draft when I don't know if I have a subject and the reader responds with a line-by-line criticism appropriate to a final draft, it angers me—worse, it doesn't help. And I have done the same thing for others. Someone shows me a draft and I respond with concerns about voice when the writer wanted to check the organization. We need to suggest the reading we need to get effective help.

Some of the readings we—and you—may need:

- "This is very rough. Don't worry about that, I just want to know if I have a subject."
- "Should this be written in another genre? Is my essay a narrative?"
- "What do you think I'm trying to say?"
- "Would anyone be interested?"
- "Is this voice right for the subject?"
- "Where does my voice falter?"
- "Am I making myself clear?"
- "Would you keep reading?"
- "Where does it bog down?"
- "Where does it race ahead of your understanding?"
- "Is there a clear line from beginning to end?"
- "Is this fully developed?"
- "Have I included too much?"
- "Do I have enough documentation? Too much?"
- "Where do you need more evidence?"
- "Where could I sharpen the language?"
- "Will you read it line by line? I think I'm done and need a careful reading."

The questions go back and forth depending on the project, the audience, our strengths and weaknesses on that draft, but the purpose of the response is to help the writer and to do that, the writer should initiate the kind of reading that will be helpful.

Techniques of Responding

Today we are fortunate to have many ways to get a response to a draft or part of a draft. I may use the post office, FedEx, or UPS to get a draft to a reader. I also have a fax and, most used of all, e-mail. The draft of this book, for example, was e-mailed, chapter by chapter, from my office in my home in New Hampshire to my editor's home office in Texas. Once the manuscript is received, the response can be delivered in a number of different ways.

Responding in Person

The ideal way for me is face to face, for example, when I meet with my friend Harvey Shepherd, a physicist and a poet, over lunch and a poem. The face-to-face meeting in conference with a colleague, a teacher, or an editor has a great advantage. We can read the tone of voice, the facial expressions, the body language of the writer and tune the intensity and the extent of our suggestions to their acceptance or resistance. We can tell when we are going too far or not far enough, when we are too detailed or too global in our comments, when the writer is taking our suggestions personally, when we are being destructive or helpful.

One of my editors, Tom Newkirk, lives across the street and we can meet over a draft on his dining room table, in my office, or, most often, at Young's or the Gateway (favorite eateries) for an early breakfast.

Responding by Phone

The reader on whom I depend the most, Chip Scanlan, now lives in Florida. Brock Dethier, the most effective reader of my academic writing, used to be a neighbor and now lives in Utah; and Ralph Fletcher, who used to live in Alabama, has moved back to Durham. Don Graves has left Durham for the mountains of New Hampshire. I also have editors in Portsmouth, New Hampshire; Boston, Massachusetts; New York City; and Federalsburg, Maryland.

Most of the responses I receive to my drafts come by telephone. My readers can't read my face and my body language but they can hear my voice—and my pauses and hesitations. They can tune their voice to my voice and mine to theirs.

Responding by E-mail

E-mail has changed how I work with my test readers and my editors. This draft, for example, was sent to my editor in Texas by e-mail and she inserted her questions and suggestions into the text and sent it back to New Hampshire. I responded to her concerns and returned it by e-mail. All my recent columns and books have been submitted, edited, and revised the same way. Such written responses have the disadvantage that the reader cannot "read" the recipient, but there are great advantages to the snail-mailed, faxed, or e-mailed written response. The criticism must be more carefully considered. It can be precise—either marked on the draft, on yellow sticky notes or tags glued to the draft, or with specific references to the draft within the response.

And the writer has the opportunity to study the criticisms carefully, over time, before responding. Often it takes me some time to accept and understand what my readers say. In teaching, I have found it helpful to employ all these methods by having individual, face-to-face conferences as well as in-class responses, and to use the telephone or writing to respond to student drafts.

Methods of Reader Response

There are many ways to encourage a reading in process that will help the writer. Writers, teachers, editors have their own ways of encouraging and controlling a reader's response and I have my own.

The Basic Transaction

- The writer explains the type of reading he needs and/or his main concern.
- The readers read the draft with the writer's instructions in mind.
- The readers tell the writer what they think works and needs work.

- The writer doesn't defend or explain but does ask follow-up questions that clarify the readers' responses.
- The readers make any other suggestions that they think will help the reader achieve the writer's intention.

Large Group Response

The whole class or large group workshop follows the basic transaction. One variation I found helpful was to have the group read the draft before the meeting.

I have found it helpful to staple several sheets of paper to the draft and have the members of the class write their responses to the questions "What works?" and "What needs work?" It is important to keep the paper moving and to get as many responses as possible so that the writer has to absorb and reconcile contradictions, taking back control of the draft in the process.

I have also found it valuable for the class or workshop to read the best papers, not the worst, to find out why the best papers were best, and to explore how they could be made better.

Small Group Response

I have found that the dynamics of small groups differ greatly according to size. Sometimes I choose the groups randomly but usually I choose the best students in the class and build the groups around them so that each group has its own "teacher" or expert practitioner. I've also found it worthwhile for the groups to stay together for a number of sessions so they see each member's work in process over time. Often I've had the groups pick the best paper and present it to the whole class, explaining why it was good. Too often we focus on the obvious failures instead of the less obvious successes.

Quintets. Five students seems ideal. It is large enough to get a variety of responses, small enough that five minutes a draft or twenty-five minutes a session can accomplish a lot.

Quartets. The even number of four too often allows an even split in response.

Trios. Three students work better than four or two but not as well as five because the number of responses is limited.

Partners. We all need writing partners. I have many of them I use when I am writing in a particular genre—poetry, fiction, nonfiction—and several I use all the time. The most important question for me is how I feel after I receive the response. If the response makes me eager to get back to my writing desk, I try to keep that partner. If not, good-bye. This has nothing to do with the toughness of the criticism; it has everything to do with whether I found that person's response constructive or destructive of me, the writer.

Teacher Response

Mort Howell, my freshman English teacher at Tilton Junior College, was my most important writing teacher, but his way of teaching paid no attention to my learning style. He criticized, marked over, rewrote everything I wrote. I hated it but respected it because what he did to my writing made it better, damn it.

After the war Carroll Towle, my writing teacher at the University of New Hampshire, held weekly conferences in which he puffed clouds of smoke at me from a vile corncob pipe and delivered clouds of rhetoric in mini-lectures I couldn't understand at the time. They seemed to have no relationship to my poem lying on his desk. But when I was writing that night—or a week or a lifetime later—I would find myself improving my draft because of something I half-remembered he said.

We have to listen to our teachers and we have to perform—let's be realistic—to their standards, learning what we can and preserving our own voices at the same time.

The late Richard Hugo, poet, mystery writer, writing teacher, told his students:

> *You'll never be a poet until you realize that everything I say today and this quarter is wrong. It may be right for me, but it is wrong for you. Every moment, I am, without wanting or trying to, telling*

you to write like me. But I hope you learn to write like you. In a sense, I hope I don't teach you how to write but how to teach yourself to write. At all times keep your crap detector on. If I say one thing that helps, good. If what I say is of no help, let it go.

Don't start arguments. They are futile and take us away from our purpose. As Yeats noted, your important arguments are with yourself. If you don't agree with me don't listen. Think about something else.

Editor Response

When I first started writing, I resisted editors. I wanted to protect the style I did not yet have against attack. I took all criticism personally. Still do too often. But I need strong editors. In the 12 years I have written my column I have had editors who never touch a line, editors who have a compulsive need to twiddle around with line-by-line trivia, and strong editors who give me a strong response. The strong response is best. I can be more daring if I know that someone is there to catch me before I make a fool of myself.

The fact is that I have to please my editors or go somewhere else. My ego now allows me to realize that if the editor misreads my draft, so will many readers, and so I must find a way by my editor, another way of saying what I feel must be said.

The Writer's Own Response

All the responses from readers by snail mail or e-mail, in large groups or small, should help the writer respond more effectively to the writer's own draft while writing, revising, and editing. Writing is a reading act. We read what we write as we write it. It is never quite what we intend and so we read it with surprise, despair, joy, discomfort and revise it, through many readings by others and ourselves until we finish the final draft and send it into the world.

Chapter 4
REWRITE WITH FOCUS

. . . if there is one gift more essential to a novelist than another it is the power of combination—the single vision.

—Virginia Woolf

Good writing takes place at intersections, at what you might call knots, at places where the society is snarled or knotted up.

—Margaret Atwood

Don't put anything in a story that does not reveal character or advance the action.

—Kurt Vonnegut Jr.

Focus is as important in writing as it is in photography. We are seduced by focus, drawn toward what the artist sees, thinks, feels. Focus makes the ordinary extraordinary. Focus attracts and instructs. Focus selects and provides significance. Focus brings meaning and clarity to the disorder of the world.

When I had writing students who went on to law school, many would come back to report that the best training they had came from my classes where they had to find the meaningful in a confusion of information. Focus is the tool that is necessary to scholarship and marketing, baseball and making love, worship and research, politics and management, hunting and art, medical diagnosis and technological invention.

Elements of Focus

To learn to focus we have to learn three skills and usually apply them in the following sequence.

Selection

The academic world often scoffs at the arts, saying that all the arts are emotional, touchy-feely, egocentric, without intellectual vigor and discipline. Not true. At the center of all the arts—painting, composing and performing, acting and directing, writing—is the essential intellectual discipline of selection. Our eyes play a continual movie in our brain while life streams by. Our eyes provide an ever-changing soundtrack. We are assaulted by tastes, smells, texture. Inside our skulls the brain produces emotions, thoughts, questions, doubts. Images, and the memories of what we have lived, studied, read, imagined.

Life would be an overwhelming confusion if it were not for the artists—including writers—who turn random sounds into music, conflict into drama, experience into narrative. Artists select what is important, what will help us survive the incredible richness and confusion of experience. As Graham Greene pointed out this is both a hazard and a help for the artist:

> *When I construct a scene, I don't describe the hundredth part of what I see; I see the characters scratching their noses, walking about, tilting back in their chairs—even after I've finished writing—so much so that after a while I feel a weariness which does not derive all that much from my effort of imagination but is more like a visual fatigue: My eyes are tired from watching my characters.*

But Greene goes on to describe the benefit for the artist:

> *Writing is a form of therapy; sometimes I wonder how all those who do not write, compose or paint can manage to escape the madness, the melancholia, the panic fear which is inherent in the human situation.*

I believe it is through the arts that we escape. The artist selects for us what is significant, what we must pay attention to, what will order our world.

Emphasis

And that leads us to emphasis. We must make sure that what is most important is clear to the reader. My friend Chip Scanlan teaches journalists to find the focus under the immediate pressures of news deadlines—*What's the news? What's the story?*—and that also applies to the research paper, the memo, the argument, the critical essay.

First of all, I must answer the question: "What is the one thing I must say?" For years—decades—I fought this, wanting to say two things or three or more. No matter what clever designs I created, what rhetorical tricks I employed, what new approaches I created, they all collapsed in confusion. In writing my column and my textbooks, my poems and my novels, my essays and my articles, I could only say one thing. Everything in the piece of writing had to lead to or away from that single message.

Focus makes sure that one meaning is emphasized, and once that is established everything in the piece of writing must support and develop that meaning.

Clarity

With a camera we select the picture to be taken, decide what to emphasize within the picture, and finally make the picture clear, bring it into focus. To do this we must anticipate and answer the reader's questions, define and document, develop and clarify word by word, line by line, paragraph by paragraph, page by page, section by section until the entire piece is in focus.

Premature Focusing

For the last two years of high school my English teacher marched back and forth at the front of the room commanding us to focus. She kept repeating, "Know what you want to say before you say it" but when I put pencil to paper I wrote what I did not intend—and that is how I have lived my life. How boring it would be if I did know what I wanted to say; how exciting that the act of writing and rewriting produces surprise. Her focus could not be mine—and of course I could not state the focus in advance of writing. The focus must arise from the draft.

Of course the page and my head are not completely blank. I come to the page with the life I have lived, all that I have seen and imagined, thought and wondered about, learned and unlearned. I have answers without questions, questions without answers, fears and hopes and concerns. Images. Fragments of ideas. Phrases. Memories.

I grab one and put it down. It is something that has bothered me but not enough to research it or think it through. It is sort of an unscratched itch. As I sit with my sketchbook open, the page empty, a scene comes to mind from the Durham Town Landing. In my mind, I see it ahead of me with a point of land marked by a tall pine jutting out from the right.

I begin to draw and my hand follows the line on the paper to see where it will take me. In drawing and writing, the act of making and creating reveals the true subject and the approach to the subject. But now the tree I see in my mind is no longer on the left, but it is on the right and it is not the tree at Durham Town Landing, but the tree at Half Mile Point in the lake at summer camp half a century ago. As I continue to draw, the tree now becomes a wind-bent pine that has survived many a storm and remains a landmark for every boat coming down Great Bay where the tidal water comes up to our town. I have brought that tree into focus the way I would if I were using a camera or if I were writing. I began thinking of one memory—one significant tree—and by allowing my mind and hand to wander, I discovered that I really wanted to explore the tree at Great Bay.

Writing and drawing are ways of paying attention and when we pay attention we learn. I discovered that pine in my drawing and in the writing above that reported the drawing.

Sometimes I come to the writing (or drawing) without intent but many times I have an intent—to begin this chapter; to write a column questioning the teachers who assign homework to prove they are demanding, not to help their students learn; to celebrate Memorial Day; to recall a scene from my war; to explore the experience of seeing a woman you have loved for 50 years grow old.

My high school English teacher and many others wanted me to write from meaning, to know the context before I began to write, to have the big picture in mind. Teacher after teacher demanded a thesis statement before I began to write. They commanded that I report on the end of the mental journey before it began. What they were asking me to do was to have a significant thought *before* I did the thinking. Writing is not reported thought. Writing is more important than that. It is thinking itself.

How to Focus

Effective writing begins with a specific detail that accumulates other specific details that grow, through the process of re-seeing and re-understanding that we call rewriting, into meaning. Writing discovers meaning and then shares it with the reader.

The List

The best way that I encourage focus to find me is the list that captures my conscious and subconscious. My lists help me focus. I write and rewrite my lists in free moments before I sit at my desk to write and sometimes when I do sit down to write. The list is made up of specific details: statistics, quotes, images, thoughts, ideas, questions, memories, whatever comes to mind. The details are not written out but captured in code words or specifics that will allow me to call them to mind if I need them.

I think I might write about graduation. It is that time of year. I have not been invited to give a commencement speech, but I wonder what I might say if I were to give one. I start with a list.

- cap and gown
- what's worn under
- see plagiarist get degree
- how will getting away with cheating affect his life?
- my father who didn't go to high school comes to my college graduation
- good teachers—three
- maybe two
- is two enough?
- first job in grocery store
- making sausage
- driving grocery truck, no license
- what learned out of school
- paper route
- collecting money from customers
- errand boy
- lectures, lectures, lectures
- who will hire an English major?
- now I can read what I want
- how to earn a tip
- how to get a raise

All my lists are private. I use code words to capture a possible focus. When I read over the list to discover what I might focus on, I ask myself three questions:

1. What surprised me?

   I thought the list would be about school but 9 of 20 were about working before and after school.

2. What connects?

   The 9 out of 20 school items connect and reveal a potential pattern that might come clear if I attempt to develop these ideas in writing.

3. What is in conflict?

There is an interesting and universal conflict between in-school and out-of-school learning.

Surprise is important because it leads me toward a new meaning. Perhaps I have something to say that is worth saying after all. In this case I am surprised by the specifics from outside the classroom.

Connections are important because they are trails that can be followed to where I have not gone before. As I look at the list I see connections there and in my mind—how did I get a raise from Mr. Miller, how did I learn to collect money for papers from people who were moving and did not intend to pay. I see myself driving the grocery truck before I had a license, arranging the grocery shelves, waiting on a customer. They all seem connected and if I write I may discover how they are connected.

To find a focus I look for a conflict, a tension, that will catch and hold the attention of a reader as I explore it. In this case it is obvious—what I learned out of the classroom has more meaning to me at this moment than what I learned in the classroom.

The Discovery Draft

The other principal technique I use to find the focus is to write a discovery draft in which the draft tells me what I should focus on in the draft. I do not write what I already know or what I expect to say, but I write what I do not know. I am thinking in writing, the most disciplined form of thought. And it is fun because I keep finding I know more than I expected, feel more than I expected, remember more, and have a stronger opinion than I expected.

Write with Velocity

I write my discovery draft as fast as I can because velocity is as important in writing a discovery draft as it is in riding a bicycle. You have to get up to speed to get anywhere. My handwriting and my typing are appallingly bad. It is hard to read what I've written at top speed but I must write with velocity to outrace the censor or to fail.

Outrace the Censor

All of us have the well-intentioned—parents, teachers, significant others, editors, the critical self—who censor what we say. It is important to write the discovery draft as fast as possible to escape them, not worrying about making sense or following the rules of language so we can discover what has been hidden in our minds.

Fail

Failure is essential to effective writing. It is the failure that instructs the chemist, the football coach, the defense attorney, the entrepreneur, the writer. An attempt is made. It doesn't work. But the way it fails instructs. Robyn Davidson, the travel writer who has written about traveling with nomads in *Desert Places,* said, "The French word for wanderlust or wandering is 'errance.' The etymology is the same as 'error.' So to wander is to make mistakes . . . allowing the mistakes to be part of the process."

Write Out Loud

The Spanish Nobel Prize–winning novelist, Camilo José Cela, says,

> *When I write I do it aloud. Many faults and cacophonies that the ear is able to catch cannot be seen on the written page. So, if it sounds poorly to my ear I can catch the error. Sometimes it takes me quite a long time to discover what isn't working, that a word is lacking or that one needs to be taken out, but I insist on searching for it and finally finding what's wrong; that there is a word missing or that a comma isn't placed correctly, etc. It comes from listening.*

We learned to speak before we wrote, and, even if we are writers, we speak thousands upon thousands of words more than we write in a day. When we write, we speak in written words. The magic of writing is that readers who may never meet us hear what we have written. Music rises from the page when we read.

We call the heard quality of writing *voice,* and it may be the most important element in writing. Voice, like background music in a movie, is tuned to the writing, supports and extends what the writing says.

Listen to master writers speak of voice:

> *I read everything that I write aloud. First, the paragraph. Then, the page. Then, the chapter. And finally, I read the whole book aloud. Because I want to hear my voice reading it, and I need it to sound natural.*
>
> —ISABEL ALLENDE, JOURNALIST AND NOVELIST

> *I hear a thousand "voices" in my head. They are the voices of my characters. They are male, female, white, brown, and yellow.*
>
> —BHARATI MUKHERJEE, NOVELIST

> *The longer you stay a writer, the more voices you find in your own voice and the more voices you find in the world.*
>
> —ALLAN GURGANUS, NOVELIST

But voice serves the writer before the reader. It is the voice of the writing that tells the writer the potential meaning of what is written in a discovery draft, reveals its emotional intensity, its importance to the writer and to readers. An eighteen-year-old college freshman might write:

> My first weekend home I expected everything to be the same as I left. The house had shrunk, the driveway was shorter than I remembered. The yard was smaller and my room had become a sewing room. My girlfriend had become a friend, a distant friend who asked me for advice about some Elmer. I gave it. As if I was some university stud, not a guy who hadn't even walked to class with a girl yet. My old friends were gone and my folks treated me like company. I was a stranger to my life and I liked it. I wasn't that kid who lived in my room. Mother came home early from the real estate

> office and we just talked as if I were her son's friend home from college. When Dad came home we had a beer and we went out to dinner with Uncle Val and my latest aunt. They treated me as if I were grown-up, dirty jokes and everything, and perhaps I was, perhaps my folks and I were friends.

I hear an individual voice, the voice of a person I'd like to know, someone who experiences the unexpected and makes something of it. I like the music of *"The house had shrunk, the driveway was shorter than I remembered," "some Elmer,"* and *"I was a stranger to my life and I liked it."* I suspect that voice has not yet been heard by the writer, but it should be. That draft needs to be developed, but it is a good first draft: a voice can be heard in a tailgating car wreck of language.

In the next draft, a student assigned to write a paper on British essayist George Orwell's "The Hanging" wrote a rough discovery draft that begins like this:

> I didn't like being assigned the Orwell essay in freshman English. I felt the instructor was messing with my head. My father is a sheriff and we believe in capital punishment and this is an English class and not political science or Liberal I. But I had to write a critical paper and read the essay one more time. It seemed to be about standing by and not doing anything, like when Joe was being made fun of I didn't join in but I didn't make friends either. After his suicide we tried to understand, I tried to, if there was anything I—or we—could have done. I remembered seeing what was happening, not knowing what would happen of course, at a distance. Orwell knew what was happening but he was a colonial officer, part of the system, and so was I, I suppose, so was I. Standing, watching, doing nothing. That coldness was scary and I guess, it was doing this English paper, that I see how Orwell did that, too.

The student has surprised herself by her second reading, by the connection with an incident in her past, and by her voice that recreates her guilt at her distance and possibly her sin of omission or her sin of passive participation. Now she has an idea for her paper and can read the essay documenting the techniques Orwell used to reveal distance.

You should—as these students did—draft your papers out loud, listening to what your voice is saying, using all your experience with speaking and listening to language, tuning that voice during revision toward a piece of writing that will be heard by readers. Voice is so central that it has its own chapter (Chapter 9). You don't have to wait until you read it. Browse through it now if you want to learn more about voice.

What if I Don't Discover in My Discovery Draft?

You have discovered something even if the discovery draft didn't work for you this time. When this happens, you have several choices. Try them:

1. Take a break, then return to the discovery draft and read it again, almost casually, as if it had been written by a stranger. When my mind wanders off in an interesting way, I note the wandering that may become my topic and go back to what caused it.
2. Do a new discovery draft. Of course it doesn't work every time. But take another run at it; see where the flow of language carries you this time.
3. Try other techniques such as brainstorming to see if they work.

It is hard for some students to write a discovery draft. They can't let themselves go, and that's all right. They have a strong sense of form or language that inhibits discovery by free-flow writing. Fine. Not every one of us thinks the same way or writes the same way.

How Do I Make an Instructor's Idea My Own?

There is a close relationship between the words *author* and *authority.* The most effective writing takes place when the writer explores a territory with which he or she is familiar.

The writer should be the authority on the subject matter, but the reality of school is that we are tested by writing exams and papers in response to a teacher's assignment. And this will continue after graduation. Our world is becoming more complex and is shrinking. There are Japanese factories in the United States and U.S.-owned factories in China. Corporations and government agencies depend on written reports sent by mail, e-mail, and fax machine. And the topics of most of these reports are not initiated by the writer. We will have topics assigned in class and beyond: in the government agency, the corporation, the laboratory, the courtroom.

As a professional journalist I have had all sorts of newspaper, radio, television, and magazine assignments; as a professional ghost writer I have written many corporate reports, speeches for CEOs, cabinet secretaries, and state proclamations. Each assignment is a challenge and the more difficult the assignment, the more fun. After I accept an assignment I sit back and perform the following tasks.

Understand the Assignment

If the assignment is written, read it carefully, marking the important points so you know what you are expected to do and how you are expected to do it. If the assignment is oral, take notes and go over them carefully. Ask questions. It is better to appear unsure now than later. Bad writing is often the direct product of a misunderstood assignment. Good writing on the wrong topic or in an unacceptable form is still a flunk.

Interview the Assignment

What is the central question to answer or the central problem to be solved? That central issue may be stated explicitly: "Explain the relationship between tax incentives and productivity growth in the automobile industry in the United States and Japan." Or it may be implicit: "Discuss the role of government in international trade."

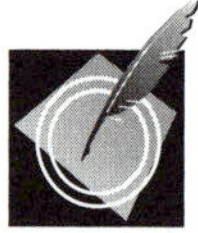

Put an assignment from another course beside these pages and use it to put my suggestions in the context of your academic life. What assumptions underlie the assignment? The instructor may assume the student will write a critical essay, report on research, do a book review but the genre is not stated. It is obvious to the teacher. The instructor may also have assumptions that are so central to the way she looks at the world that she may think it is not necessary to mention them. The political science teacher may be cynical about the present government, the history professor may think commerce is the secret to all history, the scientist may assume that theoretical research is more important than applied research. Ask the instructor what genre the instructor wants, speak to students who are majoring in the subject, or role-play the instructor and imagine what is required. In a research course in psychology or zoology, a paper probably has to have the research method described as well as the results; in a history course, the instructor will expect whatever is discussed to be placed in an accurate historical context; in a literature course, the instructor does not need to have the plot retold but the work evaluated by a critical theory.

And what documentation or evidence does the assignment giver expect? Does the assignment giver want statistics, firsthand observation, case histories, scholarly citations, or some combination of supporting information? What are the traditions of length, form, and style the assignment giver expects? Is the assignment giver impressed with length or brevity? Is the assignment, in part, a test to see whether you can write a literary analysis using the Modern Language Association (MLA) method of citation, a sociological case history, or a chemistry laboratory report?

Rewrite by Context

Each course, corporation, or government agency has its own intellectual environment. Never forget that in writing you are either an apprentice or a practicing historian, a psychologist, environmental planner, a biologist, or business manager. Each discipline has its own climate, its own expectations in written material. A writer, to be effective, needs to know the limitations of the assignment and then discover how to be creative within those limitations. Every art—the business letter, the poem, the research grant—is created from the tension between freedom and discipline.

Connect

The effective assignment writer has performed the reading and the research demanded by the assignment, taken notes that can be read, and has sources documented. Now the creative assignment writer has to think: to find a meaning, a pattern, a significance in the information the writer has collected. Often the best way to do this is to connect the topic with your own experience. You may want to describe your personal experience with divorce in documenting a paper in sociology. More often, however, your personal experience will lead you toward research questions that need answers, and you will use your autobiographical details backstage in developing a paper that is written with the objective distance appropriate to the assignment.

You will write with more authority if you make intellectual use of experiences that may have been emotional when they occurred.

How Do I Make the Boss's Idea My Own?

Every organization has its own rhetorical and style traditions. You must find out if there are formal stylebooks or guidelines for writing and you should also ask your superior for models of good company writing—what has worked in the past.

You need such information, obviously, if you plan to follow what has been done in the past, and it is just as important if you plan to depart from tradition. You cannot do that unless you know the traditions and the reasons for the traditions. The most apparently irrational rules have a history, they were imposed for a reason, and it is important you know that reason. Only then can you agree or disagree with it.

Writing on the job has a clear purpose: to sell a product, to communicate a decision or policy, to argue for support, to promote, to report. The goal is clear and it should influence the content and form of what you write. To make the boss's idea your own you must take your strength, your knowledge, your experience, your point of view and use it to help your superior achieve the superior's goal.

Role-playing your boss's situation may help: Who is above her, who does she need to impress, and how can what you know support her decision and goal? Sometimes it is a good idea to share a lead with your boss, so you can agree on the approach. But if you have a micromanager who focuses on details rather than the whole, it is usually better to hold your copy back until it is drafted, checked, and edited.

Focus Repair

When the ambulance screams up to an accident, the paramedics have to decide which patient is most gravely injured and then they have to decide what is the victim's most serious problem. There are usually cuts and bruises, broken bones, external and internal bleeding, difficulty in breathing. The medics have to decide immediately which problem threatens life and what can be done about it.

When I read first drafts from students, I must sometimes become a writer medic, deciding which section threatens the life of the essay and needs immediate treatment. From my trauma center experience with students and the professional writers I coach, the priority problem is focus.

Diagnosis: No Focus

I may see a draft that is sloppily prepared, full of misspellings (and if this poor speller can catch them, the writer is in real trouble), punctuation problems, incorrect facts, illogical structure, and an uneven, awkward style, but underneath it all is a lack of focus. An effective piece of writing says one thing and, before rewriting a draft, you should be able to state it in a single sentence. I wrote this sentence in my mind before I began this chapter: "Chapter 4 shows the role of focus in revision." I learned this from reading what John Steinbeck said he did: wrote a single sentence on a three-by-five card before he began a book. Before writing a draft a writer's mind and journals are filled with material that may fit into a meaning—or may not. Writing a single sentence, which may have to be revised as the writer proceeds, provides a point of reference, a North Star to keep the writer on course. Try it. It may begin an important part of your writing habit.

Once you have the focus, everything in the piece should relate to the focus and advance the meaning. Each word, each space between the words, each punctuation mark, each phrase, sentence, paragraph should move the reader toward meaning. There should be nothing in the piece of writing that does not do its job of carrying meaning to the reader.

Think of a camera shot. You want the viewer's eye to be led to the significant point: to see how the wedding photo reveals how close—or how far apart—the couple stands; to capture the look on the bride's mother's face; to preserve the best man's hilarious search for the ring; to see the bride's bouquet arcing through the air and the faces watching it.

The focus is the meaning of the story, essay, term paper, memo, poem. The focus captures the reader's attention and holds it through the piece of writing. It answers the reader's question, "Why should I be reading this?"

Testing Your Focus

An effective focus should be clear from the first sentence. You shouldn't have to think a long time after reading a draft to find a possible focus. Be able to say in just one sentence what the draft means. Readers will not make that effort; they will just stop reading.

To discover and state the focus, be able to answer the following questions with a specific, brief statement: a sentence or less.

What Is the Single, Dominant Meaning?

Every piece of effective writing will say many different things to individual readers. Good writing has depth and texture, but something should stand out.

The account of a beach party may include interesting material on who was there; how they dressed; how they behaved; what, and how much, was eaten or drunk; what the swimming was like; what games were played; who came with whom; and who went home with whom; but the account must have a meaning, and the meaning might be hidden in the abundance of all the details of the party. And these details may appear joyful, until the person looking back finds he is writing of a date rape.

What Is the Central Tension within the Dominant Meaning?

The central tension is what makes the focus dynamic, active, something worth writing—and reading. There should be forces at work within the focus: a question, a doubt, a conflict, a contradiction. The idea of writing a piece about Mom is not a focus or a central tension. Why did Mother keep her first marriage secret is a central tension.

The problem of date rape is a serious one, but that label will not attract, hold, and influence readers. Effective writing contains a central tension that puts everything in the article in a different perspective. That central tension might be "Beer doesn't make *no* into *yes.*" The alcoholic hilarity of the outing suddenly turns false and dark, ominous, not celebratory.

The argument might focus on the reader who thinks women say "no" and mean "yes," and therefore a few beers "to loosen her up" justifies a sexual attack: She really wanted it. The account might show how dress and behavior do not excuse sexual assault. There is tension in the topic because we discover that the attacker sees a pattern of seduction that the victim does not intend.

What Do Test Readers Say Is the Meaning of the Draft?

It is often helpful to get someone who is not familiar or sympathetic to read a draft and then tell the writer, in a sentence, what it means. I am careful about the person I choose to be a test reader. The person does not need to be an authority on the subject and, in fact, it is often better if the person is not, as my readers will not be. My test readers are not always writers, but they are people who can listen to what I want of them, and respond helpfully to an early draft. If I ask simply if they get the meaning, then they do not immediately jump in and correct my typing and my spelling. They give a candid response to the question I ask. Most of all, the test readers I return to are those who make me want to write as soon as I leave them. They may praise or criticize, but they inspire me to go to work revising the draft.

When a test reader gives me a meaning I did not intend—"Rape is OK at a beach party"—my first tendency is to say "stupid reader," but that is not good enough. The writer has to communicate to readers who are rushed and harried, not interested in the subject, or opposed to the writer's views. It is the responsibility of the writer to create a focus that will be clear to many readers, good or bad, interested or disinterested. Sometimes there are poor or eccentric readings of a draft, but most times when a test reader gives a meaning you do not expect, you can scan the piece and discover the focus is not what you meant. Then you can point the draft in the direction you want.

If the Diagnosis Is Positive

If the draft has a clear focus, then move on to the next step in the revision process. Each draft will have its own problems as it passes through revision. The effective writer moves over those stages in the process where a quick diagnosis reveals no problem.

Say One Thing

One of the biggest differences between the successful writer and the unsuccessful one is that the successful writer says one thing. One idea dominates.

The writer may have known that single idea before writing. It may have come clear to the writer during the writing. Or the idea may be discovered through the reading of the draft. But once the idea is recognized, it has to be developed and clarified by revision.

How Can I Find That One Thing?

It is vital to articulate the one thing that brings all the issues in the subject into focus. Some of the techniques I use to do this follow.

Questions to Reveal the Focus

Sometimes it is a good idea to back off, turn the draft over, or save it so it is not on the screen. Then think about the subject. After writing and reading the piece, ask yourself:

- What surprised you?
- What did you expect to read? How was what you read different from your expectations?
- What do you remember most vividly?
- What did you learn from the writing and the reading?
- What one thing does a reader need to know?
- What is the single most important detail, quote, fact, idea in the draft?
- What do you itch to explore through revision?
- What single message may the final draft deliver?

Sharpen the Focus

Once you have an answer to those questions, then you can sharpen the focus. Here are some rules for sharpening the focus:

- Use as few words as possible.
- Play with specifics from both sides of the issue that are in tension; avoid generalizations and abstractions.
- Use nouns and verbs, especially active verbs. Reveal the central tension.

Zero In on One Story

A student might write:

> My grandfather has moved in with us. We try to make it nice for him but he says nothing. He isn't cranky, just silent. I knew he had grown up in an orphanage, worked in the woods when he was a teenager, was a real war hero and, afterwards, a minister, psychologist, and he ended up in jail for insurance fraud. It is interesting to have three generations in one house and see how it affects my mother and father. My aunts and uncles are freaked out. I like to get him to tell me things, but he sits within a plastic tube of silence.

After a conference with a classmate, the writer realized that his grandfather had many stories to tell and his moving created almost as many stories. His test reader was most interested in his having been in prison. The writer decided to focus on that that but since his grandfather won't talk, he'd have to interview his father, mother, aunts, and uncles to reveal what he did that got him sent to jail. And once the student knew his grandfather's story, perhaps he would break down and speak.

Titles and First Lines

The focused meaning may, in fact, become the title. When I was freelancing magazine articles, I would start writing an article by brainstorming 100 to 150 possible titles, in fragments of time as the research was winding down. Each title was a window into the draft I might write.

To brainstorm, you have to be willing to be silly, knowing that in this freedom may lie an important insight. If I was assigned to write a paper on roommates, I might start with titles that would remind me of experiences—problems and conflicts and satisfactions—I had with roommates.

My Roommate for 51 Years
My 40 Army Roommates
Why We Had a Fistfight
My Roommate's Smell
Snores
Snores and Bores
Don't Room with a Philosopher
Familiarity Breeds Familiarity
Ten Rules for My Roommate
How to Drive a Roommate Crazy
Talk's OK—But at 3:00 A.M.?
My Roommate's Snake
My Roommate's Brother
Why I Murdered My Roommate
Why I Murdered My Roommate—and Was Acquitted
Roommate or Cellmate?
Cheese, Toothpaste, and Computers
The Music Wars
Jazz Rock Folk Classical
Rocking to Mozart
One Roommate and Four Alarm Clocks
When His Lover Stays Overnight
The Importance of Privacy
No Passion Please
Living in My Roommate's Plant Jungle
The Poster Wars
Borrow My Boyfriend, Not My Jeans
What's Hers Is Hers; What's Mine Is Hers

You could go on and on, and so could I. I may, for example, write a humorous column about my wife, my roommate for 51 years, in the form of advice to freshmen meeting their roommates for the first time. I could write a nostalgic essay, with some bite, about the roommate with whom I had a fight. I might even write about my experiences in an army barracks with 40 roommates or in a foxhole in combat with one. I am not restricted to my list. I might find myself writing about some of the office mates I've suffered and how they suffered me.

Join me in the game of titles. I used to do 150 or so at a run. And what if number 3 of 150 is the best? Well, now you know it! The discarded titles may turn up as instigating lines in the article or as starting places for other articles.

The fragments of language that focus meaning often become the first lines of a piece of writing. As a journalist, I am a great believer in writing the lead—the first line, the first paragraph or three, the first page—first. Let's see what happens if I write a few leads for that roommate column:

> As our grandchildren go off to college for the first time, those of us who have the same roommate for 40, 50 years or more should share our cohabitation wisdom.

***

> Selective vision—or elective blindness—is the first quality a student should develop in facing a college roommate for the first time. I do not see the ironing we brought from New Jersey in 1963 that adorns one corner of our bedroom . . .

***

> My first college roommate and I got along after we had a genuine, male, prancing-around, dirty-words fistfight in our closet of a room.
>
> Now, seeing freshmen arrive in cars hung with furniture, I realize their adjustment won't be to calculus, rhetoric, the philosophy of Hegel, but to fitting into a small room with a stranger who will get larger, louder, more difficult every day.

***

> I've heard of people who keep in touch with their college roommates decade by decade and I've heard of hostage victims who grow fond of their captors, but one of the good

things about getting old is that I will never ever have to have a roommate again. I hope. Perhaps in the nursing home, but I won't talk about that yet. And I am happy to have a mate, but it is fortunate we live in nine rooms, not one.

***

The first great lesson of college is that someone with a sense of humor—or sadistic need to cause trouble—has locked you and your roommate into a small space for a long year.

Now I have had a roommate for 51 years, and we are still working out all those trivial issues of territory that are so important to the human animal. As a full-grown, white-bearded sage, I have some wise counsel for first-year college students who face the first test of university life: I am supposed to live with . . .

***

~~The first great lesson of college is that someone with a sense of humor or sadistic need to cause trouble has locked you and your roommate into a small space for a long year.~~

~~Now~~ I have had a roommate for 51 years, and ~~we are still working out all those trivial issues of territory that are so important to the human animal. As a full-grown, white-bearded sage,~~ I have ~~some wise counsel~~ advice for first-year college students who face their first ~~test of university life: I am supposed to live with . . .~~ roommates.

What have I been doing? Playing my way into an essay, trying on beginning points, voices, ideas, the way you try on clothes before a party. Each lead gives me a direction in which I might go. The entire piece of writing grows out of the beginning that establishes the following:

- The question in the reader's mind to be answered in the draft
- The authority of the writer to answer it
- The direction of the draft
- The pace of the writing
- The form
- The voice

But What about All the Other Good Stuff?

There are two kinds of good stuff. One kind can be used to support and advance the focus of the story, to clarify—and communicate—your meaning. The other is material that will draw the reader's mind away from your message.

Supporting Material

Every piece of information, every literary device, every line, and every word must support, develop, and communicate the meaning. Each comma, verb, statistic, reference, descriptive detail, transition, summary sentence should relate in a direct way to the central tension of what is being written.

The melody by itself is hardly enough. The meaning, focused and sharpened, needs all the supporting material to reveal its full significance and to make the reader react emotionally and intellectually.

Distracting Material

The material you have collected through research and the thinking you have done through writing that must be cut from the draft, however, is not wasted. It is all money in the bank. You may not spend it on this draft, but it is there, to be drawn on in the future.

And in a way it is still in the draft, even after it has been cut. The marble that has been cut away from the statue made an essential contribution to the statue. It is there in the revealing.

Frame Your Meaning

You may not know much about writing, but I bet you know how to frame a picture with a camera. If you want to reveal the tranquil beauty of a flowery meadow, make sure you have not included the blur of traffic on the highway beside the meadow. If you want to comment on modern life by showing the cars rushing by unseeing, make sure you get both highway and meadow and use an exposure that will show the cars blurring past the stationary beauty of the wildflowers in the meadow. That is what the writer does. For example, you might start an essay—or a short story—in either of these frames:

> It was not the commute between home and office and hospital that made it possible for him to survive, but the ritual he followed every day when he pulled off the highway and studied the tranquil beauty of a meadow that had escaped the march of the malls. Some people liked water, but he drew strength from the ocean swell of land, the dance of wind on tall grass, the yearly explosion of wildflowers, each in its season.
>
> ***
>
> First the highway amputating this meadow from his grandfather's farm, then the subdivision behind the meadow, the strip mall on the left, the fast-food place on the right, the hundreds upon hundreds of people who raced by this last meadow, not seeing the way it changed its color, hour by hour, under wind and sky, ignoring its tranquil beauty undisturbed until the annual explosion of wildflowers, promiscuous, profligate, so much more necessary to humans than highways and burgers and cheap clothes and houses decorated with plastic possessions.

It helps us to realize how much we know about writing, without knowing we know it, when we use one art or craft and adapt its lessons, in this case focus, to our writing. Writing and rewriting go better when we can face our tasks with confidence. And we may not feel confident about our writing, but many of us feel confident with a camera in hand.

What to Leave Out

Draw a frame around the subject. You can even do this physically, by scanning the draft and drawing a line through everything that has to go. Sometimes I circle the material and mark it with an arrow heading off the page, or a question mark.

Most times the decision is easy, but sometimes I have to scan the draft a number of times to see what should go or remain.

What to Keep In

Keep in what moves your meaning forward. The remaining material must develop and communicate the focused meaning.

"But almost everything went. My draft has shrunk!"

Good. This is an important stage in the writing process. When we have found our focus, it gives us space for complete development. Maybe half the material can be saved, or only a third, or a quarter— a page? Now you have room for the material you will add during the revision process.

Revision for the experienced writer is often a far more radical process than the inexperienced writer imagines. The experienced writer knows that to cut often means to reveal. Once I cut 237 pages from a draft in response to a modest but perceptive comment by a horrified editor. It *did* improve the book. The master writer knows that what is taken out is necessary to get the draft to the place where it can be made to work. The writing that is cut isn't a sign of failure but progress toward an effective final draft.

Most of us write a first draft that skims over the surface of our topic. That's appropriate. We are searching for our focus, our meaning. Once we find it, then a lot of the material we included can be jettisoned. Over the side with it. No regrets.

Set the Distance

An important issue relating to focus that is rarely discussed in most textbooks is the matter of distance. We can stand nose to nose with our subject or back off and see it from a mountaintop, a space shuttle, or even, by writing from a historical perspective, from a distance of hundreds of years.

The focus, as with a camera, depends on how far away you—and the reader—stand from the subject. The distance cannot be set by a rule book but depends on the subject, your purpose in writing about the subject, and the reader.

When to Use Close-ups

Close-ups bring immediacy. We do not photograph the field of spring flowers but move in on one poppy, show the whole blossom, or go even closer to a petal, perhaps catching a bee stopping by for breakfast. In the close-up we don't look at the entire government but the legislature, not the House of Representatives and the Senate but the Senate only, not the committee structure but a committee, not the committee but a single senator, not the career of the senator but one revealing vote.

We can, with the close-up, expose the details of a scene, a law, a scientific experiment, a crime, a vote. We can reveal complexity and simplicity, cause and effect, action and reaction.

When to Step Back

We step back when we take a snapshot of a single wildflower and then show the fields of wildflowers that stretch for miles to the Rockies. We show the historical and theological roots of the abortion issue and the pressures that caused the senator to take a position and now reverse it. The distance shot allows us to make the generalization from the documentation: to put the anecdote, the quotation, the statistic, the scientific discovery in perspective. We can show what came before and predict what will follow. We provide a context. But what if I need to do both?

When to Zoom

You have a zoom lens. Use it. Don't just stand in one spot and try to see what's going on from there. Take your reader in close for emphasis, for clarity, for dramatic effect, to make the reader think and feel. Then zoom back so the reader understands the full implications of what the reader has been shown. In every war, photographers and writers use zoom techniques to reveal the landscape of war; they move in close to see the wounded or the dead, which reveals the price of war in individual human terms; then they zoom out again to show the larger context of war.

Don't move in and back wildly, without purpose, like Uncle Max with his new video camera at the wedding. Move smoothly in close. Draw back halfway—in close once more—then back again in a pattern that serves the reader, giving the reader the information and the experience the reader needs to become involved in your subject.

Make believe you are a movie director, as I often do when I am writing, and make a sketch showing the camera angle: what it includes and excludes. Then move the camera to different positions to see what is emphasized, included, excluded.

Interview with a Published Writer

Christopher Scanlan

I first met Chip Scanlan when I was appointed writing coach for the *Providence Journal.* He was the reporter most interested in the writing process—and the most critical. In Providence he helped create and run the paper's writing program and edited *How I Wrote the Story,* a collection of news writing accounts. Our professional dialogue remains at the center of our relationship that has grown so that if I had to choose, he would be my closest friend. We talked about our craft almost daily as he moved from the *Providence Journal* in Rhode Island to the *St. Petersburg Times* in Florida, then to the District of Columbia where he was a national correspondent in the Washington bureau of Knight-Ridder newspapers. He created the bureau's first family beat and won awards for coverage of veterans' health care and consumer issues and a Robert F. Kennedy award for international journalism for a series on hazardous exports. Chip is now director of writing programs at The Poynter Institute in St. Petersburg, Florida, a nonprofit educational institution that provides seminars for recent college graduates and newspaper professionals.

He has also been editor of the annual *Best Newspaper Writing.* His articles, essays, and short stories have appeared in the *Washington Post Magazine,* the *Boston Globe Magazine, Redbook,* and *Delaware Today.* I think his journalism textbook, *Reporting and Writing: Basics for the 21st Century* (Oxford University Press, 2000), is the best introduction to journalism published today.

What techniques do you use to find a focus before writing a first draft?

I tend to over report every story, as a glance at my desk demonstrates. Archeologists could find evidence of earlier civilizations in the layers of notebooks, reports, books, newspapers, magazines, Post-it Notes, binders, file folders that accumulate when I am reporting a story. Reporting helps me understand a subject, but after a while it begins to overwhelm me and confusion sets in. What does all this mean? What was my story anyway? What's the significance of the interview notes, statistics, observations, and descriptions I've spent so much time collecting?

The only way out of it is to push all of it aside and go to the one source that knows it all—me—and start asking the questions that help me discover the heart of the story, the single, dominant impression that every effective story conveys. What's the news? What's the story? What image captures the story for me? What quote, or better, what dialogue between more than one person, sums it all up? I try to keep in mind what Thomas Boswell, a terrific sports columnist for the *Washington Post*, once said: "The most important thing in the story is finding the central idea. It's one thing to be given a topic, but you have to find the idea or the concept within that topic. Once you find that idea or thread, all the other anecdotes, illustrations, and quotes are pearls that hang on this thread. The thread may seem very humble, the pearls may seem very flashy, but it's still the thread that makes the necklace."

Here are some techniques that work for me:

- Write your story in six words.
- Write a budget line, the sentence that promises a specific approach before the story is written.
- Ask two questions that keep track of the focus of any story: What's the news? What's the story? They address

the reader's concerns: What's new here? What's this story about? Why am I reading this?

How do you know you need to revise for focus after you have finished a draft?

I generally have two reactions to story drafts: pride or disgust. I've learned, through long and sometimes bitter experience, to be suspicious when I think the draft is good, because it won't be long before I see its true flaws. When I'm disgusted with the writing, I know I'm on the right track. If I can't stand to read it aloud, have an overwhelming urge to tear it up or hit the delete key until the computer screen is blank, then I know my focus is off. Whatever I want to say or need to say in the story is not being said, and I need to sit back and ask myself a simple question, "What is it you're trying to say?" Invariably, the sentence I write in response articulates in a phrase the central meaning of the story. It's often something I've been trying to avoid saying for some reason.

What attitudes do you find helpful as you try to focus a draft?

I was fortunate to work for eight years with one of the best newspaper editors in America, Joel Rawson, executive editor of the *Providence Journal.* I can still remember the intensity of the question that he was always asking at every stage of the process, from reporting to rewriting: "What's this story about?" Or to be more precise, he'd lean toward me and demand, "Do you know what this story is about?" Then he'd proceed to teach me the universal theme that lurked beneath the topic. Joel taught me to dig deep, to look for the universal in the specific, to make the human connection, to never stop until I knew the basic theme of my story. The attitudes needed are persistence and empathy. The focus of a story usually resides in the pit of my stomach. When I feel it there, almost like an electrical current, then I know I have the focus.

What specific process—or processes—do you try to focus a draft?

I usually begin by freewriting; that is, I try to discover the focus by writing and seeing what comes out. I am looking for words, ideas, combinations that surprise me. If I'm bored by my writing, why should anyone else care? If I can surprise myself, then I have a better chance to surprise my reader.

What tools do you use when searching for a focus?

- Questions and more questions. What's the news? What's the story? What am I trying to say? How do I want people to respond when they're finished reading the story? What's the best headline or title? Who's this story about? Why am I writing this story?
- Freewriting. Essentially I babble on my computer screen.
- Write a headline or a title.
- Talk about my story with an editor, my wife, or a good friend.

How do you know when you have solved the problem of focus?

Carol Knopes, news cover story editor for *USA Today,* says, "the job of a writer is to put elephants into ring boxes." The elephant—that immense load of reporting you've done—must somehow fit into that ring box, a space of perhaps 400 to 800 words. The focus of a story helps you decide what to leave out. If it doesn't relate to the single dominant message, then it doesn't make it.

What are the most important three things you've learned as a publishing writer that you wish you knew as a college freshman?

1. Writing is hard work, but it's fun. Keep at it. Don't give up hope. Lower your standards, as poet William Stafford advised. Give yourself a break: What you write today is what you're capable of writing. Strive to improve, but accept what you produce.
2. Good writing may be magical, but it's not magic. It's a rational series of decisions and actions that can be observed, learned, and repeated.
3. All writing is rewriting.

Chapter 5
REWRITE WITH GENRE

I always have two things in my head—I always have a theme and the form. The form looks for the theme, theme looks for the form, and when they come together you're able to write.

—W. H. AUDEN

. . . a proper tale has a shape and an outline. In painting, the frame is important. Where does the picture end? What details should one include? Or omit! Where does the line go that cuts off the picture?

—ISAK DINESEN

. . . if I saw the whole unwritten novel stretching out before me, chapter by chapter, like a landscape, I know I would put it aside in favor of something more uncertain—material that had a natural form that it was up to me to discover.

—WILLIAM MAXWELL

Genre or form is the lens through which the writer sees the subject and reveals it to the reader. It is the mission of the writer to order the confusion and contradictions of life. To do that writers use genre, applying the literary form with which they are most familiar to the chaos that swirls past us all. Novelists see novels, essayists see essays, poets see poems, journalists see news stories as they live their lives. Of course, many writers try different genres. Novelists Hemingway and Camus were journalists, essayist E. B. White published children's books that became classics, poet Shakespeare also wrote plays. We should all experiment with different genres, taking an experience and giving it narrative sequence, standing back and looking at it critically, catching the essence of the experience in a few poetic lines and then, like the golfer who chooses a club based on where the ball lies, we can record and examine experience with a tool or genre appropriate to the particular writing challenge.

Each genre—fiction, nonfiction, poetry, drama—is a continent of literature. The continent of nonfiction, for example, includes essay, argument, biography, report, memo, documentary narrative, and all the other forms of writing that use factual truth to communicate meaning.

The writer revises by choosing a new lens. What the writer thought was a personal narrative turns out to be an argument. As the writer examines the subject through the lens of argument, new elements come into focus, the lines grow sharper. Genre clarifies and makes meaning clear.

Of course one of the difficulties writers have comes from the fact that the editor or teacher assigns a particular lens, demanding a critical essay, a research paper, a personal experience essay. This limits the writer because the genre may not clarify the writer's view of the subject. Limiting the writer to a specific genre may be an effective way to teach it, but it may create more problems than solutions when the genre is inappropriate for the subject—a critical essay when the material demands a narrative, or a narrative when the material is right for a critical essay. If a writer can't get permission to take a look at the topic with a new lens then the writer must use the assigned lens, but should always be ready to rewrite with a different genre, one that will bring new insights to the experience of living.

Choosing the Genre

It is our job as writers to find the genre that provides meanings by which we can comprehend the world and our lives within our world.

1. *What do I have to say?* I try to answer that question, even if I'm writing a book, in one sentence or less, perhaps a phrase such as "the craft of revision." That simple phrase makes me focus on the methods of rewriting.
2. *Where am I headed?* If possible, I like to know the destination before I begin the trip. Often the writing takes me where I did not expect. Writing is, after all, thinking, exploration, discovery.
3. *Where do I begin?* I try to start as near the end as possible in a narrative, as near the central meaning as possible. Readers will not wade through background material they do not yet know they need.
4. *What's the length?* How much space do I have to tell my story? I live in a professional world in which the space is proscribed. No more than 800 words for a column, 300 pages for a book.
5. *How do I get from beginning to end?* What is the sequence of points that will move the reader from the first paragraph to the last?
6. *What must be included?* And what can be left out, knowing that the more good stuff I must leave out, the better the piece of writing?
7. *What genre—for example, narrative, argument, essay—will carry the meaning to the reader and allow me to deal with the six points above?*
8. *How can the traditional form of the genre be adapted to my needs?* Or how can traditional genre be combined to do the job?

Genre Provides Meaning

Genre gives meaning to your material in the same way a house, a barn, an apartment block, a supermarket gives meaning to lumber and nails, steel beams and cement. In writing, sometimes you can be the architect and design the building of meaning within the limitations of the material and purpose of the building; other times you are the job boss constructing the building you have been assigned from someone else's, perhaps a teacher's, blueprints. In each case, form shapes meaning.

The Five-Paragraph Theme

Few students escape the five-paragraph theme, the traditional introduction to the discipline of writing. It is a classroom genre, a form of writing used for instruction that rarely appears outside of school. I experienced the five-paragraph theme in class and my grandchildren move toward it as I write this.

The five-paragraph theme is taught because it is easy to learn. It has a firm and apparent structure:

Paragraph 1: An introduction beginning with a topic sentence and thesis statement that tells the reader what you are going to say.

Paragraph 2: } The topic is defined,
Paragraph 3: } developed, qualified,
Paragraph 4: } documented.

Paragraph 5: A conclusion that tells the reader what you have said.

Often teachers require a topic sentence in the beginning and a formal concluding sentence.

The intent is good: to teach form, structure, order, development. The problem is that the five-paragraph theme lives only in the classroom. It is not written or read outside of school.

Today's reader is impatient. The reader wants the writer to get to the subject immediately. The topic sentence is rarely used, and the same thing is true of the conclusion. Once the writer has said what is to be said, the writer gets offstage and does not turn around and tell the reader what it means, how the reader should think or feel. It is too late. And few subjects can be disposed of in three paragraphs—it takes the space it takes—one paragraph or twenty-five, half a page or one hundred pages.

The five-paragraph theme has dangerous implications that may reside like a computer virus in the student's brain:

- The form of the draft is more important than the content.
- Meaning can be changed to fit the form.
- There is one right way to tell all stories.
- The reader has to be told what the message will be, what the message is, what it means.

The student may well learn a great deal from writing the five-paragraph theme. I certainly did. It is, in a way, the foundation of all my writing, but then I had to unlearn it to become a professional writer and that was hard. I had to learn that effective writing grows organically: The form comes from the meaning. You may have to fit an imposed meaning—the company demands that all accident reports be written exactly the same way—but if you are reporting a hazardous situation and there is not a required form, then you can study the information and the person for whom it must be created and organize it so it delivers what the reader needs. The corporate lawyer may need to be aware of potential lawsuits, the personnel director of the danger to workers, the production manager of the loss of production. The form grows organically, naturally, from the message and its intended audience.

The Unshaped Material

The writing demonstration that follows is constructed from the facts: The writer's parents divorced and his father got married soon afterward. His mother had just remarried the summer before the writer left for college. This is a good piece of writing that dramatizes a situation faced by many young people. I am impressed at how compassionate the student is and how little he wallows in self-pity.

He does not judge his parents and he has a sense of humor. The shape of the piece is clear: a paragraph for each situation in chronological order. The purpose is to look at an autobiographical situation critically. It is a critical essay in the sense that he shows how his parents—all four—change and behave as they take on new roles.

That genre doesn't quite work at the end as he lumps in all the other family he has acquired in the last few years. This draft could be developed in the first paragraph, or it could be developed into a longer section or even an essay of its own.

> In the beginning I had two parents, then I had three, now I have four. In editing my last paper, the instructor said that "less is more." Well, in remarriage, more is more. Lots more.
>
> I didn't realize when my father moved out how much he would change—and how much our relationship would change. At first he was just angry; then he became like a buddy. He grew young. We hung out on visiting days at McDonald's, the mall, ball games, watching TV in his small apartment. He told me his troubles—me!—and asked me for advice. And he listened to me and seemed to understand the way he never did when he was my father. Well, he was still my father, sort of.
>
> Mother changed. She became SUPERPARENT. She read books and went to meetings and even signed up to coach my soccer team—and she was good. Read books on that too. When she and Dad were together, she was the easy one. Now she was Ms. Boss—and at work too, where she got promoted. My father grew young; my mom grew old. Not ancient, just responsible, organized. She became an executive mother. She gives me memos on what to do—on office forms!
>
> Then Dad married a woman who made cookies. She made like she was a Disney mother. Annie, she wanted me to use her first name, cooked whole sit-down, cloth napkin meals. She gave up her job because she was pregnant. Well, I had stayed over in that small apartment on the living room sofa before they were married. A baby was no surprise to me. It was for them! And I've become her maternity project. It was OK and I like the kid. But it was weird at times, to have a second mother and my not-real one being in a motherly phase.

Now Mom has remarried and I have an extra father. I thought if my mother remarried, I'd have some awkward guy like my friends do, who tries to kid around, be a pal, like my father before he had someone else to date. Not this guy. He had six kids before his wife died. He is in charge, and I think Mother likes that. He makes charts. We have chores. We eat around a dinner table, all of us. We have topics at dinner and I thought I would hate that, but it's fun. He really wants to be a father.

And not only do I have four parents and eight grandparents all living, and three great-grandparents, I, an only child four years ago, have three brothers and four sisters. I cannot count the cousins and the aunts and the uncles. I even have a brother-in-law.

Now see what happens as he tells his story in a different form.

Scholarship Application

I am submitting this application to the Hogue Student Foundation because my family's financial situation has changed since I last applied. My father has remarried and he has a new baby; my mother has remarried and I suddenly have seven siblings on that side of the family, only one who is old enough to have gone to college. I hope you will consider the changed status of my two families in considering this application for a scholarship.

Letter to a Friend Who Is in the Service

You talk about barracks life. Well, Mother married Mr. Fertile. I have ten people wanting in the bathroom at 7:00 A.M. I shower at school after practice. They're OK I guess but no privacy. I know what you mean about being alone. I never liked being alone, but now I have bunk beds and seven-year-old twins in my bedroom. I can't wait to go back to college and that dorm I complained about last year.

Book Report

In his book, *Role Seeking: The Sociology of Rank-Ordered Adolescents in the Extended Family,* Dr. Finley Robespierre of the Mescowan Family Research Center puts the experience of many college freshmen in a social context. At first I felt cheated of my individuality to discover I was part of a familial trend, but it was illuminating to find out that . . .

News Report

More than 50 students attended an organizational meeting of Students of Divorce at the Memorial Student Union Monday evening.

Marianne Morison of the University Counseling Service introduced Penelope Stearns-Upton, who is both the daughter of divorced parents and a single mother, and a graduate student doing a doctoral study on the effect of divorce on freshmen.

Her pilot study revealed . . .

Case History

Subject: Myles J. Turner, 18 years old, is a freshman from San Diego, who received word of his parents' separation in the third week of the semester.

Method: The subject was interviewed once a week during the rest of the first semester. The interviews lasted from one to two hours and took place in his dormitory room. They were tape-recorded.

All of his teachers this semester, the dorm resident supervisor and his hall resident, his roommate, his girlfriend, herself a child of divorce, and three close friends were also interviewed at least twice during the semester and the books and articles on the attached reading list were studied.

Discussion: The subject passed through anger, self-blame, and a beginning of acceptance during this first semester. He was able to articulate the stages through which he was passing and that concerned him, "My dad always had a certain detachment that I didn't like. Every time I screwed up he asked, 'Now what have we learned from this?' I'd like it better if he just got pissed off. I worry I'm standing back from my feelings the same way, that I'm him."

We could go on to imagine a term paper, a letter to a grandparent who is worried about him, the minutes of a meeting of Students of Divorce, a personal journal entry, a political science paper on the legal rights of children of divorce, a scene for a screenwriting class, and on and on. Each form would make its own demands because it is designed to achieve a particular purpose and serve a particular reader.

Diagnosis: Ineffective Genre

The purpose of all genres is to carry meaning to a reader. The genre you choose must fit the material you have collected and the audience who will read your piece. The genre you choose depends on the expectations of the reader. Those who give grants expect a proposal; the literature teacher expects a critical essay; the laboratory assistant, a lab report; the history teacher, a research paper; the judge, a lawyer's brief; the bereaved parent, a letter of sympathy.

The ineffective genre is one that does not deliver the information the reader needs—the poem sent in as a scholarship application, the personal letter written in the style of a sociological paper. Scan your draft, imagining it as a blueprint of the exterior walls of a building. Does the shape of the building fit its purpose? Is it a factory, a summer home, an apartment house, a supermarket, a medical clinic, a fire station? Is it an argument, a narrative, a case history, a report, a poem, a review, a lab report, a critical essay?

Turn yourself into the reader of your draft. Does the material fit the tradition—the reader's expectation—or break the tradition and increase its effectiveness? Would you, as a reader, respond the way the writer expects you to respond? Is this the most effective way to attract and hold the reader's attention?

Does your draft, for example, follow the "building code" of an argument? Does it define and clarify the key issue? Does it make your position clear? Does it anticipate and respond to the opposition's arguments? Does it place your own arguments in increasing order of importance? Is each argument supported with objective documentation? Is the source of each piece of documentation available to the reader?

Such questions are obvious for each genre. Imagine you are the reader, and list the questions that must be answered by the shape of your draft and the information delivered within that shape. Your account of an automobile accident can be shaped by the task: filling out an insurance report, dictating your account to the police, giving a lawyer material for a brief, preparing a eulogy for a victim's funeral, writing a letter of sympathy to a parent or a personal letter to a close friend.

In scanning your draft, determine whether the genre is appropriate. Does what you have to say fit the tradition, the form the reader expects? Many times in school or work, of course, the genre is ordered ahead of the material: It will be a term paper, a corporate memo, an argument, a case history. Then the focus will be on collecting the material that will satisfy the genre.

If the genre used in the draft is appropriate to the material and to the audience, you can move ahead to the next stage in the rewriting process. If not, then you may have to choose a different genre, turning a report into an argument, an argument into a personal essay.

When the genre is required by an instructor or an employer, the writer can only adjust the genre—switching the point of view, reordering the evidence, casting the traditional form in a manner more appropriate to the message being delivered. Even when you cannot choose the form, you can still make it yours by the way you develop it.

Genre Communicates Meaning

The genre helps to communicate our meaning. A house invites us to live in it; a field house invites play; a factory invites productivity. *Story* says there is a beginning, a middle, and an end; action between people shapes events. *Essay* states there is significant information worth critical commentary. *Lyric poem* implies there is truth to be found in image and song. *Description* declares there is something important to describe; *report,* that something has occurred that needs to be reported to a reader; *argument,* that there is something to be argued for or against.

Discovering the Genre for the Draft

To build a house of meaning, a structure that delivers significant information and a critical opinion of that information, you have to choose an effective form. Just as each type of building has a different purpose and a specific structure to serve its purpose, so does each genre.

The Internal Genre

Most writers try to find the genre hidden within the draft. They read the draft to see how the information they are collecting dictates the content:

The Writer Discovers	The Possible Genre
A significant pattern in ordinary information that the reader needs to understand	Expository essay
A significance revealed by a series of events organized chronologically	Narrative
Facts that contradict a law or regulation	Argument
A situation that needs study	Grant proposal
A book that readers need to discover	Book report
An individual who has made important changes in the way we live	Biographical profile
A personal experience that will give the reader helpful information	Autobiographical essay
Solution to a problem at work	Memo

In the cases just listed, the genre may not be clear until the writer has completed a discovery draft. The writer may begin thinking that the material will become an autobiographical essay and it may turn into an argument or a memo; the student may begin to write an argument and discover that the material demands a humorous memoir.

I respect my material and listen to it for what shape it seems to be developing. A writer should respect the integrity of the specific pieces of information collected, especially if those details contradict what the writer expected; a writer should respect the patterns into which this material arranges itself—meaning that arises from the material—especially if it is traitorous to the writer's intent. A writer should respect the message from the language—the music of the evolving text, its voice—especially if it does not say what the writer thought it would say or was saying during the writing of the draft. It is the material, in the best writing, that determines the form.

The External Genre

Of course, much of our writing must fit an external genre that is established by tradition or reader expectation. We are not allowed to look into our material to find an essay, story, poem, history, research paper, but must fit our material to an assigned form such as a lab report, corporate memo, critical essay, history term paper.

In these cases we follow the tradition. We manipulate the genre we are given so that it delivers a meaning to a reader. We can, and should, be given a model to follow when we are assigned a form that is new to us. If we aren't, we can ask the teacher or the employer for an example or look one up. We may, to our surprise, discover we know more about the form than we realized. That conscious seeking of tradition will connect with the subconscious knowledge of which we are not aware.

Tradition

When facing a writing task you have not attempted before, find out what genres have been successful in the past by looking at books that analyze and explain argument, business writing, screenwriting, science writing, writing for nursing and police reports, news writing, fiction and poetry writing, scholarly writing, writing criticism, and speeches. Such books conduct autopsies of successful writing in that genre, revealing the conventions, the tricks of the trade, which have worked in the past.

It is also possible to take a piece of writing you like—or one the audience you are trying to reach trusts and respects—and analyze it to see what the author has done. Let me give you an immediate example of writing and rewriting from my own professional experience. Many high schools are returning to a system of tracking students that I hated when I was in high school.

We were given intelligence tests and placed in tracks from 1 to 13—1 was honor college-bound students; 13 was male shop. I wanted to point out that, in fact, we were tracked by the economic, social, and ethnic status of our homes and forced into ghettos.

> Looking back, I realize with horror how tracking affected our lives out of school. We were separated—tracked—from junior high on: college track students never attended class with business students. They never went to class with home ec and shop students. When the economic differences were reinforced by dividing the classes by I.Q.—10-1, 10-2, 10-3 in college and then all the way down to track 13-"general," who were expected to drop out anyway—we hung out with people in our own track. We dressed according to track. I could tell a 1 or 4 or 8 or 13 track student by how they dressed, the slang they used, the jokes, each level's protective snobbery. Our parties often seemed tracked.

This paragraph is from a column I wrote arguing against tracking in school because of the effect it has on students, citing my own negative experiences with tracking. The paragraph worked and was published. But in analyzing it, I realize I could put it in a larger social context.

> When I go back to my hometown I am struck at how accurately the program that tracked us into college, secretarial, commercial, vocational, and general classes predicted what we would be decades later. The program even predicted an amazing number of our dating and marriage patterns. I wonder what would have happened had we not been tracked. Would the factory worker have become the doctor, the doctor the druggist, the engineer the car mechanic, the housewife the lawyer, the judge the housewife? Did some test, full of social/gender/ethnic/economic bias, predict our lives because we accepted the school's evaluation of our worth as our own?

No magic. Just a careful reading of a draft, asking what the writer is doing, paragraph by paragraph. An effective piece of writing, one that works, will stand up to this type of scrutiny and instruct a writer who needs to understand the form.

Reader Expectation

The experienced writer anticipates the reader's expectations and makes use of them, developing, pacing, and voicing the draft to the reader's desires. If the boss wants specific facts, the writer delivers specific facts; if the reader expects understanding, the writer understands; if the company president will only consider an argument that appeals to the brain, the writer serves up thought; if the reader wants emotion, the writer provides emotional material; if the reader is busy, the writer is brief.

The writer becomes the reader, imagines what the reader expects, and delivers in many forms of writing. Each form the writer uses has its own pattern of reader expectation, and since we are readers as well as writers, we can predict those expectations.

Writing against Expectation

Some of the most effective writing, however, is written against the reader's expectations. The reader expects a sermon and receives a humorous story; the reader expects humor and receives a government report filled with facts that the reader slowly discovers is hilarious; the reader expects an emotional argument and is delivered a list of hard, cold facts; the audience expects a high-flown political speech full of grand clichés and hears a quiet, honest piece of autobiography; the reader of an annual report expects statistics and is taken on a walk through a manufacturing plant.

You can work against reader expectation when the draft communicates significant information in the manner most appropriate to that information; but it is important, in some way, that you let the reader know that you know the reader's expectations and are contradicting them on purpose.

You may be able to accomplish this more subtly, but readers who come to the page with an expectation—and all readers do—deserve a response to their expectation. If you don't anticipate their expectation, they will go away early and go away mad, and you aren't an effective writer if your readers leave and don't turn the page.

The Essential Narrative

We humans are the beast who records and shares the present, remembers the past, and predicts the future in narrative. We are storytellers, using the narrative's beginning, middle, and end to order the river flood of confusion and contradiction in which we struggle to survive.

We study all the variations of narrative in short story, novel, stage, screen, and television drama, but rarely examine the narrative that is imbedded in all effective writing—the proposal for a new marketing plan, the essay on health care, the insurance investigator's report, the sermon, the college scholarship application, the restraining order appeal, the memorial service remarks, even the lab and book reports. All are built on that sturdy and time-tested foundation of narrative.

If we are to become successful writers and rewriters we must develop the craft to create and then hide the narrative that underlies most effective writing. The reader does not need to see the narrative any more than we need to see the intestines of the writer, but the narrative and the human organs both must be in place and working.

As you start to study narrative, much of it will sound familiar. It should. You have been a story listener and a storyteller all your life. You were read Bible stories or *The Little Engine That Could*. You started to read stories yourself but before then watched stories on television, on VCRs or DVDs, at the movies.

Then you started to tell your own stories, some made up and some real, that allowed you to make sense of life and sharing that meaning. You became a storyteller and joined the human community.

Narrative's Clock

Story runs on time. This is not the time that is measured in the story—the last four minutes of the game, the life sequence of a biography, the pace of historical events, the time it takes to get the hero bedded and unbedded—but the unseen clock that runs behind the story. Narrative time is the time it takes to tell the story and move the reader through the story.

When we write narrative we distort time as life distorts time: I found that infantry combat is weeks of boredom interrupted by minutes of terror. The fundamental skill of narrative is to be able to expand time to reveal those moments, in which characters interact with such revealing actions as what must be said that isn't and what cannot be unsaid, that move the story forward, then move quickly through time to the next revealing, dramatic moment. The clock of narrative never ticks evenly but is sped up and slowed down.

When I write narrative I always attempt not to leap backwards, out of time—"meanwhile, back at the ranch"—and to have the events in the novel occur in a natural and revealing sequence. But when I have to use a flashback to recover material from the past, I must be aware that the narrative clock is running, timing how long it takes me to tell the flashback.

Questions Answered; Questions Asked

Beginning, middle, and end are in each narrative even if the writer begins in the middle of the end and then moves back to the beginning. Story implies sequence, one thing leading to another. There are many ways to think of this sequence, but the one that works best for me is an answer-question-answer-question-answer-question chain.

Each answer, each problem solved, brings with it a new question to be answered, a new problem to be solved.

> *Answer:* Kim decides to ignore her parents' command and go out with Bruce who is married but separated.
>
> *Question:* Kim has only known Bruce at work. What will he be like when they are alone away from the office?
>
> *Answer:* Bruce doesn't whine about his marriage as Kim fears or gossip about the office, but tries to find what Kim is like when she is away from her computer.
>
> *Question:* Kim is charmed at Bruce's attention to her but she can't get him to talk about himself. She knows him no better when he takes her home than she did when he picked her up.

And so the story is revealed as the narrative clock ticks. And the same sequence or narrative can underlie a marketing report.

> *Answer:* Corporate management has approved the promotion budget for "When It Itches," the new CD by The Minority of Eight.
>
> *Question:* How should it be spent?

Answer: This is the band's second CD. The first did well in its home area—Seattle and the Pacific Northwest—but not nationally. We should reinforce the band's regional popularity and plan for a national tour for CD three.

Question: How do we increase the audience depth in the Pacific Northwest?

Whatever names you give to narrative order, it should be familiar. You are the storytelling animal.

Walking Beside the Reader

When I tell a story in a novel, a newspaper column, at a party, or in a textbook such as this I like to imagine I am walking beside you, the reader, and that we are experiencing the story together. I am not ahead or behind you, above or below you, but at your side. We experience the story together.

This morning, for example, I started to write about the essential narrative. I knew it existed but I had never explored it before. As I have investigated this concept I have been aware of you by my side as we order and consider what we know about storytelling.

Reading the Listener

The oral storyteller is constantly surveying the audience, noting who is listening and who is not and how the balance is changing. This reading of the audience is essential to the writer. When we tell the story to a live audience, the reading is immediate. When we write we must predict the audience's reaction, anticipating the reader's questions and answering them at that moment; we must deliver a satisfying meal of information, not too little or too much; we must keep an eye on narrative's clock and move forward at a pace that allows the reader to comprehend and consider what we are saying.

Entertaining the Reader

Do you mean that the writer of an accident report, a petition to the court, a business plan, a proposal for a scientific grant, a scholarly essay re-examining the critical response to Emily Dickinson should all "entertain"?

They'd better, or the reader will turn to a writer who does entertain the mind or the emotions. The entertainment may be in a critical essay on the comic George Carlin or in a medical article on new research in atrial fibrillation. It may appeal to the mind or the emotions, forcing the reader to think or feel—and sometimes both simultaneously.

This isn't done, of course, with rhetorical dances, with words unconnected with meaning, with playing tricks on the reader, but by providing information the reader needs in an order that leads toward meaning. George Carlin or Garrison Keillor have an embedded narrative in their performances that reveals a significant commentary on the human condition, and so does the article on new methods of cardiac treatment of atrial fibrillation.

Design Your Own Genre

One of the delights of writing is to design your own genre that carries your individual information to your own reader. Many writing tasks do not fit a traditional genre or they combine traditional genres: description and argument, book review and essay, narrative and memo.

The experienced writer soon learns to design a genre that fits the task.

The Discovered Genre

To discover the organic or natural form that lies within a draft, read the draft quickly, trying to visualize the outlines of the piece, its horizons or boundary fences. There may be several genres in a draft. It may tell a story and use narrative techniques; try to persuade the reader and use some of the strategies of argument; relate facts in a manner appropriate to a scientific report. All these techniques might be used in a magazine article on an environmental problem. But the overall genre would be an investigative piece of magazine journalism.

Your job is to discover the genre that contains and communicates the message effectively.

The Invented Genre

The invented genre is created from the three principal elements:

- Message
- Purpose
- Reader

Once those elements are identified, the process of invention is usually a matter of simple logic. At first the inexperienced writer writes drafts and eventually discovers the need to invent a genre to do the job; the experienced writer sees the need ahead of time, but the process of design is the same.

Message

What is said comes first. The message itself, "I need money," is a force in determining the form. Each message may need a special container that will carry it efficiently to the reader.

Purpose

The purpose of the writer is another force that shapes genre. The purpose of the message "I need money" may be to get sympathy from a friend, to delay a lawsuit from someone to whom you owe money, to make someone pay up who owes you money, or to negotiate a loan from a parent, bank, or college financial aid officer.

Reader

The one who is to receive the message also exerts a profound influence on the genre. An appeal that works with a mother may not work with a father. A friend who owes you money may not be influenced by your good grades, but a financial aid officer may be affected by that information.

Create an Effective Design

It is a simple, logical matter to create an effective design, a genre that is custom-made to communicate a message to a listener and accomplish a clear purpose. Remember, you have been using speech to persuade, report, entertain, communicate since before you started school. You know many of the genres of our literary heritage, you simply don't know the names that scholars use to describe them, and that doesn't matter in the designing process.

Put the following headings across the top of a sheet or pad of paper or at the top of your computer display screen.

Message ⟶ Purpose ⟶ GENRE ⟵ Reader

Write a brief description of your message in the left-hand column; add a statement of purpose in the second column; then jump over GENRE and write a brief description of your reader. Now consider the forms that might deliver that message to that reader and accomplish your purpose. It may be the genre you have used in the first draft, the genre you used with some modifications, or a genre you have read and written before. It may also be a way—new to you—of delivering a message to a reader.

Here are some examples of how this method might work.

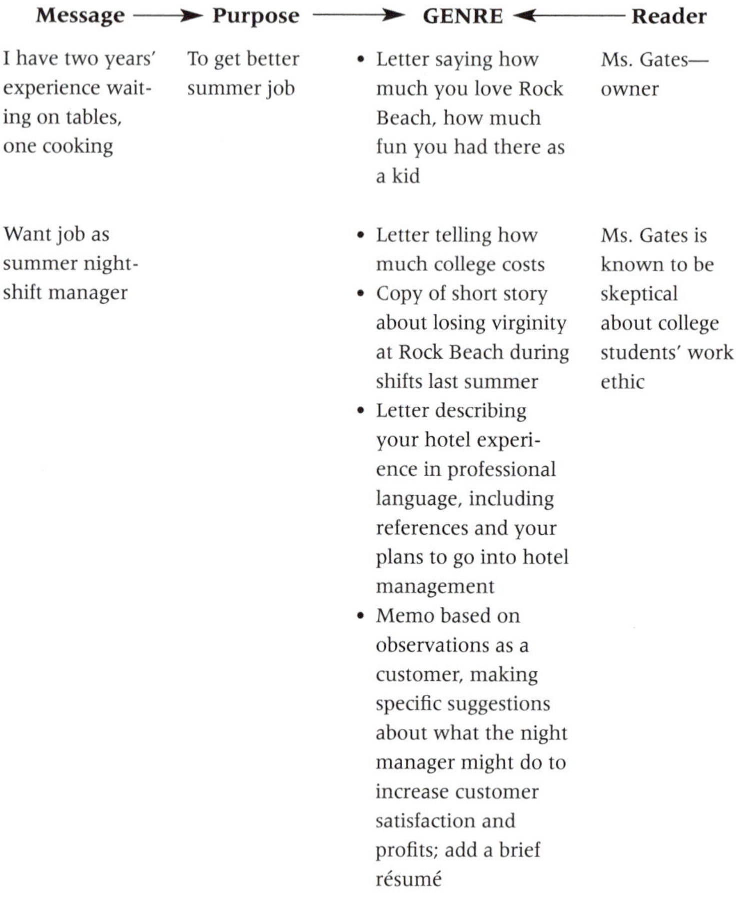

Message →	Purpose →	GENRE ←	Reader
I have two years' experience waiting on tables, one cooking	To get better summer job	• Letter saying how much you love Rock Beach, how much fun you had there as a kid	Ms. Gates—owner
Want job as summer night-shift manager		• Letter telling how much college costs • Copy of short story about losing virginity at Rock Beach during shifts last summer • Letter describing your hotel experience in professional language, including references and your plans to go into hotel management • Memo based on observations as a customer, making specific suggestions about what the night manager might do to increase customer satisfaction and profits; add a brief résumé	Ms. Gates is known to be skeptical about college students' work ethic

What Is Saved

All that is saved in the draft is the material that gives the genre shape and meaning. Each detail, each word, phrase, line, paragraph must move the meaning forward. When revising, the writer must, with a cold eye and an icy heart, examine each piece of information the writer has collected, each lovely phrase the writer has created, and save only those that clarify, develop, support, communicate the meaning.

What Is Discarded

Consider writer Isaac Bashevis Singer's wastebasket. He said, "The main rule of a writer is never to pity your manuscript. If you see something is no good, throw it away and begin again. A lot of writers have failed because they have too much pity. They have already worked so much, they cannot just throw it away. But I say that the wastepaper basket is a writer's best friend. My wastepaper basket is on a steady diet."

What is thrown into the wastebasket is not wasted. The material not used—that fascinating specific, the unexpected quotation, the phrase that once seemed to illuminate, the concept that once appeared to bring all the elements together—led to what was used and what is in the process of revealing meaning, as well as what will be shared in the final draft.

Go through a draft and make a plus mark in the margin opposite what must be kept and a minus mark opposite what might be cut. Cut and see if the draft becomes stronger. Usually it does, partly because you have the space to make the best parts better.

Remember that all genres not only help you see, they force you to look at the world in a particular way. The genre may limit your vision. I like to imagine my subject as it would be seen through the lens of other genres so that I do not miss important elements that must be dealt with to serve the reader effectively.

Case History of a Student Writer

Maureen Healy

Many Freshman English departments are divided in a civil war. On one side the scholars, armed with footnotes and bibliographies demanding all students write "The Research Paper" and on the other side, the writers, armed with anecdotes and specific details demanding all students write the personal narrative. The war, fought with rolling barrages of rhetoric, volleys of e-mail, and bombs in the form of memos and reports, can be threatening, boring, or amusing depending on the vantage point from which you observe the war but, of course, writing is writing. Personal narrative can require research and research requires personal experience.

It is important to learn the discipline of the research paper. It is vital in the academy where scholars depend on ordered, documented information to increase the resources of knowledge we have in every field from literature to hotel management, philosophy to engineering, agriculture to political science. The research paper provides the discipline that is necessary in the corporate marketing report, the medical research paper, the legal brief, the insurance investigative report, the stock offering proposal, all the many forms people use to persuade.

It is also important for students to learn to examine their own personal experience in a documented way, standing back from their immediate feelings to examine the life they are leading and to place it in a meaningful context.

Maureen Healy, a student at Boston College, was encouraged to make use of her personal experience in a research paper by her instructor, Mary Hallet. She is both an undergraduate learning to write with the discipline demanded of academic discourse and a person coming to terms with a serious illness. The paper allowed her to explore the subject with detachment and to apply what she learned to the intimate details of the life she was living. The well-written and well-researched result has the strength of both forms. It has the power of personal experience and the authority of scholarly research.

Here is an example from her first draft:

Learning

I was diagnosed with Juvenile Rheumatoid Arthritis when I was ten. At that age I had no concept of what the disease was. I felt pain, I knew I was slower than most children, but emotionally I denied something was wrong with me. I tried harder, I worked harder to measure up to healthy kids my age. I did not want to be better, I just wanted to catch up and do what the other kids could do. I didn't want anyone to know I had arthritis.

I later started to take a medicine called Methotextrate, which is also used to treat cancer patients. It is still commonly used today and has been proven to be effective medicine. However, when I was on this medication scientists were still testing it, and I was one of the youngest patients to try it. The result was negative. The medicine did help my body tremendously, yet it also made me feel as though I had the flu. This was my first experience on medication. I began to fear the disease I had. I could not understand that this medicine, the purpose of which was to make me better, could make me feel worse. From that time in my life, I had the notion that I may not be able to be helped.

As I aged, the arthritis in my body progressed, I had tried different types of medicines, but none of them were effective. The doctors were of very little help. I went to see a specialist in the Boston Floating Hospital, which was where I was diagnosed. Each trip to this hospital meant close to two thousand dollars without insurance (they did have a payment plan, fortunately) which included ultrasounds, x-rays, blood tests, seeing the specialist for approximately five minutes, and some intern telling me I had to exercise to get better. By that time I had been playing field hockey for four years, among other sports. What else could I do to get better?

I was around fifteen when I made the decision to not see a specialist for my arthritis. I did not want treatment anymore. I was committed to helping myself. I continued to be involved in sports for several more years, which was a great benefit to my long term health. However, it also caused injuries that now have progressed into bone and cartilage deterioration. But that I have always remained active is what has kept me going for almost twenty years. Though my body has not changed over the past ten years, I have not gotten worse since I was diagnosed. I have maintained my strength and all the ability I have.

After five years I finally chose to see a doctor again. I was recommended to a doctor who had dealt with women my age with rheumatoid arthritis. I am happy to say that she has helped me a lot. I am now in recovery, as I like to call it. Now I am making up for those years. I do not regret not seeing a doctor for that period of time. I chose this because I did not want to be on medication my entire life. And while I knew I had the strength, I decided to manage with the pain without help. Now, I can no longer take the pain. I have also realized that there are many new medications with fewer side effects, medicines that have done wonders for many people. There may also be a chance that if I start to take a medicine now, and in later years if the medicine has been effective, and I have improved, I can stop taking medicine entirely. With a new medication, I may also go into remission. The outlook looks good right now, with all the new medications and the advancements in the medical field.

The main achievement for me by going to this doctor was that I finally decided to learn about arthritis. I wanted to know about the medications I should or could be taking. This way I knew all the side effects, information I lacked when I first started taking medicine. It is important to me now to have a conversation with the doctor and not have everything explained to me. I wanted to understand what I have in store for me for the next five years. I have not found all the answers, but I know a lot more than I used to. For this research report, there is a lot at stake for me as an individual learning not just about some disease. I am learning about myself, what arthritis has done to me, and what I can do about it.

The hardest part of the research was finding the right information. I will explain that there are different arthritis diseases, and mainly focus on Rheumatoid Arthritis (RA) and Juvenile Rheumatoid Arthritis (JRA). The most common form of arthritis is RA. The Center for Disease Control and the Arthritis Foundation estimates that there are forty-three million people with RA (Wilcox, 37). More than seventy percent of women are effected (Wilcox, 38). JRA is one of the most prevalent chronic childhood diseases. Arthritis effects more than 285,000 children under the age of 17. JRA effects 71,000 children (Arthritis Foundation).

There are three different types of JRA. Pauciaticular (effective four or fewer joints) onset accounts for about half of all cases. Polyarticular (effectiving five or more joints) accounts for about 40 percent and Systematic (effecting the entire body) accounts for the remaining 10 percent. Although about two thirds to four thirds of all JRA patients experience a disease remission with little disability, early diagnosis and comprehensive therapy are important to minimize deformity and maximize normal growth and development (American Juvenile Rheumatoid Arthritis Organization).

Mary Hallet, Maureen's English instructor, confronted a common but always difficult problem in teaching writing by the conference method: How far should she go in encouraging a student to write about personal topics—the place where the best writing and the best learning about writing takes place?

When I first talked with Maureen she seemed a little discouraged. She had started, but then had to drop, a writing course the previous semester because of illness in her family. When I assured she could use some of the material she had written for that class, she finished and submitted a piece she had begun for that class about Juvenile Rheumatoid Arthritis (JRA). I found out from Maureen that she had much at stake in writing about this topic, as she herself had JRA.

I also sensed that this was a topic she wanted to continue to explore. So when it came time to write her researched narrative, I suggested that she continue to write about JRA. She told me her parents had some material on the topic at home, and when the class went together to the library to use the online catalog, she looked for other sources and searched the Internet for pertinent Web sites.

In gathering her sources, Maureen started a double-entry journal method of note taking but in the end seemed more comfortable with a kind of hybrid breed of recording information, simultaneously reflecting on what she had read and copying what she needed from her sources. As she wrote, she also synthesized directly from materials in front of her—articles, books, Web sites, etc.

When I read Maureen's first draft, I noticed that the moving story of her diagnosis, which had comprised the bulk of her personal narrative, was missing entirely.

She told me that she still wasn't sure how much of that story was appropriate to include in a research "report." I told her that this was the writer's dilemma when researching a topic "close to home," but to include as much of her personal experience as she wanted, at least to begin with.

In the second draft, she added her researched piece onto her personal narrative. This gave the paper more depth and a sense of Maureen's voice, but seemed disjointed where the personal experience ended and the research began. By simply adding one piece to the other, the essay also repeated certain information. The researched part of the narrative, for example, had included some facts and commentary that had already been addressed in the personal portion. We talked about ways she could synthesize the two pieces and cut out repetition.

Now Maureen Healy has invited us to join her on the intellectual and emotional journey of researching and writing her paper. We will hear her reflecting on the research and writing process as well as talking to herself in her daybook as she takes this trip into medical science and into her own life. In her account of the paper's research and writing, Maureen Healy documents the impact that writing can have on your life.

Maureen's Account of Crafting Her Essay

The topic for my research paper came from the personal essay that I wrote earlier in the semester. Exploring the topic personally was a good beginning. I had an understanding of what it meant to me, and I decided that I would like to learn more about it. I was also motivated by going to see a specialist for the first time in almost ten years and discussing new medications. I wanted to have a better understanding of these medications and my condition.

I started my research with materials I already had. I also found resources in the bookstore and in the library. Then I found the Arthritis Foundation, the National Arthritis Research

Foundation, and the American Juvenile Rheumatoid Arthritis Organization on the Internet. These Internet sites were very helpful. I had thought of interviewing my doctor, but I have no insurance, and it's $80 a visit and she allows only fifteen minutes a visit. So I did not use her as a significant source.

It was difficult finding information on JRA and teenagers because it is more common in younger people who grow out of it. There is little information on people my age (nineteen) with JRA because the actual number of people with this condition is small. So, because JRA and Rheumatoid Arthritis (RA) are so similar, I focused on RA as a description of the disease and then discussed what I knew and what I felt concerning JRA.

It was not difficult writing about myself, and talking about my experiences. Learning the specifics about the disease, though, was sometimes hard because now I realize the seriousness of it. However, finding the research gave me hope of a vaccine and gave me a better outlook.

When my teacher told me I could include my personal narrative into my researched narrative, I ended up adding the whole thing into the paper. This made the paper a lot stronger, but also longer. I then decided I had to organize the research better and add my thoughts about some of the information I found, and also discuss how it related to me. So the first complete version was mainly just research that was not structured well. The second had a major introduction, including a part of the original personal narrative about my first experience going to the hospital, which tied into my research. In the final draft, I cut out sections where I repeated myself and reorganized the research and writing so that it held together better. I also took out extra words or thoughts I repeated and smoothed out the writing.

I am very proud of the final version. It is an account of my life, my struggles and my future. This is the first paper I have ever written that conveyed so much about my life and also helped me discover so much about myself. I learned more than I expected and came away from this experience with a greater knowledge and confidence about this disease. So, all in all, writing this paper was never a chore. I was engrossed, involved and excited about the research. Every time I learned something new I called my Mom and told her about it. I felt great just knowing.

What follows are some of Maureen Healy's daybook entries:

7/13/99
Details, focus on the hospital experience itself, the doctors, the tone, my feelings, bitterness, smell of hospital, walls, decor, etc. DETAILS! Make it an analysis, go with structure already have but add more and give more.

7/15/99
I am just finishing my eighth page of my research narrative. Right now I feel really good about it. I just was on a roll. Reading my notes and putting my thoughts into it. It just flowed out and that made it so much easier to write. I am still going to the hospital library tomorrow. So if I find any more resources I will have to fit them in somehow. This was really a work in progress but I am proud. I feel as though I need more resources but I am at eight pages. I still should re-work it. I will copy out a draft to go over tonight.

7/20/99
More details—revision will involve more. The experience of being at a hospital, smells, walls, people, what they look like, doctors, nurses, etc. How did it impact me? What can I remember of the actual experience? Remember the look on my parents' faces? What was the doctor's expression? What did it feel like to be a patient for the first time? More details—analysis.

8/3/99
Portsmouth Hospital library, research arthritis there, large hospital library, hospital websites, Yale, Boston, etc. . . . Best suggestion so far has been to go to Portsmouth hospital to research their library. So far five pages written, need to outline it better and organize these thoughts. And go through all the information that I have. Need to restructure the paper. The opening is about my own thoughts and why I am writing it. May leave that and either add or shorten it. Need to find more info specifically on Juvenile Rheumatoid Arthritis.

Going well so far. I think I can get more info. I am enjoying this research and am enjoying it a lot, learning about myself, getting a better understanding.

8/16/99

- E-mailed Arthritis Foundation and also joined the organization
- E-mailed and joined the American Juvenile Rheumatoid Arthritis Foundation
- Found many websites
- Received some new information
- No success at library
- Found out that Portsmouth hospital library has medical journals that would not be comprehensive to the untrained eye, basically I would not understand the lingo
- Do not know how to document website, do not know how to site it on work-sited page
- I don't have any authors of research from websites. I only have the websites themselves
- Go back and find names of authors?
- It was a general bulletin board

8/17/99

Well, I am about to hand this in. Just wanted to write one late note. The research went well, I did have a hard time finding info. However the information that I did find worked well with the narrative. I learned a lot. I am really glad I was able to do this report. I will remember this research for a long time. It has really helped me. Anyways, its done!

Now we can read Maureen Healy's final draft:

Learning: Coping with Juvenile Rheumatoid Arthritis

Maureen Healy

The sign said Floating Hospital for Infants and Children, New England Medical Center, with a small arrow pointing left.

This was my first visit to Boston. As we waited in our car for the light to turn green, I stared at the tall buildings and business people in suits and sneakers in a rush to get somewhere. Since we crept along in a traffic jam for quite some time, I concentrated on everything around me. Mostly I saw people in a hurry, indifferent to their surroundings and other people. They seemed not the least bit confused by the loud noises of construction and car horns, the sewer smells of the street, or the homeless men asking anyone and everyone for change. They crisscrossed the streets among the countless cars backed up for blocks. I was not even in the hospital yet and I was already scared and shocked.

Finally, we reached the high-rise parking garage and drove up and down its floors for a half-hour waiting for someone to leave. Almost late for our appointment and with no time for lunch, we rushed to an elevator connecting the hospital entrance. My mother held my hand and my dad kept glancing back to make sure we were keeping up with him. As we followed all the signs and walked through an endless maze of hallways and people, I immediately recognized the unique and disturbing smell that reminded me of sterilization and the sick even though I had been in a hospital only a couple of times. The hallways and reception areas were crowded with people of all ages. Parents with children ranging from eighteen-year-olds to newborn infants filed into centers labeled by disease and medical specialty. It seemed as though everyone except us knew where they were going. The doctors were in a rush and detached; the nurses tried to help people from lab to lab. Some children were in wheelchairs with smiles on their faces; others struggling along on crutches; still others held the hand of their parents looking just as scared as I felt.

When we found our waiting room, my dad and I sat down as my Mom stood in line waiting to check in with the receptionist. The seating area seemed no bigger than my bedroom. Kids were playing with toys, reading books, bumping into each other, and a few tired ones were fighting. The really young children supported by their brothers or sisters were having a wonderful time annoying their parents and wreaking havoc on the room. It was total chaos.

I did not know then that the Floating Hospital, founded in 1894 as a hospital ship to help ill children, had some of the best child specialists in the world. The people in this waiting room came from distant places; they stayed in hotels nearby, often for days at a time. (We only lived two hours away so we were considered lucky.) This room, as well as the cheerful and helpful receptionists, therapists and nurses, for most families became an important and familiar source of comfort. However, Boston Floating is a teaching hospital, so most doctors stay only for the duration of their specialized internship. Patients usually are assigned a new doctor each appointment, with only a few minutes with the director of each center who checks the diagnosis of the student doctor. Parents must recite their child's medical history over and over, reconfirming what previous physicians have observed, as well as results of various tests and therapy sessions. Somehow there is never enough time to read the medical history in the patient's thick folder.

Throughout the waiting room I saw parents slouched in chairs with tired and distracted looks on their faces. I was overwhelmed by how their children took over the spaces in between, as if it were their own playground. Amidst what I took as a war zone, these parents were unconcerned about those of us who just wanted to sit in peace. My dad impatiently paced through the hallways while my mother sat next to me, shielding me from the surrounding noises. My dad is nervous in hospitals. He says he hates the sight of blood, but I really think his dislike of hospitals has to do with some kind of phobia. For him to come this day with us meant my visit to the doctor was serious.

My Mom is a calm person in any situation, especially the tough ones. This time I knew would be no exception. She dug out of her purse a paperback novel and quietly read. She got so absorbed in her reading that even when I said her name several times it did not penetrate. Eventually she looked up and asked if I said anything. By that time I had forgotten what was so desperately important. I was a little mad that I was not given the same attention as this novel. Once, though, I caught her glancing away from that novel and concentrating on a wall poster that said: "What chronic disease does your child have?" And also: "How to talk to doctors about your child's disease."

I could sense that there was more to this doctor's visit than I had been told. I was particularly sensitive to my parents' behavior, although they tried desperately to act normal. I needed them now more than any other day of my life. I had never seen a specialist. I was rarely sick and almost never got the colds and flu that went around school. My Mom always told me I was healthy. As soon as I had entered the hospital, removed from the curiosity and awe of the big city, I felt contained and not able to relax in any way. Nervousness is a trait inherited from my father, something I often feel when confronted with something new and different. I still get nervous just thinking about this trip. Everything that surrounded me was frightening in a way that I had never felt before. It was an uncontrollable feeling. I did not belong, I never would feel, in any way, at ease in all my time spent there.

I sat very still, my mother across from me in a chair reading, and my dad pacing and often disappearing from sight. A little girl who must been five or six kept screaming "no" over and over. The entire waiting room heard her loud piercing cry that I interpreted as a desperate plea for help. I saw concerned parents glancing at their children and hoping their daughter or son would not be the next one screaming. I felt numb with nervousness, and I became terrified. I sat in the same state for four hours.

Shortly after four o'clock I heard my name called. Eyes lifted. Heads turned. Everyone looked as if they had been awakened from a deep sleep. After waiting for that long, I wanted nothing more than to be out of that waiting room. My mother and I gathered up our things, and maneuvered through all the playing children. We could not find my dad; he had disappeared once again in the anonymous chaos of the main hallways. My mother waited for him by the reception desk as the nurse took me away. All alone I followed her into a small side-room with no door. The nurse was really nice, so for a moment I felt assured that I would not have to scream. I was weighed and measured. She took my blood pressure and smiled gently. She asked if I was nervous. I said yes. My heart was beating so rapidly, my whole body was shaking. She then led me to another room. First she politely knocked on the door and after hearing a response opened it. It sounded as if my parents were having a serious talk with the doctor. I felt betrayed, left out, unimportant. I was told to sit on an examining table. The room was painted dull pale green with a frayed poster of Monet's "Waterlillies" on one wall. There were two old wooden chairs; my father stood up and the doctor and my mother sat down. The room was small, cramped, cold and sterile.

I was introduced to Doctor Jameson. She was in her late twenties, and I quickly decided she was inexperienced. She asked me many questions about how I felt in the morning, during the day and when I went to bed. She wrote everything down and nodded her head absentmindedly each time I answered her. I could not understand why such information was important to her. It seemed so insignificant. She kept pushing her hair aside and appeared to be more involved with her hairstyle than us. Kids were yelling and running around outside the door. We had not escaped the chaos. The doctor seemed cold and distracted, and I did not know what I was supposed to say. I did not know why I was there. I only knew that I was different. I could not do somersaults like all of my friends and that I had stopped growing for a year.

After all the questions, I was told that I had to have tests. I had never had tests before, except a blood test in my family doctor's office. We were given instructions to go to another section of the hospital. After searching from floor to floor, and getting mixed up on the elevator, we found another waiting room. The hospital was closing soon and the hallways became very quiet. I felt a little more relaxed not having to hear screaming children and not bumping into frantic doctors and lost visitors like us. I was led to another examination room, and I had to put this blue starched robe on, sit on a freezing metal table and have x-rays taken of my elbows, knees and hips. This required me to be in the most awkward positions and have to explain to the technicians that my arms could not straighten and my hips were stiff.

Next, I had an ultrasound that examined just my elbows. A glob of cold and sticky gel was spread on my arms to lubricate the instrument the doctor used so it could move freely about my arm. This is what the doctor said, although I had no clue what it all meant.

With test results in hand, we finally were taken back into the first examining room. By now the hospital seemed very familiar, but I was exhausted. My Mom was almost finished with her novel of roughly two hundred pages. My dad had bags under his eyes and yawned continuously. It was about 6 P.M.

Hearing a loud knock on the door, we looked up to see Dr. Jameson come in with two new doctors. Doctor Jameson introduced the head of the department, Doctor Schaler, and assistant head, Doctor Thomas. Doctor Schaler looked over the papers in my file and then set them aside. She was tall, stately, serious and seemed very much in charge. She focused on me with a smile and took a deep breath; I think she was trying to remember my name; she began the conversation with me. Dr. Jameson was concentrating on Dr. Schaler's every word and would turn her head towards me and smile every once in a while, almost as a courtesy. Dr. Thomas was busy writing and reading results and notes, ignoring our presence, as if she were separate from the discussion. Dr. Jameson again became very involved in her hair, tossing layers back with her hand while trying to concentrate on Dr. Schaler's analysis. I felt like a nameless patient.

"The test results indicate Rheumatoid Arthritis," Dr. Schaler casually stated. As she continued her speech, I tried to spell the words out in my head. She explained to my parents that I had to see a physical therapist and should be on medication. Nothing the doctors said made sense to me. I looked to my parents who appeared to be just as confused as I was. My mother gazed down at the floor, looking almost relieved that it was not worse. My father's glassy eyes stared blankly at the doctor. He seemed to have heard nothing, and looked slightly in shock.

There are many different arthritis diseases, but I am mainly concerned with Rheumatoid Arthritis (RA) and its relative,

Juvenile Rheumatoid Arthritis (JRA)—my disease. The most common form of arthritis is RA. The Center for Disease Control and the Arthritis Foundation estimates that 43 million people have RA (Wilcox 37). More than seventy percent of these are women. RA also affects more than 285,000 children, 71,000 of whom have JRA, one of the most prevalent chronic childhood diseases. The distinguishing factor between the two diseases is that JRA is a condition one is born with, while RA affects people later in life, usually between the ages of 20 and 50.

JRA can take one of three forms: Pauciaticular onset (affecting four or fewer joints) accounts for about half of all cases. Polyarticular (affecting five or more joints) accounts for about forty percent. And Systematic (affecting the entire body) accounts for the remaining ten percent. Although about two-thirds to three-fourths of all JRA patients experience a disease remission with little disability, early diagnosis and comprehensive therapy are important to minimize deformity and maximize normal growth and development (American Juvenile Rheumatoid Arthritis Organization).

In all these types of arthritis, the immune system, for unknown reasons, attacks a person's own cell inside the joint capsule. White blood cells that are part of the normal immune system travel to the synovium and cause a reaction. This reaction, or inflammation, is called synovitis, and it results in warmth, redness, swelling and pain. During the inflammation process the cells of the synovium grow and divide abnormally, making the normally thin synovium thick and resulting in a joint that is swollen and puffy to the touch. As the disease progresses, these abnormal synovial cells begin to invade and destroy the cartilage and bone within the joint. The surrounding muscles, ligaments and tendons that support and stabilize the joint become weak and unable to work normally. All of these effects lead to the pain and deformities often seen with rheumatoid arthritis and JRA. Doctors studying rheumatoid arthritis now believe that damage to the bones begins during the first year or two the person has the disease (Wilcox 97).

Arthritis can attack any joint. However, rheumatoid arthritis usually affects hands, wrists, elbows, shoulders, knees, ankles and feet. This usually happens in the morning; patients tend to feel pain and stiffness when they first wake up. A hot shower or bath can sometimes warm the joints and patients start to feel better and have less pain (McIlwain and Bruce 56–57). An article I read, for example, tells about how a six year old child with JRA soaks in hot baths for a few hours every morning before school. The child also has twin younger brothers with JRA. All three have inherited the disease from their father. Caring for such children is an emotional and draining task for parents, and sometimes these children get to school late. "Sometimes they do not make it at all" (Edgar 28).

Other problems associated with arthritis include swelling of the joints, fever, loss of weight, and skin rashes. Internal organ disease may also coincide with arthritis and affect kidney, heart and other organs (Tucker et al. 34) To add to that, most medications that treat arthritis have harsh side effects for major organs such as the kidneys and liver. Dr. Doyt L. Conn, in "Scared by Side Effects," says, "After reading the pharmacy sheets listing side effects of the medications I take for rheumatoid arthritis, I can't help but wonder if the cure is worse than the disease. . . . No medicine is completely safe." However, the dangers of untreated RA, in most cases, far outweigh the risks of the drugs used to treat it (Conn 58–59).

Some medications treating arthritis, such as aspirin, are used purely for pain relief (McIlwain and Bruce), others to reduce inflammation, and a third type called "disease modifying antirheumatic drugs," or DMARDs, are used to slow the course of the disease. The third are the strongest type, and includes the drug Arava that I will begin taking soon, and Methotextrate, my first medication (Dunkin 27). Currently, I am taking Plaquenil, which reduces inflammation. I will continue to take this medication when I begin Arava because some medications work jointly with greater results to fight the disease. So far Plaquenil has been successful in reducing swelling in my hands. However, I suffer from bone deterioration in my elbows, causing swelling and pain. Potentially, Arava should prevent more deterioration.

As children grow, arthritis can cause bone deformities and also slow growth and development. When I was seven, my family doctor decided that I should see a specialist because I had stopped growing for an entire year. When I was referred to a specialist nearby who could not understand my symptoms, I was sent to the Floating Hospital in Boston. There I saw one of the top specialists in the country. At that time, I did not have swelling in my joints. However, I was incredibly stiff. Because of a history of arthritis in my family, especially a grandmother who had the disease in her twenties, the doctors determined I had JRA.

Family history definitely plays a role in my disease (Dunkin and Reese 42). My father has rheumatoid arthritis; he had it at the time I was diagnosed. He was fifty at that time. My father remembers that my grandmother also had some form of arthritis, most likely JRA. By the age of forty, the disease had crippled her. She had played the piano her whole life and taught my father as well. What my father remembers as most devastating was the way her hands became so crippled she could not play anymore. And when he was a child, she could not care for him because of her loss of mobility. (Her sister-in-law took care of my father most of the time, but he tells me he "got away with murder," because his mother could not run after him and his aunt had to look after every one else too.) Doctors eventually treated my grandmother with a common painkiller of that period (we believe Morphine). It is fair to assume they knew relatively little about its harsh effects. My grandmother died from high doses of this medicine, her organs finally deteriorating.

My father was my age when his mother died. He has told me that I look and act much like her. I too play the piano and knowing these stories about my grandmother has been my motivation to get well. I feel like I know her. I feel as though she is with me, helping me persevere. In over ten years of playing the piano, I have not stopped. It gets a little harder every year, but somehow I can always play for hours. She is my only link to this disease. My father has eight children, and I am the only one with JRA.

It is likely that if I have children my gene for JRA will be passed down (Tucker et al. 101). It would be devastating to see my own child have to deal daily with pain as I do. While my arthritis is by far not as bad as most, many children and young adults have to use crutches and wheelchairs because their bodies are deformed. During my experiences at the Boston hospital, I saw children in the most agonizing pain, having no strength, extremely thin, joints red and swollen. It was an awakening for me to witness this at such an early age. Just seeing these children gave me motivation to strive for improvement. The most difficult struggle I see in my future is raising my own child with this crippling disease. My mother always says to me that she wishes there were a way she could absorb my pain and take away my fears for the future. I know her feelings of helplessness and frustration. Someday I may also go through those exact emotions with my own child.

I have always felt in my heart some kind of inner strength that resists any urge to give up; this does not allow me to give in to my pain. I often remember those children I observed at the hospital and know always that it could be worse. I have made it this far, and I have got the rest of my life to live. There is no better time than now: That is my motto. For five years I remained off medicine because I knew I would have to depend on it in later years. I wanted to spend some of my life without that risk while I knew I had the strength. But I do not feel as though I am giving in by using medicine again. I am simply getting older.

Recently, I have been looking into the new arthritis research on the Internet. Learning about these advancements has given me hope for the future. The Arthritis Foundation has been promoting their new research on finding a cure for arthritis. There is talk of a vaccine that could prevent arthritis. Researchers are also studying genetic factors that predispose some people to developing RA, as well as factors connected to the disease's severity. The aim to identify genes involved in RA has become a major effort. NIH (National Institutes of Health) and the Arthritis Foundation have joined together to support the North American Rheumatoid

Arthritis Consortium. This group of 12 research centers around the U.S. is collecting medical information and genetic material from 1,000 families in which two or more siblings have RA. It will serve as a national resource for genetic studies of the disease.

Researchers are also exploring why so many more women than men are developing rheumatoid arthritis. They are studying female and male hormones and other elements that differ between men and women—for example, possible differences in their immune responses. Researchers are examining why RA often improves during pregnancy. Results from one study suggest that the explanation may be related to differences in certain special proteins shared between a mother and an unborn child. These proteins help the immune system distinguish between the body's own cells and foreign cells, which may change the activity of the mother's immune system (Arthritis Foundation).

This information is plentiful. The hardest information to find, however, is about teenagers with JRA. I found only one article directed at teenagers. I am nineteen, a young adult, but these years are determined by hormone changes. The research confirms that hormone changes can affect arthritis in either negative or positive ways. I hope that the medicine I will begin taking will help me as I go through these changes. And I have to try different medications in order to know what works (American Juvenile Rheumatoid Arthritis Organization).

It is frightening to have to accept at age nineteen that I have arthritis. It is difficult to explain to someone my age how hard it is just to get up in the morning. People rarely look at me and know I have this disease. It is getting easier to explain as I get older, but, at the same time, I hate to be reminded of it. I have learned to understand and accept my condition, slowly, day by day, knowing that what I feel comes from the disease, not from a lack of trying.

When I left that hospital nearly twelve years ago, I did not know that I had a chronic terminal disease. I felt pain almost all the time. I knew my bones were small; I knew I was slower growing than most children. But emotionally I denied something was wrong with me. I tried harder, I worked harder to measure up to healthy kids my age. I did not want to be better than them; I just wanted to catch up and do what the other kids could do. I did not want anyone to know I had arthritis.

I wish that, back then, someone had taken the time to explain to me what the disease was. The fright and anxiety from not knowing why I was at the hospital is indescribable. I had no experiences with illnesses or medications. I did not understand pain or tolerance. The doctors were cold and the hospital was frightening, and from that day forward I was scared to go back there, or to any doctor, and even more worried about what the doctors would find out.

Six months after the hospital visit, I began taking a medicine called Methotextrate, first used to treat cancer patients. It is an effective medicine commonly used today both for cancer chemotherapy and arthritis. However, when I started this medication it was only in its experimental stages for children with arthritis. Doctors did not always know the impact high doses would have on someone my age. For many the results were good; for me, it was negative. The medicine did help the joints of my body, yet it made me feel as though I always had a bad case of the flu. This was my first experience on medication. I began to fear arthritis.

I could not understand how this medicine, the purpose of which was to make me better, could make me feel worse. I began to get the notion that I could not be helped. During my teens, the arthritis in my body worsened and progressed to other joints. I tried different types of medicines and physical therapies but none of them were effective, and the doctors were of very little help. I continued to see a specialist in the Boston Floating Hospital. Each trip to this hospital cost close to two thousand dollars (my father had retired without long-term insurance and new plans excluded my arthritis so we were without insurance). These visits again included ultrasounds, x-rays, blood tests, seeing the specialist for approximately five minutes, and some intern telling me I had to exercise to get better. By that time I had been playing field hockey for four years, as well as other sports and physically demanding exercise at school. What else could I do?

I was around fifteen when I made the decision to stop seeing a specialist for my arthritis. I did not want treatment anymore. I was committed to helping myself. I continued to be involved in sports for several more years, and I have always remained physically active. This, more than anything else, has kept me going for almost my whole life. Though my body has grown over the past ten years, I have maintained my strength and physical dexterity since my first diagnosis.

This spring, however, I finally decided to see a specialist once again. I was recommended to a rheumatologist who has experience with women of my age with rheumatoid arthritis. I am happy to say that with her help and new medicines there have been less swelling and pain. I am now in recovery, as I like to call it. But I do not regret not having seen a specialist for so long. I did not want to be on medication my entire life; and natural methods of handling the pain, such as massage therapy and herbal baths, can make the symptoms more bearable (Wilcox 55). I also knew I had personal strength, so I decided to manage the pain without help. Now, however, I can no longer take the pain, and I have learned that many new medications with fewer side effects have helped others. There may also be a chance that if I start to take medicine now, and in later years if I have improved, I can stop taking it entirely. I could go into remission.

I pray for a cure, but if there never is one, I have at least lived my life the best way I know how. I have taken control and helped myself. Learning about arthritis through research has been the most rewarding experience in dealing with this disease. I have finally found answers to the questions I have had for almost my whole life. It is remarkable the comfort you can gain through knowledge. I finally know what I am up against.

Works Cited

Arthritis Foundation. Atlanta, GA. 16 August 1999. <http://www.arthritis.org>.

American Juvenile Rheumatoid Arthritis Organization. Atlanta, GA. 16 August 1999. <http://www.arthritis.org.>

Conn, Doyt L., M.D. "Scared by Side Effects." *Arthritis Today.* Jan.–Feb. 1999: 58–61.

Dunkin, Mary Anne. "Arthritis Today's Drug Guide." *Arthritis Today.* July–Aug. 1999: 27–48.

Dunkin, Mary Anne and Krista Reese. "Your Heritage, Your Health." *Arthritis Today.* Jan.–Feb. 1999: 41–45.

Edgar, Kathy A. "My Three Sons." *Arthritis Today.* Jan.–Feb. 1999: 28–32.

McIlwain, Harris H., M.D., and Debra Fulghum Bruce. *The Super Aspirin Cure for Arthritis.* New York: Bantam Books, 1999.

Tucker, Lori B., M.D., et al. *Your Child with Arthritis.* Baltimore: Johns Hopkins University Press: 1996.

Wilcox, Deborah A. *Arthritis Relief! Breakthroughs in Natural Healing.* Michigan: Rhodes and Easton, 1998.

Maureen's teacher wrote:

> ***In the final draft, Maureen used her personal experience and commentary as a frame for the research, keeping some of it in the beginning and moving the rest to the end, embedding most of the researched portion in the middle. She also eliminated some repetition, and used extra spacing as transitioning devices. Then she edited to pare down and smooth out some sections.***
>
> ***I think the most difficult part of this project for me was dispelling the student's idea that research and personal narrative were two discrete and different genres. If we had extra time together, I would work with Maureen to more seamlessly weave her personal experience into her research. Still, Maureen's final draft is passionate and compelling, and her engagement with her work and her real stake in finding answers affirmed for me the importance of encouraging students to see how research can be both academically and personally significant.***

Chapter 6 REWRITE WITH STRUCTURE

A novel is a piece of architecture. It's not random wallowings or confessional diaries. It's a building—it has to have walls and floors and the bathrooms have to work.

—JOHN IRVING

Has a drinking song ever been written by a drunken man? It is wrong to think that feeling is everything. In the arts, it is nothing without form.

—GUSTAV FLAUBERT

Plot might seem to be a matter of choice. It is not. The particular plot for the particular novel is something the novelist is driven to. It is what is left after the whittling-away of alternatives. The novelist is confronted . . . by the impossibility of saying what is to be said in any other way.

—ELIZABETH BOWEN

Readers should be drawn into a piece of writing so they will follow a trail that leads to meaning. During the revision process, the writer clears and marks that trail. The effective writer creates paths of continual seduction that keep readers interested.

Readers are in control. Readers can leave the writing at any time and will if they don't have a sense of progress. They may not be told explicitly where the writing is taking them, but they need to have a sense that they are moving toward meaning.

Rewriting effectively means reading what you have written with a stranger's eyes to see if there is a clear, seductive trail of exploration that runs through the draft. That line may be clearly marked by headings or it may be hidden within the material, but readers must sense a sequential order in what they are reading or they will put the writing down.

Diagnosis: Disorder

In diagnosing a draft, there may be many signs of disorder. For example, the writer may start out describing the drinking policy on campus, then suddenly switch into the history of fraternities and sororities and anti-discrimination laws, return to the drinking policy, then go into the author's own high school drinking history, and swerve back to the college alcohol regulations. The reader loses track of the topic and the writer's opinion, and stops reading. Disorder is not attractive in a kitchen, but it's fatal on the page. Here are some of the signs of disorder in a draft:

1. The trail through the draft is based on a sequence of false assumptions or assumptions that are true only to you, the writer. Count the false assumptions in the following example. I count three whoppers.

   EXAMPLE

   We should not send good tax dollars to foreign countries. Other countries do not have the moral standards of the United States. Better to use those bucks at home, in our cities, for example. Even if people cheat welfare at least it is on the economy. At least if you make a bad loan it should be to someone in the family, then there's no trouble.

2. The writer tells us the emotions the writer wants us to feel, but we need less emotional direction and more details that make us feel for the writer and the writer's father. The reader should have the emotions; the writer should inspire those emotions from what is written on the page.

   EXAMPLE

   I was so overwhelmed when I saw my father, after all this time, and in a hospital bed. It was so sad, I almost cried. In fact, I did cry, the hospital bed and everything. I remembered him young and he was so suddenly old. All the feelings of hatred and resentment and anger and loss surged up within me. And yet he was my father. It was tragic, so sad for him and for me.

3. The draft was written by a kangaroo who takes great leaps for reasons the reader does not understand.

EXAMPLE

If we are going to do something about the deficit we should start by paying ball players less. The owners of professional teams make money, and so do universities from football, but the workers earn more than is appropriate in a nation that has a foreign trade imbalance and a national debt to reduce. Taxes on sport tickets might help.

4. The writer is lost in the accumulation of information that seems to have no context, no fascination for anyone but the writer, no order.

EXAMPLE

I have put a new Pentium 120 chip Lexus 480M in my computer, but I don't need to in my laptop, new, that already has a Pentium Q400 STA, with lotsa ram—188 mg—and even with memMaker and Qemm. I get General Protection Faults but that's probably my scanner or Omni-Page if it isn't my 4 quad CD-ROM, but the Zip drive is great.

5. The writer wanders off the trail to examine wildflowers, butterflies, and mountain streams that are interesting but have nothing to do with the subject at hand.

EXAMPLE

Trust is the most important element in a relationship. I certainly discovered that after the accident in the sculpture studio last week when my roommate trusted her partner and lost three fingers to a power saw a classmate said he knew how to operate. I wonder about the role of trust when people perform dangerous jobs in the military, as lumberjacks or as farm workers, especially children.

6. The rewriter asks, "How does this piece of information advance the reader's understanding of the subject?" and finds there is no answer.

EXAMPLE

Automobile manufacturers have adapted vehicles to the needs of their customers and to the dreams of their customers. They may live in an urban area but they like to drive adventure vehicles, four-wheel drive and all, as if they were pioneers. These vehicles allow the driver to sit up high and they are ready to ford rivers, up canyon arroyos, whatever, drive through snowdrifts in the Sunbelt.

7. The sequence is unnatural, because the reader has to leap back and forth in time or logic for no artistic reason, going from A to F to C to G to K to B.

EXAMPLE

There are things I know now about college sports recruiting that I didn't when I needed to. I can't blame my parents. They never went to college, to high school. What my high school coach told me was all wrong. I can't believe what he said. And it wasn't just this school. I was made promises like you can't imagine. And no one told me what would happen to me if what happened. Now I know and it's too late. But maybe the appeal will help.

8. The draft reads like Swiss cheese—it is full of holes.

EXAMPLE

The latest treatment for diabetes, at least in tests, is far better than current practice and will be appropriate for all kinds of diabetes, although the treatment will differ unless new technology is developed, as has been announced, and its cost is cheaper than what patients have to pay now, a substantial figure at best.

9. The reader's questions are not answered the moment they are asked. The effective writer can predict when

the reader needs a definition, documentation, an example, more description by hearing the reader's subconscious questions: What's that word mean? How come? Who says? So what?

EXAMPLE

We were supposed to have M-1s but we were issued Enfields on which we had not been trained and had to hold our positions against the enemy even though we did not know how to use the pieces since were trained on the others and the difference was great as you can imagine.

Answer the Reader's Questions

I have found one organizational technique more effective than any other in revision: anticipate and answer the reader's questions. Any piece of writing is a conversation with a reader who interrupts to say:

"How come?"
"How do you know that?"
"Says who?"
"I don't get it."
"What do you mean?"
"I'd like to know more about that."
"No kidding."
"Why'd she do that?"
"What'd he do then?"
"Tell me more."
"Stop it. Enough already."
"Get to the point."
"Whoa. Back up, I don't understand."
"Whatta you mean 'gaseous diffusion'?"

Inexperienced writers—and some experienced ones—do not hear that half of the conversation. All effective writers hear the reader's questions and *answer them the moment they are asked*. In an essay on civil rights, here are the questions the reader might ask about your draft:

- Who is most responsible for the passage of the Civil Rights Act of 1964?
- Who was for it? Against it? Why?
- What federal civil rights laws—if any—were in place before the Civil Rights Act of 1964?
- What did it accomplish?
- Why was it needed?
- What did the law say?

I usually find that there are four to six questions that must be answered to satisfy the reader. They are the simple, obvious questions that someone who is deeply involved in the subject may forget, but the common reader will ask. They may even be questions the writer does not want to have asked, but there is no escape: Those questions will be asked—and they must be answered.

After the writer has determined the questions, the order in which they will be asked can be anticipated. The question third from the end in my example should be last and the one second from the end should be first (and the third question can be incorporated into it).

- Why was the Civil Rights Act of 1964 necessary; weren't there laws against discrimination?
- Who is most responsible for the passage of the Civil Rights Act of 1964?
- Who was for it? Against it? Why?
- What did the act provide?
- What did it accomplish?

Can you use this technique *before* you write the first draft? Of course. I still have to use it in revising and in editing other people's copy. A version of this that I have used in revision is to write the reader's questions that the writer is answering in the margin of the draft and then reorder the piece to anticipate the sequence in which the reader would ask them.

Outline After Writing

Outlining is normally considered as only a planning activity, but my most helpful outlines are often made *after* the first draft. To do an effective outline in advance of writing, the writer has to have a firm idea of what the draft is going to say. And many times, since writing is thinking, it is impossible to write anything but a brief sketch outline—a guess—ahead of time.

It is, however, always helpful to outline during revision to reveal the structure of a draft, and then to design the structure that the draft must have to satisfy the reader.

Expose the Structure of a Draft

Here are some of the ways the writer can strip away the language from the draft and reveal the structure underneath:

- Ask the reader's questions as described earlier.
- Read through the draft and make a formal outline to visualize the structure of the draft.
- Use the movie writer's storyboard and put each topic you come to on a slip of paper with a reference to the page and line in the draft ("statistics on rural poverty p. 3, L 13–22"). Then rearrange the slips of paper into a logical sequence.
- Create, on the computer or by drawing, a tree that shows the sequence of major points in the draft in the way that computer programs display directories and subdirectories.
- Draw a graph with a computer program or on graph paper that shows how the major issues rise, fall, and interact with other issues in the draft as graphs show the rise and fall of the stock market.

- Write a quick, shopping-list sketch of the main points in the draft.
- Make a computer printout of the draft on your screen; underline or otherwise mark the key phrases; then cut away the rest of the draft to see the structure revealed.

Outline After Writing

- Write out the questions asked by each section, and then look to see if they are answered in the sections that follow.
- Write down the major section headings to see the line—the logical order—that is the skeleton of the draft.

Adapt the Structure

Once you see the structure of the draft, you can often imagine the structure the reader needs. It may be easy to adapt your draft to the needs of the reader by moving sections around, perhaps creating new ones and eliminating old ones. Such moves may be suggested by test readers—classmates, workshop members, instructors, editors, friends, family—who, because of their need to understand and their distance from the writing of the draft, see a potential new structure clearly.

Redesign the Structure

Many times the structure of the draft has to be abandoned; it just doesn't do the job of producing a draft that can be understood by the reader. In this case you have to design a new trail through the material.

This is a good time to work backward:

- Write down at the bottom of a page what you want the reader to think and feel after reading your draft.
- Pick a starting point in the material that is as close to the end as possible while including all the information

the reader needs to arrive at the conclusion you have written at the bottom of the page.

- Note the three to five pieces of information the reader needs, in sequence, to arrive at your ending.

Interview with a Student Writer

Kathryn S. Evans

Kasey Evans, now a doctoral student at the University of California, Berkeley, was a 20-year-old English major and a junior at Princeton University when she responded to these questions. She graduated from Oyster River High School in Durham, New Hampshire, where she received the Yale Book Award, the Valedictory Medal, the faculty Honor Key Award, the Robert Byrd Scholarship, a National Merit Scholarship, and several departmental awards.

With a grant from the Princeton Plasma Physics Lab, Kasey held a 1995 summer internship, teaching math, science, and English to middle-school students from the Trenton public school system. In the summer of 1996, she worked as an intern in the production department of Heinemann Books in Portsmouth, New Hampshire.

At Princeton, where she studied under Russell Banks and Joyce Carol Oates, Kasey was the editor-in-chief of *The Princeton Eclectic,* a writing magazine for which she also served as contributor, copyeditor, and fiction editor.

What techniques do you use to plan or outline information before writing a first draft? How do you adapt it during the research, drafting, or rewriting process?

Prewriting—in both the amount I do and the strategies I use—depends on the kind of writing I'm doing. I begin essays by writing stream-of-consciousness notes. I start with obvious citations, or a rehashing of class discussions, and free-associate. Certain ideas or themes reappear. I connect these with arrows, or asterisks, and continue writing about how or why the two instances of the idea connect.

Why does Dante use the same phrase to describe himself, at the beginning of the poem, and the false prophets down in lower Hell? Plato's idea that we are all degenerate versions of a single perfection—why does that same idea appear in Boethius? And then again in Augustine? And then Milton, and then Faulkner, and then . . .

These notes aren't in full sentences, and end up looking like annotated road maps. Once I think my road map contains enough information to complete the assignment, I start to translate it into an outline. I write an approximate thesis idea at the top of a clean sheet of paper. This thesis—which usually lacks a verb, and so is still mostly a vague idea that will, hopefully, give rise to a thesis—names what the arrows stood for in the map: "Dante's anxiety about his own sin" or "degeneracy: human life as turning away from the 'real.'" (The would-be thesis usually sounds pretty incoherent at this point—it's not just that I've given poor examples.)

Then I start to list the passages or quotations that started me on my road mapping in the first place, trying to group them into some kind of order. After I write each quote/idea, I write how that evidence relates to the idea at the top of the page. I'm still thinking at this point, not just reorganizing; I'm still trying to make connections that will flesh out a thesis.

By the time I've slogged through the instances that I included on the road map, along with any others I've thought of while writing, a theme has hopefully developed, one that will supply a verb to that thesis idea at the top of the paper. Then I can go back and revise that heading:

> "Dante's anxiety about his own writing makes him feel sympathy for the false prophets."

If I feel confident about this outline, I'll start drafting on the computer from the notes that I have. If the connections still seem tenuous, if I'm not sure that my evidence really says what I want to make it say, then I go through again, making more notes, drawing more arrows, revising the thesis, until I have a more secure outline.

The fiction writing that I've done hasn't required similarly formal prewriting. I carry a daybook/journal in which I write down the stuff of my day: bits of dialogue, anecdotes, descriptions, topic ideas, smells, and anything else that seems as if it could provide fodder for later writing.

Because the assignments I've had for fiction classes are permissive (i.e., "write something this week"), I don't plan so much as I plunge. If I begin with a voice of a character I think I want to use, I'll write in the first person for a while and see what comes of it. If I liked the girl behind the counter at the coffee shop, then I'll write a scene about what she did when she got off work and see where it goes.

When writing fiction, I use the drafting process to discover my story and to surprise myself. I'm not willing to be surprised by my essays, for the most part (especially when I'm writing them at three o'clock in the morning of the deadline, as I am wont to do). If I haven't learned something in the process of writing the essay, then I have written a terrible essay. The things that I learn in the process of writing essays, though, work within the structure that I have planned for them. The things I learn when writing fiction are more drastic: That character isn't actually his sister; she's his girlfriend, and she can't appear until the fourth chapter.

This discrepancy means that I rewrite most of the fiction that I draft, and I merely revise the essays.

How do you know you need to revise and switch to a different tactic or reorganize a draft?

I need to reorganize when there's nothing to say. If I find myself avoiding a piece, or starting 17 new stories so I don't have to go back to an ongoing one, I can be pretty sure that I need to make substantial changes in the draft that will make it appealing again.

The most common substantial change I make in fiction pieces is a voice change. I get bored if I'm in first person and want to know what the other characters are thinking, but can't; I get lost and overwhelmed if I'm in third person, trying to understand how all 37 characters understood their night at the beach when Bob is the only one who seems to be having an interesting night. Voice change is also a somewhat safe place to start reordering a draft, because it doesn't require that

I give up the entire premise of a story. I don't have to admit to myself, "Well, maybe this one isn't going to work." (At least, I don't have to admit it yet.) I can keep the concept, keep the dialogue, keep the setting: I just have to rethink the way I go about telling it.

What attitudes do you find helpful as you order your raw materials or reorder a draft and what specific process—or processes—do you use to reorder a draft?

The most difficult, and the most important, thing for me to remember when revising is to be willing to abandon what I've done. I try to rehearse in my head: "You are capable of writing well. To say that, however, does not mean that just because you have written it, it is written well." I think often of Anne Lamott, in *Bird by Bird,* when she wrote about an editor who rejected a novel she had written. "Your problem," he told her, "is that you think that everything that has happened to you is interesting." Not everything, I remind myself, is interesting just because it comes from your brain.

As a guideline, to keep myself from becoming too wedded to my first drafts, I try to cut at least a third of what I've written. I literally take a word count, and cut until a third of that number is gone. This sounds arbitrary and silly, but I've never had to cut any keystones. The way I draft, I can easily cut a third of my first-draft words without losing the heart of a story.

To lessen the pain of making major cuts, I keep a document on my computer entitled (strangely enough) "cuts." When I start to agonize about whether to cut a paragraph/page/section/dialogue/ description, I cut it and paste it into the document. Pasting it somewhere makes me feel as if I haven't completely abandoned it, and makes me less reluctant to cut. (I have never, incidentally, pulled anything back out of the "cuts" document and reused it.)

I try also to remember that the stories have all been told before. I'm never going to entirely create something—I'm just going to inherit a story that's already been told about 100 times (99 of which told the story better than I will). People have told me that they think this is a cynical attitude for a writer to adopt. I disagree. If the stories have been told before, then what I am doing is proposing that I have something to lend to them. I have a voice, or the capacity to adopt a voice, that no one else could give to those stories. I have confidence that my voice and my vision are a valuable asset to hundreds of years of telling the same story.

This attitude is a helpful one to keep in mind when revising because it keeps me honest, and (hopefully) unpretentious. "Kasey," it reminds me, "you don't have anything new to say. You aren't going to create anything new today. So why don't you just relax? Why don't you just say what you mean, and say it the way you mean it? Why don't you stop using big words and images that don't make any sense? Why don't you just say what you mean in the best way that you know how? Because that's what you have to offer—a vision of something that a hundred thousand people in the world have already seen. Have faith that your vision is worth telling, and tell it with clarity."

How do you know when you have completed the reordering process?

I don't.

I'm not trying to be facetious, but I've never finished a story. I cannot read anything that I've written without cringing and wishing that I'd revised it 75 more times before I let anyone read it.

I think, though, that at some point I have to agree to let things go. I have to agree to let the piece be imperfect and to start something new. When I'm rewriting or revising, I am learning new things about my characters. It's obvious in the drafting process that writers learn what their characters do. In most interviews, or books on writing, that I've read, authors say that their characters surprise them all the time. If their characters don't surprise them (look at that! she's leaving her husband to run away with that single mother from the daycare center! and you didn't even know!), then the characters aren't real, the story is dead, and the writing is worthless.

For me, this process of discovery continues all the way through revision. I cut that section, and reread, and all of a sudden I know what goes in place of the section I cut: The waitress has to go find that guy who left the $100 on the table instead of $10 (look at that! and I didn't even know!). Once this process of discovery is dead, and the changes I'm making during revision aren't teaching me anything new about the characters, then it's time to let go.

What are the most important three things you've learned that other college writers might find helpful?

1. Be honest. Don't say things you don't feel or don't understand. Your dishonesty will show. Writing dishonestly won't make you feel good about your writing, either—won't make you feel compelled to go back to the piece.
2. Be willing to let go of what you write. Don't hold drafts as sacred. Don't be afraid of destroying and rebuilding.
3. Write every day.

Chapter 7
REWRITE WITH DOCUMENTATION

My task . . . is, by the power of the written word, to make you hear, to make you feel—it is, before all, to make you see.

—Joseph Conrad

I would want to tell my students of a point strongly pressed, if my memory serves, by Shaw. He once said that as he grew older, he became less and less interested in theory, more and more interested in information. The temptation in writing is just reversed. Nothing is so hard to come by as a new and interesting fact. Nothing so easy on the feet as a generalization.

—John Kenneth Galbraith

I could keep myself busy for months without moving from one spot, just by leaning now to the right, now to the left.

—Paul Cezanne

Writers don't write with words.

Writers write with information: accurate, specific, significant information produced by effective research. We think of the scientist as a researcher but the effective writer is also a researcher—one who researches life to discover what can and should be said. Information has to be documented. If it is not documented the reader will not believe it. The reader must be convinced that what the writer says is true by fitting the information into the reader's subjective life experience or by objective documentation as cited in the writing or—ideally—by both.

It is essential to the craft of revision to consider the information communicated in the draft. Words are the symbols for information, and when there is no information behind the words, the draft is like a check with no money in the account: worthless.

Effective research helps the reader discover the information the reader can use to understand the world, to think more clearly, to make better decisions, to learn, to act, to appreciate and enjoy life, to become an authority in the eyes of those around the reader. The list of reasons why readers want and need information is long. Effective writing is constructed from sturdy bits of information. Beginning writers can easily understand the necessity for specific information in nonfiction articles designed to communicate information—the research paper, laboratory report, minutes of a meeting—but they have less understanding of the need for information when writing about ideas or feelings. Yet specific information is absolutely essential in both forms of writing.

Which of the following examples from a history of World War II would you read?

> Tech-strategists retroactively engaged in cognitive studies of an interdisciplinary nature theorized that the late entry of U.S. forces, the very lack of preparedness that was so castigated, was, in contradiction to all expectation, a situation that produced positive, if unexpected, tactical and strategic results.

or

> Hitler was prepared for war, and when his Stukas and Messerschmitts overran the low countries of northern Europe, the U.S. Air Corps could not have flown with them even if the United States had been in the war. Ironically, those who mobilize last will enter combat with the "latest" equipment. If the enemy can be held at bay, the later entry will fly planes, as we did, that are technologically better than the German planes that seemed invincible a year or two earlier. Some scholars have argued that poor preparation is the best preparation for war.

I try to write of my feelings about being unable to help my 20-year-old daughter when she became ill and died. Which example is more effective?

> A parent always wants to protect a child and never, no matter how irrational it is, stops feeling guilty if a child is killed or dies from an illness, feeling there must have been something the parent could have done.

or

Lee

Remember me not
when I was kept from you
in the waiting room, not
when I sat in an office signing
your dying, not
when I pushed you on the swing
higher than you had ever flown
and you looked back as I grew small,
certain I would always be able
to save you.

Effective writers of nonfiction, fiction, and poetry do not tell the reader how to feel but give the reader the specific information to allow the reader to feel.

Diagnosis: Too Little Information

The draft will tell you what additional information is needed if you listen to its commands. Quickly read through your draft and put a check in the left-hand margin whenever you give the reader specific, accurate information. Then go through it again and put a small arrow where you could give the reader specific information that would help the reader think, feel, experience the draft.

Some of the forms of information the reader may need are revealing detail, fact, statistic, direct quotation, anecdote, firsthand observation, precise definition, attribution, and authoritative citation or reference. Information may take many forms, of course, and may be incorporated into the draft. A book about the writing process might be written on the basis of research reports and have many footnotes and other forms of attribution; this textbook is written from personal experience and has few references to other sources. Neither way is right or wrong; each is appropriate to the forms of writing.

There is no quota on the amount of information needed in a given piece of writing, but if you have pages or paragraphs without checks, then you should read the draft to see if the reader needs more specific information.

The Writer's Eye

The writer is a researcher of life constantly on the lookout for specific details. The more specific the detail, the more it resonates, revealing other specific details that begin to connect, leading writer—and later, reader—to meaning. The writer is never bored. The writer sees significance in the commonplace. For example, I saw "American Chop Suey" on the blackboard at Ron's, our favorite breakfast/lunch eatery, ordered it, and started to write a column.

The column, published in the *Boston Globe* on January 12, 1999, began in my taste buds as I munched on the greasy, slimy, tomatoey American Chop Suey and remembered the first day, in the school lunch line, when I allowed this "foreign" dish to be piled on my plate. I heard a mock-heroic inflated voice that might be amusing and wrote:

> I remember it as one of those crystalline moments of great daring that I would reflect on when I was old, knowing that the courage I displayed at that moment would forever change the course of my life.

I go back to a specific description, placing myself and the reader in another time and in a situation most of us share.

> It must have been in 1939 when I was fifteen and in the ninth grade, ready for great adventure but still riding a bike no hands in front of Sheila's house, showing off and hoping for what I did not yet really know.

> I was in the school lunch line—fifteen cents a day, seventy-five for the week—when I again smelled the hot, greasy, seductive, mystery of American Chop Suey.

I build the column from specific details that inform me.

> I had resisted it for years. I knew it was not for me. I was a Scots Baptist and we ate American food. They couldn't fool me by calling it American. Chop Suey was Chinese. "We" didn't eat Chinese.
>
> Later I was to learn that my mother, secretly with her friends, away from my father, would eat Chinese and in my adult years we had some of our best moments when I bought her Chop Suey and Egg Foo Yung for lunch in Harvard Square. We never told Father.

I am amused by the secret life, and this may have turned my mind toward the secret, rebellious life we will discover during the writing and reading of this essay.

> But this moment was long before I knew of Mother's secret restaurant life, before I even knew she'd eat a dill pickle away from home, even though I did witness a sudden burst of feminism when Mother ordered the salad my father didn't approve of when she took me along with her friends to Filene's Restaurant for lunch.
>
> I studied the pan in the hot lunch line. It had pasta—I'd say "paster" and still do. I'd had canned ravioli but this looked better and the red must be the mysterious tomato. I hoped the ground meat was safe ground beef. Well, in for a penny, in for a dollar. My voice squeaked but I got the words out, "I'll have the American Chop Suey."

I am writing with concrete details and one of the great wonders of storytelling is that as I describe my mashed potato home, the reader will remember a home where far different foods were served.

> It was another step in leaving my mashed potato home where we did not have pepper on the table or vinegar in the

> pantry since they might arouse the emotions. We ate white bread, beef and lamb, haddock and cod, tinned peas, and for adventure, brussels sprouts.
>
> I sat down with my buddies, who did not know they were witness to an act of culinary daring, and took my first bite of American Chop Suey, hot and flavorful and greasy and wonderful. Minnie Mae will rarely make it but when it is on the menu at Ron's I always order it. The flavor of adventure remains in every bite.

It was great fun to write this and now the draft took an unexpected turn. The experience of eating a food that would never be served at home is placed in a larger context to my surprise and delight.

> I've been a college professor and I always vote for the school bond issue, but we probably have good reason to fear the schools. If I'd been taken out of school at fourteen as my father had I would never have tasted American Chop Suey and I might well have never left home gastronomically or philosophically—I might even vote Republican.
>
> When I finished that single serving of American Chop Suey, I began to doubt my parents.
>
> I tried pepper and vinegar. They didn't seem to affect my already aroused emotions, but they sure made things taste better.
>
> I tasted Velveeta cheese—yum-yum good—and found there were other cheeses tastier and sharper and smellier. Seventy years later I am still exploring the world of cheese. If I win the lottery, I will fly to Bologna and find that cheese shop hung with a thousand cheeses, each different, and slowly, happily nibble myself to death.
>
> Once I tasted American Chop Suey, I became daring. I discovered West End Blues and then the William Tell Overture, wore peg pants and learned to jitterbug, read Tolstoy and Dreiser, argued politics and religion with my father. There was no apparent limit to the power of American Chop Suey.

Again notice the strength of the specifics.

> I do not eat Chinese Chop Suey today, but I eat Szechwan at least once a week, Japanese—unagi, smoked eel, is my favorite sushi except, perhaps, yellowtail. I eat Korean and Thai and Brazilian and Mexican and Kosher and Arabic and Italian and Czech and German and Russian and Cuban and French and still revel in Scot's Minced Scallop—boiled hamburger poured over mashed potato.

I put the experience of American Chop Suey in a still larger context.

> The moral of this story is clear. If you send your children to school they may eat and dress and learn and think differently than you do—and have more fun as well.

Imagine this piece written without specifics: "When I ate funny food at school I left my parents' way of eating and voting and thinking." The writer's eye provides the specific information that produces lively writing that will be read—more important, it ignites the thinking that is communicated by lively writing.

The Importance of Information

It is normal for inexperienced writers—and some not so inexperienced—to become infatuated with words. The condition is called "word drunk." The writer staggers down the page, spouting words that may, accidentally, sound wonderful but say nothing. Most readers do not want a word-drunk writer any more than they want a shaky-handed surgeon. Here are some of the reasons that it is essential to write with information.

Provides Reader Satisfaction

Readers are hungry for information: *In infantry training I was taught to run* toward *machine gun fire because the barrel rose as it was fired.* Readers want such images and facts, revealing details and interesting quotations, amazing statistics, and insights that make them see, feel, and know their world better than they did before the reading.

It helps to understand the reader's desire for information when you realize that one reason you read is to become an authority. The information-rich writer makes the reader an authority, and the reader, in turn, becomes an authority. The reader broadcasts new information to family, colleagues, friends, and gains status in the process. A good piece of writing ignites a chain reaction of communication. Most of the writing that satisfies us as readers has served us an abundance of information.

Establishes Authority

Readers believe specific information: *The driver hit the curve—and the tree—at 77 miles per hour, according to the state police radar.* If you want to lie, lie with statistics. Precise information makes the reader believe that you know your stuff. But serve up one piece of precise information that the reader knows is wrong and the reader won't believe anything in your draft.

Accurate information is the reason that readers trust the writer; inaccurate information is the reason that readers mistrust the writer. Readers test the draft by noting the information that relates to their world. When I read something about a newspaper or a university—both are places I've worked—I am especially critical. If I think the writer is on target, I trust the writer's comments about institutions I do not know well; but if the writer's comments do not fit my knowledge of newspapers or universities, then I suspect everything the writer says.

Produces Lively Writing

"How can I make my writing lively? It is dull, dull, dull."

"You told me the Republican elephant—a real one—sat on your father's car."

"Would that make the campaign parade story more interesting?"

"It sure did for me."

Lively writing is specific, not vague, abstract, and general. It builds the generalizations on the page and in the reader's mind from specific pieces of information that surprise and delight the reader. Often I remind myself of the importance of specifics by taking a piece of writing I particularly like and circling the specific pieces of information.

The Qualities of Effective Information

Effective information is information the reader uses successfully. A manual tells the reader how to solve a problem with computer software; an editorial makes the reader change a vote; a biography puts a historical figure in perspective; a literature textbook illuminates a poem; the poem makes the reader see the woods the reader passes every day with increased perception.

Accuracy

Readers respect specific information because the author takes the risk of being specific. Much of what pours through our ears is purposely vague, general, abstract; the writer uses political language that can't be nailed down, information for which the writer is not accountable. Specific writing is unusual, and readers like it, but it must be correct. One slip, as we have said, and the reader will not trust anything the writer says.

Factual Accuracy

The first accuracy is the truth of the fact: the number of miles in the marathon, the cost of the school bond issue, the date of the Battle of Gettysburg, the ingredients in the formula and their precise amounts, what the president actually said in the speech. All must be right. These facts can be checked with authoritative sources and should be. Often the writer will check the source with another source; just because a fact is in print doesn't mean it is a fact.

Here are some questions that you can ask of a fact, and then check and recheck if the answer is not "yes":

- Does it make any sense?
- Does it seem possible from what you know of the subject?
- Is it consistent with other facts you know are correct; does it fit the pattern?
- If this fact is true, does it change other facts in the draft—or the meaning of the draft?

Of course, the most interesting and significant facts will not get a simple "yes," but those pieces of information will have to face the skepticism of the reader. They deserve to be checked and rechecked.

Contextual Accuracy

The writer has the responsibility to make sure the information in the draft is accurate in context. Your campus may have had 73 sexual attacks reported last semester. That statistic may be accurate in fact, but the context may change the impact of that figure. A historical context may reveal that there were 214 attacks two semesters ago and that an educational program on campus safety seems to be working. Or the 73 attacks reported may be up from 36 but reveal that women are now willing, because of a new reporting procedure that protects their identity, to report sexual attacks. You may have 2,000 students or 45,000, which affects the importance of 73 attacks even though there should not be any sexual attacks.

The context reveals the significance of information. That is a far more difficult, and more important, task than just checking the number of pork pies at a church supper. Here are some questions that may help you test the contextual accuracy of a specific piece of information:

- What does this detail mean to the reader? What message does it deliver to the reader?

- What does this specific detail make the reader think? Feel?
- What impression is conveyed by this specific detail and the information that surrounds it?
- What is the pattern of meaning being built by this piece of information and the specifics that come before and after it?
- Is this piece of information accurate in context?

You are using specific information to construct a meaning, and you have the obligation to make that meaning true.

Specificity

Think about the kitchen during the holidays. The oven opens and the smell of turkey brings the taste of stuffing, gravy, sweet potatoes, and white peas, creamed onions, cranberry sauce, and pies—mince, blueberry, squash, pumpkin, and apple served with a slice of sharp cheddar. Such specific information because it catches our eye, or ear, or nose, sets off chain reactions of memory or imagination; gives us something to play with; makes us think and feel.

The Disadvantages of General Information

Writers—and politicians, corporate executives, educational administrators, bureaucrats—often use generalizations to avoid responsibility. Politicians avoid saying how many were killed and use a detached phrase such as "body count" to avoid responsibility. You can't nail a generalization down. Watch a political press conference. Either party will do.

Meanings, feelings, ideas, generalizations, theories, abstractions are all important. We use them in writing, but we are fortunate when we can cause them to happen in the reader's mind because of what we have said on the page. The details are arranged in a pattern, and that pattern makes the reader construct a meaning or experience a feeling. We cannot usually construct a meaning from generalities. Nothing is there to cause a thought. There is just someone else's thought to be accepted or rejected. It is given to us without documentation. We can't see backstage to discover—and evaluate—how it was put together.

Undocumented generalizations, those not built out of accurate, checkable, specific information in front of your eyes, are weak, flabby, vague, dull. And the writing is as well.

The Advantages of Revealing Details

A revealing detail is a specific that says more than one would expect. *"The additive may cause genetic problems"* sounds specific, but notice the difference when you read *"Urgatative, a normal food additive, may cause nerve damage in a pregnant woman and her child—and her child's child."* Revealing details expose the subject; they connect with other details to construct an opinion, argument, theory, poem, story, report that can be studied, challenged, tested.

The details themselves have power. *"The mayor won"* is not equal to *"The mayor won five votes to her opponent's one."* And details can make the reader think beyond the end of the sentence: *"The first African American to be elected mayor won with 71% of the white vote."* Or make the reader feel: *"In her victory statement she thanked her husband, her children, her parents, her campaign workers, and then lifted Soozie, her Seeing Eye dog, up on her hind legs so she could acknowledge the cheers of the mayor's supporters."*

Significance

Effective information is significant. If the new mayor had a dog named Soozie, that would mean nothing, but the fact she is a Seeing Eye dog makes a statement about the possibilities for the disabled— a term the mayor never uses—and implies that her administration will pay attention to that minority as well.

Resonance

A powerful detail has resonance; it radiates with implication. Resonance means that when the reader absorbs the information, it increases in importance. Resonance causes the reader to begin thinking, taking the text of the page and exploring its implications.

"The newly elected mayor reminds the audience that she went to school in this city, but that although each year the white high school students elected a mayor who served for a day in City Hall, she was not allowed to serve when her African American classmates elected her their mayor." That piece of information resonates. The reader can imagine how she felt then and how she feels now; can imagine the struggle that put her where she is now; can imagine how many other talented citizens did not and do not have the chance to serve; can imagine the changes that allowed this to happen and the changes that need to take place.

Connection

The information you choose should make significant connections in the writer's mind and in the reader's.

With the Topic. The information should relate to the topic and advance its meaning in the reader's mind. Often writers collect interesting information and they can't let go of it. The more interesting it is, the more it draws the reader's mind away from the message you are delivering. Each specific should amplify, clarify, extend the topic. *"On the wall behind the mayor's desk is her certificate when she was elected high school 'mayor'—and the letter telling her she could not serve."*

With Other Information. The specific details should work with the other pieces of information in the draft. They should build toward an increased understanding of the meaning that your draft is delivering to the reader. Some details will increase the impact of the other details; other specifics will qualify or limit the meaning that is building up. During revision you have the opportunity to check on these relationships. *"When asked about a picture on her desk the mayor says, 'I'll never know her name. She died in the Holocaust but she needs remembering.'"*

With the Reader. The information you choose to use should relate to the reader. Both the type of information—statistics, anecdotes, quotations—and the meaning the information bears should appeal to the reader. What will persuade one reader may turn another off. It is your job to select appropriate information from which to construct your draft. *"I tell students to read newspapers. When I was growing up they were all about a different world—the country club and such—and I wanted to know that mysterious world."*

Fairness

A doctor once told me he became a different—and a better—doctor after he had been a surgical patient. I became a better journalist after I was the subject—the victim—of some news stories. I want to be fair to the reader and deliver the news—good and bad, joyful and painful—but I also want to be fair to my subject. Writing is power, and it is too easy to use the printed word like a machine gun.

The best way to evaluate the fairness of a draft is to stand back and become a person in the piece of writing or someone who is affected by it. What would you think if you were in the piece or if your reputation were affected by its publication?

We need to be fair to our sources: Are we citing them in context? We need to be fair to ourselves: Are we writing something we will be ashamed to read in print later? We need to be fair to the evolving text: Does this information belong in this story?

As in all ethical questions, the answer lies in the situation. It may be accurate, but not fair, to say that my doctor considers me overweight if you are writing about me as a textbook author, but it may be fair and essential if I have written a diet book.

The Basic Forms of Information

We deal with information all the time, but we don't think of it as information we might use to construct a piece of writing. It may be a good idea to remind ourselves of the common forms of information.

Fact: A precise piece of information that can be documented by independent sources. Linda J. Stone was *elected governor.*

Statistic: A numerical fact. The governor received *5,476,221 votes.*

Quotation: The direct statement by an individual speaker or writer or from a document, book, article, report. *"The first Monday of every month the door to my office will be open to any citizen who wishes to see me."*

Anecdote: A brief story or narrative that documents the point a writer is making. The parables, such as the story of the loaves and fishes in the Bible, are a form of the anecdote. *"Governor-elect Stone drove the family car, a five-year-old Ford station wagon with 137,422 miles on it, to election headquarters herself."*

Descriptive Detail: A specific that reveals a person, place, or event. "She held high the *old-fashioned wooden clipboard* on which she had made notes during the campaign on what individual citizens told her during the morning coffee meetings she held in private homes, offices, schools, and factories."

Authoritative Report: A document that is accepted as accurate by a responsible organization such as a court, corporation, or academic discipline. "In her acceptance speech, Governor-elect Stone cited the *Newkirk Report, which called for small classes in the public school system and a paid-by-the-state system of summer retraining for teachers."*

Common Information: Information the reader can be assumed to know: three strikes and you're out; the president outranks the vice-president. *"The governor-elect of this state is immediately given a state police driver and an official limousine."*

These are just a few of the most common forms of information. There are obviously many more, and I have used a journalistic example common to all of us. Each academic discipline, each corporation, each profession, each government agency will have its own basic inventory of information forms. Most of them will, however, fit these patterns. The literary scholar will have many quotations from the work studied and from its critics; the economist will cite many statistics; the physicist will have many facts, mostly in the language of mathematics; the environmentalist will build a draft with many descriptive details; the historian will make good use of authoritative reports; the caseworker may have a great deal of anecdotal evidence. In every case, however, the most effective pieces of writing will be constructed with specific information.

Where Do You Find Information?

One of the reasons I am glad to be a writer is that I am forced to continue to learn. I have to search my world for the specifics I can use to discover what I have to say. The process of writing is a process of thinking, but if the thinking is to be effective—and if readers are going to read and use it—it must be built from information. And to get that information I have to study my subject.

Memory

We fear that writing will prove us ignorant. But writers discover how much we know by writing. I don't think I remember what it was like when my father, during the Depression, was fired again and again. Then I write about one of the times and begin to hear him blaming others, never himself, bragging how he told his boss off, how the reason he was fired was that he would be replaced by a "college man." I find out that I remember more than I thought I would, and I also realize I can now begin to recreate my doubts and questions about my father, how I felt, how I would try to live my life. Writing reveals how much I know. Of course, writing may reveal my childhood, but it will never reveal nuclear physics, no matter how many drafts I create. Drafts reveal the knowledge of which you were unaware, not the knowledge you do not possess. If your draft did not show you how much you knew, you may need to take a step back and discover what you know that you didn't know you knew.

Before Writing

I start withdrawing information from my memory bank by brainstorming a list, putting down everything I know about the topic I am going to research. Or I fastwrite a "what-I-know" draft to surprise myself.

During Writing

While I am writing the draft, I encourage the connections I do not expect by writing fast, without criticism. I continuously make use of my writer's memory, which is stimulated by the writing act, making me aware of what I didn't remember that I knew. I try not to know too well what I may write, allowing the discovery drafts to lead me. I also may make notes in the draft or on a pad of paper of things I suddenly discover in the writing: references to other writing, connections between facts or ideas, new patterns of meaning, sources I have to explore.

Observation

In the academic world, direct observation is often overlooked, yet it can be a productive source of significant information. If you are writing a paper on criminology, visit a police station or a jail; on health care, spend a few hours sitting in a hospital waiting room; on economics, walk through a supermarket or a mall; on literary studies, browse through that part of the library in which your subject is preserved; on government, attend a meeting of the school committee, town or city council.

When you observe, make notes. That activity will make you see more carefully as well as preserve what you observe. Note your first impression of a place, a book, a person. Make notes on what is and what is not; what is as you expected and what is not. Look for revealing details: how people interact, where things are placed, what is happening. Use your senses—

sight, hearing, smell, taste, touch. Take account of how you feel, react.

Internet

The first source for external information for many of us now is the Internet. We move the mouse and enter a universe of information. We can browse in libraries around the globe, explore other data sources, join interest groups, send out messages seeking the information we need.

The ability to use the Internet has become a basic intellectual tool essential to anyone who intends to be informed. The explosion of information in my lifetime has been a revolution of such magnitude it is hard to comprehend. When I was an undergraduate at the University of New Hampshire after World War II, we were denied a Phi Beta Kappa chapter because our library was so small. I had to go to Boston and sneak into Harvard's Widener Library to complete papers in elementary literature courses. Now, through my laptop, I have instant access to millions—perhaps billions—more pieces of information almost instantly.

Interview

Live sources should not be overlooked. If you are writing about schools, interview students present and past as well as teachers, administrators, school board members, parents. Read the books and articles about schools, but also go see the people in the classroom.

Good interviewers are good listeners. Few of us can turn away from a quiet, receptive listener who makes us an authority by asking our opinions. Try not to ask questions that can be answered with a simple "yes" or "no." Not "Will you vote to make professors sing all their lectures?" but "Why do you think it is important that professors sing their lectures?"

I like to prepare for an interview by listing the questions the reader will ask and expect to have answered. There are usually five questions—give or take one—that must be answered if the reader is to be satisfied.

"Why is tuition being doubled?"

"How will the money be spent?"

"How do you expect it to affect students?"

"What are you doing to help students who cannot pay?"

Listen to the questions and follow up on the answers to your questions: *"We are raising tuition because the faculty is underpaid." "What evidence do you have that the faculty is underpaid? Can you name faculty members who have left because of pay? What positions are unfilled because the pay is so low?"*

Note the answers to your questions, but check the ones you have any hesitation about or the ones that are most dramatic and surprising: "We are raising tuition so we can build the first-class table-tennis stadium our students demand." Journalists rarely check back with the person they interviewed, but I usually did. The purpose of the interview is not to trick the person being interviewed but to get accurate information to deliver to the reader.

Library

We live in an increasingly complex world. We need information on toxic wastes, traditions in Italian politics, Arctic survival techniques tested in Siberia and Canada, Norwegian exchange rates, the discovery of a new strain of AIDS virus in Africa and a treatment developed in Paris, the translation of the work of a Nobel Prize winner who writes in Arabic. The list goes on and on. Libraries are the intellectual closets of humankind where information is stored until we need it.

Search Techniques

Can we find the information? Not on my desk, I find myself answering. Fortunately, humankind has librarians who organize information so that it can be recovered.

Your library will be changing and increasing its access to sources of information. Go to the reference desk, but do not ask reference librarians only to help you get information on your topic; ask for instruction on how to use the library so you can do your own research. That is a skill you'll need as a lawyer, salesperson, police officer, politician, social worker, doctor, scientist, teacher, nurse, retail store manager.

The starting point for all the resources available to you—books, reference guides, monographs, articles, reports, audio- and videotapes —is your librarian. Use the librarian to learn how you can tap into the abundance of information you need to draw on to write— and think—effectively.

Effective Note Taking

It is important to have a system of note taking so that you have accurate, readable notes with the source clearly indicated.

File Cards. Most writers find that the most efficient system involves note cards—three by five inches, four by six, or five by eight on which most information can be placed, one quotation or piece of information to a card, together with the source. The cards can be easily carried to the library and ordered and reordered into categories as the research develops. It is easy to check back with cards and to line them up for reference while rewriting.

Computer Notes. More and more people are typing their notes into a computer, using software programs that do a spectacular job of organizing, ordering, and reordering information.

Printout, Photocopy, Scan, Fax. The electronic world in which we live has changed the way in which we collect and take notes. I do a great deal of photocopying when I research, making sure, however, that I write where it came from on each photocopied page. I either place these notes in a file folder—with the same heading as my computer file—or scan them into the computer. I also get printouts from computers or have a direct computer transfer of information into my computer files. Those are either placed in the stationary file or the computer file. Other material comes in by fax and I treat it the same way. It is vital that you know where each piece of information comes from at every stage of the research and writing process.

Creating the Bibliography

The inexperienced library researcher pounces on an enticing piece of information and forgets to note where it came from. It is useless. It is no longer a piece of important information if it cannot be cited with an accurate attribution and checked by you and a reader.

Use a system of file cards—usually organized by topic and within that, alphabetically by author—to record the complete title of your source, the author, the publisher, the copyright or publication date, the edition, the library reference number, the page on which you found the reference. Take down all the information you or a reader may need, and record that information in the way demanded by your discipline or in a way that will best serve anyone trying to find and use that reference.

It is hard for those who have not used scholarly materials to understand the necessity of footnotes and bibliographies. It is not just to establish the authority of the writer, but to serve the reader who is doing research, to let that interested reader follow the trail of scholarship that led to your writing. It is a matter of more than etiquette. Footnote references and bibliography are a duty if you are to participate in the intellectual world, adding your knowledge to those that went before, so it is possible for those who come after to build on your contributions.

Plagiarism

Plagiarism is using someone else's ideas or writing as if they were your own. Plagiarism is theft. But plagiarism can be avoided if the writer takes accurate notes that indicate precisely which of the author's words are being cited and which are the words of the researcher summarizing what the author said.

Of course, many students do not know the difference between quotation and paraphrase. Here is the difference:

Quotation is using someone else's exact words. Those words are enclosed in quotation marks: *President Franklin Delano Roosevelt said, "The only thing we have to fear is fear itself" in his 1933 inaugural address.* They are attributed to the person who said them by a direct attribution in the text, a footnote, or both.

Paraphrasing is putting someone else's idea in your own words. *President Franklin Delano Roosevelt spoke of the insidious effect of fear on the nation in his 1933 inaugural address.*

Attribution

Attribution connects information with its source.

> No attribution: *Alcoholism is a problem on the campus.*
>
> Attribution: *Alcoholism is a problem on the campus, according to Chief Ruth Grimes of the university police.*

The reader deserves to know where the information comes from: "Who sez?" The reader ought to be skeptical, questioning the text, challenging its authority. And we have the obligation to answer that challenge.

Unstated

All the information in the draft has an attribution. That information without footnote or reference is attributed to the writer. We must remember this and make the information we use on our own authority accurate, specific, and fair.

Stated

In formal academic, research, or scholarly writing, the attribution is provided by clear statements in the draft, together with a footnote, or with a footnote alone. The footnote style may vary in a history, psychology, physics, zoology, or mechanical engineering course. Make sure you know the style that each instructor expects.

Should your chosen style be less formal, it is still important to provide, in the draft itself, a reference—*as President George W. Bush said in his televised report to the nation on the state of the economy on July 23, 2002*—that will allow the reader to look up the original document.

Reader-Granted Attribution

There is a third form of attribution, the one granted by the reader. When you write to a particular audience—police chiefs, supermarket managers, colonial historians, college undergraduates, town managers—you can refer to common experiences, express common opinions or frustrations, articulate the thoughts and feelings of your audience, and if they recognize and agree with what you are saying, that act grants you authority.

You may not have to attribute common knowledge, but you should indicate the source of any surprising or unusual information. This is a gray area, and I would lean over backward, when in doubt, to make sure your reader knows the source(s) of information central to a piece of writing that depends on research. *"In 1980, only one in four college students was over 25 years old. In 1990, the proportion had nearly doubled, to four in ten," according to Sam Robert's* Who We Are—A Portrait of America Based on the Latest U.S. Census *(Times Books, Random House, 1994).*

Discover Sources with a List

I am a great list maker, and it takes only a few minutes to brainstorm the sources that you might overlook without the list. *Try it.*

Our campus is having a problem with alcohol, and if I decide to write about it, here are a few of the sources I might use:

Students at a bar

Students not at a bar

Campus police

Town police
State police
State liquor commission's enforcement officers
District attorney
Judge
Campus infirmary
Local hospitals
Alcoholics Anonymous (AA)
College counselors
Local therapists
Psychology professors
Sociology professors
Bartenders
Beer and liquor stores
American Automobile Association
State motor vehicle agency
MADD—Mothers Against Drunk Driving

The list can go on. Try it. Then, of course, you have to select the sources you can contact within your time limits.

Writing with Information

Once the writer's information inventory is full, the challenge is to use selected information gracefully and effectively. Inexperienced writers believe that effective writing is constructed with words—especially adjectives and adverbs—but experienced writers use words to communicate the information with which they have constructed their writing.

The Craft of Selection

Writing—and every other art—involves the craft of selection. A great deal of good material, information the writer worked hard to collect, will be left out. That is the mark of a good piece of writing. And, in a sense, it is all there. The reader feels the abundance of information behind the page. The draft is not thin. It has depth and weight; it is worthy of attention.

Style

The style you will use to write will depend on the message or information you have to convey, the reader to whom you are writing, the occasion of writing, the publication in which the writing is to appear, the genre in which your message is carried, the voice of the draft; but there are some basic techniques to consider.

Word

The individual word carries information to the reader; and to write lively, information-laden prose we should make sure that each word carries an adequate load of information to the reader. The words that can carry the most information are nouns and verbs.

Each case depends on the situation, but consider the information contained in the simple words *house* and *home,* a choice worthy of consideration. Carry it further:

She lived in a house home.
shack.
mansion.
hovel.
palace.
tenement.
prefab.
trailer.

And look at a simple, active verb:

He	walks	into the house.
	slams	
	strolls	
	darts	
	charges	
	saunters	
	dances	
	tiptoes	
	marches	
	clumps	

The list can go on. Notice how much information a noun and a verb can convey in a simple sentence:

They	walked	into the	house.
	slammed		home.
	strolled		shack.
	darted		mansion.
	charged		hovel.
	sauntered		palace.
	danced		tenement.
	marched		prefab.
	clumped		trailer.

Notice how simple but different nouns and verbs change the information and the message.

Phrase

The phrase, that fragment of language less than a sentence, is often an effective way to communicate information. *He walked the streets* is a sentence but it becomes more powerful with the addition of a phrase *like a soldier on patrol.* And the writer can go on, adding more phrases: *He walked the streets like a soldier on patrol in fear of each shadow, listening to his own footsteps . . . seeking the safety of shadows . . . aware of who was following him.*

Sentence

The simple sentence—"Jesus wept."—can carry more information than we might expect, but we can load up the sentence with a great deal of information:

> A university has been described, by Grayson Kirk, as a collection of colleges with a common parking problem, but I am struck, after returning to the university I attended, at how resilient an institution it is, welcoming unexpected thousands of veterans on the GI Bill after World War II and changing its curriculum, year after year, in response to society's need for study and research in many fields unheard of when I was an undergraduate: computer studies, space sciences, women's studies, black studies, environmental sciences.

Paragraph

I think of paragraphs as the trailer trucks of prose that carry a heavy load of information to the reader:

> I wonder if my post-World War II generation will be known as the generation of the single-family house. I dreamt of living in a single-family home because I was brought up in rented apartments where I was shushed by the fear that the neighbors upstairs or down might hear. Hear what? Anything. Music, fights, kitchen clatter, the Red Sox game, bedsprings, bathroom flushes, burps, curses, footsteps, doors shutting, drawers opening. And then an uncle bought a single-family home in East Milton, and I knew that was what I wanted. A house of my own, far enough from the neighbors to thump a ball, yell back, play my music at proper volume, flush the john after midnight. And I made it, one of the veterans who gloried in urban, suburban, and exurban sprawl. But my daughters, both successful, making more money than I did at their age, may never be able to afford a single-family home.

There are many other ways to carry information to the reader such as illustration and graphics, but most information is communicated by word, phrase, sentence, and paragraph.

Remember that the reader is hungry for information. That is the principal reason we have readers. They want to read the specific, accurate, interesting information that will turn them into authorities on our subjects.

Interview with a Student Writer

Jennifer Bradley-Swift

Jennifer Bradley-Swift is now a graduate student at George Washington University in Washington, D.C. Previously she was in the Peace Corps in West Africa and was a student at the Residential College, an interdisciplinary college within the College of Literature, Science, and the Arts at the University of Michigan. At the University of Michigan she concentrated in international social sciences, French, and photojournalism and was a staff photographer for the *Michigan Daily,* the student-run paper independent of the university. Jennifer considered "the *Daily* just as much of my education here as I do my classes."

What techniques do you use to collect specific and significant information before writing a first draft?

Before writing a first draft, I start sketching (more in the form of a casual mind map than an outline) the categories of information I will need: For a paper built around a thesis, these categories are each of my supporting arguments; for research and personal pieces, they are each of the elements used to build my story. The next step is then to start the actual collection process. In any paper where I am using sources other than myself I will go through each category and pull out all of the information nuggets available—quotes or passages or facts. For most papers I collect these info-bits by copying them onto index cards: one card for each bit, complete with bibliographic info (especially page number so I can go back and remind myself of the context) so that I can easily credit my sources once I begin writing. On each card I also write my thoughts about that particular infobit—why I think it is important for my argument, how it relates to the other bits I've collected. Using this technique, organization of the paper is simply a matter of arranging the cards. And to supplement the cards, I sometimes use a notebook on which I sketch a more fixed linear representation of the argumentative organization.

What different techniques do you use when initiating a topic or when responding to an assigned topic?

When initiating a topic, I will do preliminary info searches first to find sources and then within those sources, skimming through to get an idea if there will be enough meat with which I can create a sound and convincing argument or story. Responding to an assigned topic, I have no choice and must then do my best, finding info within the sources available for that topic; in this way I will turn more quickly to the card technique, often making notes as I read along in an assigned reading if I know beforehand what the focus of the resulting paper will be.

How do you know you need to collect more information to revise a draft?

When diagnosing problems within a draft, I look first at whether the problems arise from within the syntax and organization. I check to see if these problems are simply a matter of poorly constructed sentences that are innocently bad, or if they have the ulterior motive of trying to hide a deeper weakness within the paper. If I don't have enough information in a certain passage, I often initially try to patch the hole with redundancy and wordiness. As my mother (born an editor, I think) has taught me through years of a relentless red pen, I shouldn't use useless sentences, even the ones that may sound quite nice at first. If I'm afraid to let such a sentence go, often that fear stems from the realization that I'll have to go out once more and either collect more information or abandon my argument for lack of legitimate support.

More generally, if outside readers are not gaining the meaning—whether that meaning is an argumentative persuasion of something based more on fact, or on emotion—then either I'm simply not expressing myself well (in terms of sentence structure, expression of the information) or there aren't enough tangible infobits for them to sink their teeth into. This can be determined by analyzing the roots of each poorly understood passage (in the manner just discussed).

What attitudes do you find helpful as you try to collect information?

When collecting information (especially when just starting), I try to remain open to all possibilities, avoiding initially discounting something that might prove useful later. This attitude is essential for me as a journalist, when both reporting and photographing. In most journalistic cases, there is no going back later to catch something I missed the first time around; if I missed it then I'm usually out of luck. Therefore, I am continually reminding and then forcing myself to ask all of the questions and take all of the pictures (from all of the angles and using all of the lenses and all of the light, shutter speed, and depth-of-field possibilities) first, and then to question, edit, and organize later. When writing papers, this means I often have index cards left over, which is a much better fate than not having enough and scrambling around when I really just want to be writing.

There are many reasons why I might be at first hesitant to take a picture: time restraints, questions of appropriateness, of being too obtrusive, fear that the shot will take too much energy to put together. But I never want to feel I have limited myself and my expression of the subject in question simply because I didn't take that one shot. These concerns are especially relevant when creating a photo story, a series of pictures that explains a subject through images; often that one shot becomes the foundation for the whole story.

For example, shooting the Ann Arbor Blues and Jazz Festival, I had unlimited press credentials and therefore found myself on stage with guitar great Luther Allison. During what would be the last song of his set, he switched to a cordless guitar and stepped from the tall outdoor stage to the speakers below in order to get closer to the crowd. As his guitar continued to wail the crowd wailed along with him, eating up every note. Allison then proceeded across the speakers, and was then suddenly below, with only a fence between him and the crowd. But he didn't stop there, instead he continued to walk around past the edge of the stage and past my field of vision. Since I was still up high on the stage I wasn't sure what I should do—wait for him to return or somehow follow. While I hesitated I looked out and saw just what was happening: Allison had gone all the way around the edge of the fence and was now "in the crowd," still wailing as crazy as before. I realized there was no more time to hesitate, and if I wanted the shot I would have to act immediately. So I jumped from the stage (about ten feet up) and ran as I have never run before—yelling and pushing my way through the crowd. With three shots left on that roll of film I got the shot—Allison lifted on the shoulders of some stranger in the controlled chaos of the moment—crowd and performer united in the appreciation of the music. It was the primary shot of the festival's photo story, and I wouldn't have felt I had done a complete job of expressing the story without it.

What specific processes do you try to collect the information?

When collecting information I most often start generally and focus down to the specifics. This means thinking about the types of sources I'll be using, finding those sources, figuring out which parts of those sources I need, and which infobits within those parts. By source I mean books, periodicals, Web pages, essays, class notes, interviews, conversations, memories, depending on the type of writing. In journalism, collecting information means getting background info and then going to the people most appropriate for the topic, the ones who know the most (taken from the list of those willing to talk). It means asking the right questions and being respectfully persistent in order to get the best answers. In photography, it means being able to evaluate a situation or person and trying to capture and express the right information (in the right way, considering angle, light, etc.) that will most effectively and honestly tell the story.

What tools do you use when searching for information?

When searching for information I use the actual tools of our library's computer system for book and periodical sources; the Internet is also proving very useful and if I'm not using it myself, other people are very kind to send me bits of information I might find interesting. I often use the people around me as resources. If I know someone (a professor, classmate, friend, parent) who has experience with the current task I am undertaking, he or she often has useful insight on how to get started.

When I'm reading something (either as one of several sources for a paper or a novel/play, etc., on which I'll be writing), I always read with a pen in my hand. It reminds me that I am reading for information, and that at any point of discovery I can underline or jot down a note at a moment's notice.

How do you know when you have an adequate amount of information?

I know I have an adequate amount of information when my audience gains the meaning I wished to have expressed in my paper/story/poem/photograph. Or, I should say in the case of more emotionally based pieces, when the audience has gained an equally strong (if not the same) meaning as that I am expressing.

What techniques or tricks of the photojournalism trade help you as a writer?

It is essential to be aware of the entire setting and subject matter when setting up a shoot or trying to capture the existent moment. It is an equally important thing I try to remember as I am writing. I never want to leave out an essential bit of information (an inch or two in the frame), or include too much so that it muddles the piece (photo) and the subject is lost or inaccurately portrayed. I need to have enough information about what I'm shooting (and if a photo goes along with a written article, knowing the angle taken on that article) so I can be most effective in choosing which information I will need (and in what way it should best be portrayed) for the assignment.

The difference between an assigned topic and a personally initiated one holds true for my task as a photographer at the *Daily* as it does my role as a writer: When shooting an assigned subject I must do my best to shoot what I've been assigned. But when the task is for me to come up with a feature shot (to stand on its own) or a photo story, I am responsible for making sure there is enough information available to make a good photograph, both info that makes something newsworthy and visual info that makes something a photograph.

What are the most important three things you've learned that other college writers might find helpful?

1. Never try to write something (or I should also say, defend something you've already written) when there simply isn't enough information to back it up or to give it meaning. Instead, although it will mean more work (and sometimes an element of pain), it is always worth it to find the holes and fill them instead of trying to patch them with duct tape.
2. Don't be afraid to take initiative when collecting information. Often the juiciest bits come from the hardest and most risky collection endeavors, but these are the pieces that make the story.
3. Initial steps toward organization (although they might seem silly or unnecessary at first) most often pay for themselves many times over. (Those little cards can really be a godsend.)

Chapter 8
REWRITE TO DEVELOP

Talent is a question of quantity. Talent does not write one page; it writes three hundred.

—JULES RENARD

The importance of a writer . . . is that he is here to describe things which other people are too busy to describe.

—JAMES BALDWIN

For me the initial delight is in the surprise of remembering something I didn't know I knew.

—ROBERT FROST

The most critical difference between poor, unread writing and fine, well-read writing is development. People imagine that a creative idea—the more eccentric the more creative—is what marks good writing. But there are few if any new ideas. The creativity and the quality comes in the development of a piece of writing.

Fine writing makes the writer's vision of an idea, a place, a person, an event clear to the reader with a rich blend of revealing specific details, observations, references, patterns of thought—all the forms of information appropriate to the subject.

It is also the richness and fullness of the draft that gives the writer authority and makes the reader trust the writer. The writer recreates experience—with texture and in depth—so that the reader sees, feels, thinks.

Diagnosis: Superficial

Undeveloped writing is difficult for the writer to diagnose because the draft is fully developed in the writer's mind: It just isn't on paper.

The writer writes, *"It was a terrible accident,"* and sees the victims trapped in the car, hears their cries for help, hears the sirens, is bathed in the flashing light, sees the rescue workers using the Jaws of Life, sees the blood, the body rushed to the ambulance, bags with intravenous tubes held high, sees the next victim wheeled slowly to the next ambulance, a blanket over the head. The writer has only delivered a blank check to the reader, expecting the reader to imagine what might be terrible.

Another writer says, *"It's a good idea to raise gasoline taxes,"* but the reader asks, "Why?" and finds no answer in the text. An intern writing a marketing memo says, *"There are obvious markets other than youthful ones that CompuGames should exploit,"* but does not go on to identify the markets and how they could be reached by the reader.

Those readers will not read on. The writer has to develop the ability to stand back and create a distance between writer and draft so the writer can read the draft as the reader—hungry for information—will read it.

The signs of an undeveloped draft are many:

1. No news. It is predictable, telling the reader what the reader already knows.
2. No voice. It could have been written by anyone, or a computer.
3. No individual vision. The reader does not see the subject through the eyes—the brain—of the writer. Anyone could have written it.
4. No information. The draft lacks an abundance of revealing details.
5. No documentation. The draft is full of generalizations without evidence.

Take a piece of your writing and write "more" in the margin wherever you would like more information. Do the same with published and unpublished writing you like and do not like to see how a well-developed piece of writing serves you and an undeveloped one does not.

Techniques of Development

An effective piece of writing has depth that goes below the surface and a richness of texture that attracts and holds the reader. *"We suffered a flood"* becomes *"I expected a huge, sudden tidal wave, wind, rain, but what we experienced was worse, the quiet arrival of the river that usually was a mile away, first a trickle, then streams and puddles, then the quiet, continuous rising of water as far as I could see, my horizon rising and trees, telephone poles, houses, barns all sinking out of sight, quietly, certainly."*

Three basic problems with many early drafts can be solved by development: (1) there is little information, (2) the reader doesn't know if the information is authoritative, and (3) it is not clear what the information means. Solving these problems, however, does more than satisfy the reader; it educates the writer.

Develop with Information

Never underestimate readers' hunger for information: specific, accurate, lively information that informs readers and allows them to inform those around them. Readers want to gossip, to pass on information they have just learned.

Reveal with Specifics

The writers we read, enjoy, trust, the writers who inform and stimulate us, write with information. Nonwriters think they write with words, brightly colored balloons empty of information, but words have no value unless they are loaded with information. Words are nothing in themselves. They are devices to carry information, the way a check is a device to deposit, withdraw, or transfer money in the bank. No money, the check bounces; no information, language bounces.

An empty paragraph: *Newspaper editors are masters at displaying what has occurred so that readers will know what has occurred that should, or may be, of interest to them so they can increase their stored information.*

A full paragraph: *Newspaper editors take thousands of stories every night and display them so the reader can see their significance instantly. Page 1 news is the most important news and the most important stories are at the top of the page, with the largest headline. The most important single story is in column 1 at the right-hand side of the page. Then the editors break the stories down by section: foreign, United States, local (metro), home, business, sports, using the same top of the page and right-hand column 1 to indicate the stories that readers should consider reading.*

Write with Abundance

Meaning, form, order, voice lie within the material. Developing a draft is an intellectual act of enormous importance. We don't think or write with telegraphic summations—*"environment should be saved"*— but with a rich plenitude of information—about a specific threat to the wetlands—and the details of complex problems that might result from a specific solution.

Here's an example of a developed paragraph on the topic just mentioned: *"Building a dam solves the flooding problem that can damage or destroy the important wetlands, but the dam is, of course, a permanent flood that causes damage upstream, burying important biological features underwater and changing the patterns of wildlife above the dam forever."*

Develop with Authority

"Who sez?" is one of the most significant questions academic and other readers ask. Readers should not believe the writer is the authority on everything in an article or book. The reader will demand that the writer attribute significant pieces of information to an authoritative source.

Convince with Authority

It is specifics that give the writer authority with readers. Readers are impressed by an abundance of information that convinces them the writer knows what he or she is talking about. Instead of *"Mozart composed a great deal of music,"* I might write, *"When I feel in need of a symphony I choose the Linz by Mozart; when I'm in a piano concerto mood, I reach for the 15th or 16th by Mozart; if an opera is in order it will probably be* Cosi Fan Tutte *by Mozart; a string quartet, one of the Haydn Quartets by Mozart; a piano trio, by Mozart; clarinet or bassoon or French horn or flute or organ, it will be Mozart."* The reader should say, "He knows his Mozart."

Persuade with Evidence

Most writing is argument. We want to persuade the reader that our vision of the world is true; the reader should share our opinion, follow our leadership, vote for our proposal, buy our product. To persuade the reader, the writer must deliver evidence that the reader will believe.

Personal Documentation. Some of the evidence may be personal. In writing about date rape, a student could describe what happened to her roommate, a friend from home, a sister, herself. The reader needs to know where the documentation is coming from. Attribution is vital in persuading the reader, who should be suspicious of information that is not connected to an authoritative source. For example, *"I know. I went out in college with a guy I'd known since sixth grade and was raped."*

Objective Documentation. Most evidence comes from impersonal sources. The reader of the article on date rape demands—fairly or not—to know if this is a problem of that particular writer or if it is a widespread problem. For example, *"The Atwater Report of 2002 documented that date rape occurs on this campus, in our dormitories and our fraternities, as well as in off-campus housing."*

The writer should build her case with an abundance of information that comes from campus and local police reports, medical records, campus housing administrators, sociological studies, case histories of victims. Again, attribution is vital. The reader needs to know from statements within the text or footnotes where the writer has gotten the documentation.

Develop with Clarity

What we write is often correct, but the reader doesn't get it because it is not clear. We need to develop our drafts so the meaning is not only clear to us but to a skeptical reader.

Description

Description is the mother of all writing. With words we describe our worlds, physical and intellectual. We describe observations, ideas, theories, people, events, concepts, experiments, emotions, processes—the range of human experience. Two essential elements of effective description often forgotten by inexperienced writers include dominant impression and natural order.

Dominant Impression. The description has a focus, and everything in the description supports a single impression or meaning.

> Everything in the operating room was sharp: piercing light glinted off stainless steel equipment with clean edges; the sounds of machines echoed brightly off the tile walls; the eyes of masked doctors, nurses, and technicians probed the patient; a tray held a battalion of knives, each sharpened, pointed, waiting.

Natural Order. The reader should receive the description in a natural order, a story built on chronology, time passing; a description of an argument moving from the weakest to the strong points; a place seen in the order the narrator would see it.

> The first thing she felt as they wheeled her into the operating room was the sharp piercing light that glinted off stainless steel equipment. Then she became aware of the clean, precise edges of the equipment, the clatter of tools and the

pulsing beat of the machines that would breathe for her, the piercing eyes of masked doctors, nurses, and technicians, and before the mask came over her face, a glimpse of a tray with a battalion of knives, each sharpened, pointed, waiting.

Put Meaning in Context

Many writers deliver information—facts, quotations, case histories, reports—that are interesting but cause the reader to ask, "So what?" Pure information is not enough; that information has to be put in context. The anecdote or personal experience must be in a larger context for the reader to understand its full meaning.

For example, consider an interesting bit of information without context: *"The homicide detective said, 'We always start at the same place—the victim knew the person who killed him.'"*

Now, with context added: *"During my research into the causes of murder, I talked to a homicide detective who told me, 'We always start at the same place: the victim knew the person who killed him.' I added 'or her' and realized that murder was an intimate crime. I had to move in closer, escape the charts and statistics, and talk to murderers and the families of their victims to understand the causes—and effects—of murder."*

Since it is easier to see what someone else's writing needs than your own, take a piece of writing by another writer on a subject you know well, and mark in the margin how each paragraph or section that needs it could be developed.

Rewriting Starts with Rereading

The writer first has to reread to see what is on the draft's page, what is not, what should be.

The following e-mail message from Christopher Scanlan, a writer who teaches journalists at the Poynter Institute, to a student reveals a writing teacher at work. It was written in haste but it is packed with practical information on revision and development.

> Hit the print button on whatever you have and take it downstairs, outside, anywhere outside of the newsroom and read it first quickly. Don't mark it up. Just read it fast like a reader might, groggy at the breakfast table.
> Then take a pen and this time, start making marks in the margin.
> As you read ideas will come to you: I could move this.
> I need more here.
>
> This could
> be an
> ending, a
> lead. This
> word is
> spelled
> wrong.
> I need her correct title.
>
> Little things, big things. Make note of all the things that you think you need to do.
>
> Most of all, focus on the story, just the story. Not your belief that it sucks and by extension so do you.
>
> There's a stage in childbirth (I know this as a witness) called transition where the mother-to-be is convinced this baby ain't never coming. She's ready to cash it in, call it a day, forget the whole thing. It's the darkest moment and of course is followed by the brightest.
>
> That's where, if my experience is any measure, is where you probably are.
>
> So just focus on the words on the page because all of
> the answers are there on the page. The text is your
> editor. Listen to it (I know I'm beginning to sound like
> Yoda here.)
> Let the text instruct you. It will tell

you the things to work on. And
that's all you have to keep doing:
work the text.
When you've done that, I guarantee you will feel a bit better
because you will have some direction. Then go up to the
computer and start making the biggest changes.
Move whole grafs around. Don't worry if they fit yet,
you can smooth them out later. Every time you fix
something, draw an x through that mark on the
page.

Try to make every change possible.
Then print it out again.
As directions say,
Repeat as needed.
Good luck. You can make it. The child will be born today.

Read Fragments

Often potential meanings are hidden in a word, a phrase, a line. I have had to teach myself to read fragments, and so should you. When we read our drafts we are like the archaeologist who finds a fragment of a bowl, the preserved ashes of a fire, a sharpened piece of stone, and then uses a trained imagination to create a civilization.

Many forms of fragments reveal meaning. Here are some that I frequently discover.

Code Words

These are words that have a private meaning for us. I read "basement," an ordinary word, and suddenly remember that was the word in first grade that took on a new meaning and a terrifying, seductive mystery. When I went to first grade the basement was where you were sent when you raised your hand and said, "I have to go," and it was where other little boys told you . . .

Revealing Detail

When I had my heart bypass, I was part of a machine for 91 minutes. That we can survive while surgeons manipulate such a vital organ as a heart opens the door to the poems and columns I have written about that experience. That revealing detail could lead, in my hands, to a novel; in another writer's hands to a screenplay, a nonfiction book on heart surgery, a play, a biography of a surgeon, or an autobiography of the patient.

Significant Phrase

In New England, we all look forward to Indian summer, those days in the late fall when the weather suddenly turns warm. But the phrase was born in fear. In colonial times, the pioneer farmers worked their fields with musket nearby and huddled at night in crowded forts where they could protect their families against attack by Indians. When it started to get cold, the Indians would not attack and the families could live in their homes beside their fields. Then the weather would change and the Indians would return, surprising individual families. That phrase has for me two hidden meanings, meanings that have a tension filled with possibility for writing.

Haunting Image

After we buried my father, I went into my parents' bedroom and found my mother sitting alone on the edge of their double bed that had been worn to the shape of their double forms. I am haunted by that image. We all have those snapshots of memory that carry enormous loads of meaning we may choose to explore and share by writing.

Read What Isn't Written

I think it is important to read positively, to recognize the potential within the draft, but there are drafts in which no potential is apparent. It is neither on the page nor in the world from which the draft was written. Beginning writers must read to see what is not even in the rough draft. Drafts without apparent potential usually display some or all of these deficits.

Problem: No Territory

The writer has not created a world of people, events, or ideas the reader and the writer need or want to explore together. An inviting world has a richness and a complexity that interest the reader.

> *Before:* Often the U.S. Supreme Court has to rule on ethical as well as legal issues.

Solution

Move the location of your article to a place where you are familiar enough to know the simplicities and the complications that interact to make good writing. A paper on ethics might be moved from the Supreme Court, where you haven't served, to the football field, where the coach has just asked you to cheat by faking an injury. On the other hand, it is equally possible to write about faking an injury in the context of National Collegiate Athletic Association rules, emphasizing research rather than personal experience.

> *After:* I am only able to go to college because I have a football scholarship, but I'm not a star. I'm special teams on kickoffs and punt returns; I hold the ball for the place kickers; I carry the ball in certain short yardage situations; and, although we are a religious school, I am the quarterback's retaliator and the guy who fakes an injury on the coach's command.

Problem: No Surprise

The reader reads only what the reader expects. The reader knows what is coming next. There is no challenge, nothing that provokes a thoughtful or an emotional reaction from the reader. There is no suspense.

> *Before:* Research into the nation's early history may change the contextual environment of our mythic beliefs.

Solution

Look over your notes, written and mental, to see what surprises you, what you learn, what you question, what your reader needs to know, what runs against expectation, to find a subject that will interest a reader.

> *After:* We think of "Indian summer" as a delightful return to summer in the autumn before winter sets in, but the term had a different context in colonial times. Then settlers feared the unexpected warmth because Indians, who did not attack in cold weather, suddenly returned to raid isolated farms.

Problem: No Writer

The reader does not sense the presence of a human being behind the draft. The draft does not breathe; there is no individuality. There is none of the essential human music we call voice that is essential to the individual act of one person, a writer, meeting another person, a reader, on the page.

> *Before:* One is rather overwhelmed when one arrives on a university campus from a small community for the first time.

Solution

Read the draft aloud and tune it until you find a voice that sounds like you and is appropriate to the meaning of what you have to say. This may mean writing in the first person—I—or in the third person—he or she. Whoever the speaker, the reader needs to sense a single human intelligence behind the words on the page.

> *After:* I chose this university because I came from Eagle Pass, population 105, and was graduated second in a class

of seventeen in a county high school. I wanted to escape. I knew everyone and everyone knew me. Watch out when your dream comes true. Here I know no one and no one knows me. I'm doing solitary.

Problem: No Respect

The writer does not respect the subject matter, the reader, or him- or herself. The writing task is not taken seriously, but kissed off, dependent on superficial tricks that call attention to themselves, not to the subject. The writing cheats the reader. It is dishonest.

Before: In an election year, politicians talk of entitlements, but nothing is ever done to cut off these payoffs to freeloaders.

Solution

You are revealed when you do not take the subject seriously. Find a topic that you can take seriously and write with your heart as well as your head. Look for a way to respect your topic, to have compassion for the people involved, to respect opinions you may not share.

After: I know there is welfare fraud, but last weekend we put my grandfather in a nursing home. He worked hard all his life, voted Republican, even refused his veteran's bonus after his war, but the care he needs costs $3,500 a week, without extras. He worked as a truck driver. Now his bill will be $182,000. He needs Medicare, Medicaid, Social Security, anything he can get.

Problem: Too Little

The reader is given nothing but generalities. There is no information, just emotional or intellectual generalities that pass over the surface of the subject. There is no evidence that allows me to think with the writer. There are no revealing, resonating details.

> *Before:* New zoning regulations may be needed in a college town, but they should not be aimed at students.

Solution

We often feel that writing is most intellectual when it is full of generalities, but theories must arise from fact. Readers are hungry for an abundance of accurate, specific information that allows them to do their own thinking.

> *After:* Zoning regulations in a college town should not be aimed at students but at behavior—the number of people who live in an apartment or a house, the number of cars parked outside, the noise made by boom boxes, the activities that are lumped under the term "party." The people whose behavior upsets the neighbors may be students or not. The target is not any group of people but the actions of people that affect those within eyeshot or earshot.

Problem: Too Much

The writer floods the reader with too much information of equal importance, or pours so much rhetoric on the page that the reader drowns in language.

> *Before:* The party started early, before the football game, at lunch, with beer and then the guys got booze into the game in hip flasks and then we all went out to the lake where Flynns serves the best steaks but it was crowded and we had to wait an hour and a half in the bar, where, of course, there were girls and they'd had a few. We did eat lots of peanuts and I saw my priest there but I don't think he saw me. He was pretty red-faced. Well, that's not the point. The point is

that Rafe outdrank us all. He always did and there was no talking him out of driving, never is. Two dead.

Solution

Whether you are writing a term paper, an essay, or a story, be careful not to load up on so much specific information that the hearing of each piece is lost and your writing becomes a jumble of unrelated information. Decide on your single, dominant message and then cut anything that doesn't move it toward the reader.

> *After:* Saturday I lived a TV commercial against drinking and driving. We drank from 11:30 in the morning until 10:45 at night, when the police, the wreckers, and the ambulances arrived at the intersection. Two stretchers left with the sheet over the faces of two of my best friends.

Problem: Too Private

The writer is so close to the subject that the reader has no idea what the writer is talking about. The writer produces a mumbling monologue of code words and phrases that may mean something to the writer but are obscure to the reader. Private writing is a particular problem when the writer becomes, at least in the writer's own mind, an expert on a subject, such as the Internet, honeybees, systems engineering, the history of the *Dred Scott* case.

> *Before:* When I added a 120 Pentium I could boot my computer and get a GPF faster than ever before.

Solution

Put your writing in context. This can be done with a short paragraph, sometimes with a sentence, sometimes with a phrase.

> *After:* When I turned on my computer with a new, far speedier chip, I found that I could get to a problem message telling

me I had a memory problem faster than ever before. I had not solved the problem. I had just gotten to it faster.

Problem: No Significance

The information the writer provides is not put in perspective. There is no emphasis, no clear point. The writer is just delivering information. There is no evidence that the writer has thought critically about the subject and what it means.

Before: A foxhole in infantry combat holds just one person. Close together, makes you vulnerable to mortars, hand grenades, mines. Extended order means you march with several yards between you. Taking cover from each other, you disappear from your own army. Greater firepower means a single soldier can command a large field of fire.

Solution

Writing is always a form of critical thinking. The reader expects more than "Just the facts, ma'am." The details must add up to something that affects and involves readers, making them think or feel—or both.

After: Infantry combat is lonely. In the movies, soldiers huddle together where the camera can see them interacting. In combat, the soldier is alone in the foxhole, dug far enough apart that one shell hits only one foxhole. Each soldier's first enemy is loneliness.

Problem: No Connection

The draft is neither placed in a larger context—political, historical, sociological, psychological, scientific—nor does it connect with the experience of the reader.

Before: Poverty is terrible. Bad housing crowded together. People sitting an afternoon away on doorsteps or staring out the window. Kids playing without toys. Hopelessness.

Solution

References can be woven within a draft to connect with the reader's experience, using business examples and references for a readership of businesspeople, sports references if the readers follow sports.

> *After:* Studies by Murray (1999) and Morison (2000) have demonstrated that television has brought the poor into intimate contact with the affluent, so the "have-nots" are forced to see how much the "haves" possess—or are invited to purchase—many times in each hour. Starobin (2003) has confirmed what Nestelberger (1980) theorized: the poorer the home, the more hours the television is likely to be turned on.

Rewrite within the Draft

When writers revise their drafts they are tempted to look beyond the page to identify problems and solutions. They try to remember what their teachers or editors have said about this form of writing, they study their notes and look into writing texts, and they consult with friends, family, classmates. But once the writer is within the draft, the most important place to look is within the draft itself. If you read the draft as a stranger, reading what is and what is not on the page, the draft will often tell you what it needs.

Here are some examples of student writers engaging in a dialogue with their drafts:

> High school was, to me, even more boring than home. I'm only in college because of the job I had. That really changed me.
>
> > ***How was school and home boring? What job? What changed?***
>
> Memo to Manager SuperDooper Supermarkets: Kids could man busy checkout counters. In the Liston Avenue market the checkout lines build up in the later afternoon. I used to work at Bell Road. But it is SooperDooper policy to have

high school kids fill shelves when they come on in the afternoon. Older workers could fill shelves.

> ***Straighten out the chronology. How about going through a day?***

Paper route, 1:26 A.M. papers, used fifth-hand Pontiac I bought from Uncle Jim who was in the Coast Guard, married to my mother's younger sister, she was band director, went to that before school, played tuba cause I was the small guy, I suppose, tuba with feet they said, big noise, played jazz tuba, too, don't laugh, and then school where I had math first period, teacher had a rug, no rugs, he was redhead-blond-prematurely gray, it depended, his wife was the shop teacher, had six fingers—on both hands—no, two on one, four on the other, and . . .

> ***Whoa. Slow down. What do these specifics mean? Where are you taking me?***

Development during revision is often a matter of working through the draft, paragraph by paragraph, line by line, sanding, fitting, rebuilding, shaping, caulking, adding, cutting according to the demands of the line.

Boring? No. Because as you develop the draft it grows and changes, teaching you what you don't expect about your subject.

Emphasize the Significant

In developing a draft, make sure you give the proper emphasis to the information you are adding so your meaning will be made clear. In accumulating an abundance of information there is a danger that the draft will be piled up with so many lists and heaps of information that the reader will not be able to see its significance.

Emphasis, of course, is provided by the dramatic nature of certain pieces of information, by the vigor of the writing, but, most of all, by the placement of the information. Where you place the most important information in the sentence, the paragraph, the section, the article, the book is important.

This can be seen most easily in the map of a paragraph:

Often the most important information is buried in a paragraph, and the reader zooms right over it. When you have information that you must emphasize, the reader remembers best what is at the end of a paragraph, next best what is at the beginning, and least what is in the middle of the paragraph.

Second Point of Emphasis
(Important information that will attract a reader)

Third Point of Emphasis
(Attribution and other pieces of less interesting information that need to be included)

First Point of Emphasis
(Most important information; will stay in reader's mind and make reader want to continue to read)

This 2-3-1 principle works in key sentences and in larger blocks of writing, but it should not be followed all the time or each sentence, paragraph, and piece will sound the same: ta-boom, ta-boom, ta-boom.

In revision, I consider the 2-3-1 question when I read significant pieces of writing that must be clear to the reader and are totally confusing. Often the important material is buried in the middle and moving it out to the edges will clarify the writing.

Make a photocopy of a page or two of your or someone else's writing, and then cut the paragraphs up, separating the material in the beginning, middle, and end of the paragraph. Then move them around to see how you can deemphasize and emphasize the information being delivered to the reader.

Remember, there may be good reasons to put the key information in the middle of the paragraph or at the beginning. Do not follow this advice slavishly, but consider it if test readers are confused.

Pace and Proportion

Two important elements in writing that are often ignored by writing textbooks are pace and proportion.

"Pace" is the speed at which the writer causes the reader to move through the text. One way to speed up the pace is to use short sentences and sentence fragments, what one person calls "the English minor sentence": *"Now is the time to vote. Not in the next election. Not tonight on the way home from work. Not during lunch. Right now. On your way to work. This day. This hour. Right now."* The pace can be slowed down by longer words and longer sentences with clotting clauses: *"It is understandable that citizens with multiple responsibilities procrastinate and wait to vote at a later time period that never comes. There is always a meeting, an overdue assignment, a deadline project, a crisis, real or imagined, that delays the electorate until the vote that affects their lives, and the lives of their families, cannot be counted because the polls have closed."*

"Proportion" is the relationship of the parts to each other. Description may need to be balanced by dialogue, facts with people, theories with evidence.

Here is a case where the description overwhelms the dialogue:

> "As town manager, why do you think the town should set aside its zoning regulations to allow a fish processing plant a hundred yards off Main Street?" The town manager, a neat man with a precise manner, adjusted his rimless glasses, swept his left hand through the head of hair he used to have, tapped his pencil on the hearing table, then opened his old-fashioned leather dispatch case. Outside the hearing room, a siren grew loud then faded as it screamed past and in the hearing room those who were for and against the fish plant, neighbors in arms against each other, grew impatient. He found his folder, snapped the case shut, ran his pencil down

> the right side of the paper then stopped. He looked up and said, "Sixty-five jobs."

And in this case the dialogue overwhelms the description:

> "As town manager, why do you think the town should set aside its zoning regulations to allow a fish processing plant a hundred yards off Main Street?"
>
> The town manager looked up and said, "Sixty-five jobs."

Neither is right or wrong. It depends on what you have to say. The first might be a profile of the town manager, the second a simple report of the hearing.

As you develop your draft, you will confront two key questions: How fast is fast enough? How much is enough?

The issues of pace, the speed with which the reader moves through the draft, and proportion, the length of each section of the draft in relation to the other sections—all have to be solved together. When you speed up or slow down a draft, you alter the length of each section, and when you decrease or increase the length of a section, you speed up or slow down the reader's pace.

Proportion is a matter of length, but what is enough exposition or description is affected by the length of other parts. A detailed description of a manufacturing process might allow a detailed analysis; a quick anecdote about the designer of the process might limit a quotation to a sentence. How much ketchup depends, in part, on the size of the burger.

The writer wants to give the reader all the information the reader needs and no more. If there is too little, the reader will stop reading, and if there is too much, the reader will stop reading.

Pace is influenced not only by length but by the way the piece is written. Long sentences and paragraphs slow readers down, short ones speed them up; dialogue increases velocity, description slows it down; verbs and nouns accelerate, adverbs and adjectives apply the brakes.

There is no right pace. It depends on many factors, such as how familiar the readers are with the subject, how specialized their knowledge, how much the writer wants to entertain or inform, appeal to the brain or the heart.

Length

Making a piece of writing dramatically longer or even more dramatically shorter has been common in my writing life. The reason for this is rarely the quality of the writing itself or the quality of the research, but a question of the space a publication has available. Of course I have grumped at times but I have found almost always that another look at the draft with a new length in mind has helped the draft by either developing or compressing it.

What follows is the first draft of a column for the *Boston Globe.* I do not have an assigned space as some columnists and therefore do not have to hit a specific number of words or lines, but my target is 600–700 words.

> Approaching 80 and no longer teaching but living in a college town, I watch the students return with amusement and nostalgia. First the football players with no necks; then the prematurely smooth campus politicians followed by tanned sorority and fraternity officers; next the faculty who are often library or laboratory pale with the haunted look of those who have not yet published what they promised; finally the freshmen, the boys young, gawky, who tumble over each other puppy-like and the co-eds as young but women, poised, and tightly garbed to prove to all they are indeed fully developed women: and overnight the undergraduates and graduate students acting as if they own our town which they do.
>
> As I watch them, I realize that some are overloud and others profoundly silent, but all are aware of each other, seeking to discover, what's in, what's out, what costume shall I try this semester?
>
> I do not scorn this trying on masks or ridicule it. I remember my own efforts at sophistication by emulation. Away from their parents and their hometown classification,

> they face themselves. Many have no dreams and they confront their purposelessness, but I found that those who had dreams confronted a special terror when a professor like myself said, "You have the talent, but I don't know if you have the energy. If you do, your dream of being a writer will come true."
>
> I remember the elation and the burden I felt when my English teacher, Mort Howell, submitted an editorial from the student paper at Tilton Junior College to the *Christian Science Monitor,* where it was published.
>
> "You'll be a writer when you come home from the war." And he was right. Three years at war, two more in college, four years in the City Room and I was writing three editorials a day.
>
> I had made, in a few short years, my dream my reality, I had paid my own way to college and escaped my family's expectations. I was living a life they could not comprehend or approve of when they shook my hand—we did NOT hug—as I went off to college, a world they never knew.
>
> Now I watch the students flood my streets and wonder who will become a lawyer, scientist, politician, surgeon, entrepreneur, scholar, artist, actor, composer living the life they chose at college when they were unsure the life they tried on would fit.

The column is short. I run the word count on the computer and find it is 403 words, two-thirds of the length it should be. Now I have to expand it by at least 200 words. There are a number of things I can do:

- Read the column fast to see if there is anything to develop. What is the draft trying to say? The focus? Is it worth developing? Will the reader be interested?

  The draft attempts to celebrate—and explain?— the opportunity college students have to design a new life. [Insert something about how college may distance students from parents, class, race, or ethnic background or is that another column?]

- Do I need to stop and do more research? What documentation will the reader want?

  This is not a research piece on how many students change their life direction in college—and where would I find such statistics anyway. This is a subjective essay based on my personal college experience as a soon student and/or professor. The authority will come in part from the reader who will connect this piece with their own college or career history.

- Is the genre appropriate? Should this be an article, a poem, a story, an argument?

  I don't see a poem in this but it obviously could be a short story, a novel, a memoir, but I think it is appropriate for a column called Now and Then which reports on the aging process.

- Does the structure work? Does it support the meaning? Does it carry the reader towards that meaning?

  I'll keep an eye on this as I rewrite and develop the draft. I feel that it does support the meaning and lead the reader toward a meaning, but other readings [and perhaps readers] will confirm this. And my editor will be instinctively asking all these questions.

- Is the voice right for this topic and my readers? Does it support or work in harmony with the meaning? Is it consistent?

  I will tune the voice in the final read through as I always do but I think the voice suggests an appropriate distance as an old man looks at the students returning with some bemusement, an increasing nostalgia, and a discovery that what can happen in college—and happened to him—should be celebrated.

- Is it ready for a line-by-line reading for clarity, accuracy, and grace?

  No. Not until the draft is developed into a completed column.

How I Developed This Draft

First I read the draft it to see if it says what I think it does—something even better. I reread the draft and think it rings true. Students *do* design their own lives in college to the horror or the pride of their parents, or the horror and pride of their parents. Indeed, many students make their dreams come true. That's the center of the piece, but I have failed to show it happening. I can describe, in specific detail, how I came to be able to write that editorial or I can describe the process students pass through to make their dreams come true. I have told my story in the past, it may be time to report how I show students develop.

The changes I made in **upper and lowercase italic type** were inserted after my first reading; the ones in italic **CAPITAL LETTERS** after my second read through.

> Approaching 80 and no longer teaching but living in a *THE* college town *OF DURHAM, NEW HAMPSHIRE,* I watch the students return with amusement and nostalgia.
>
> First the football players with no necks; then the prematurely smooth campus politicians followed by tanned sorority and fraternity officers; next the faculty who are library or laboratory pale and often wear the haunted look of those who have not yet published what they promised; finally the freshmen, the boys young, gawky, who tumble over each other puppy-like and the co-eds as young but women poised, and tightly garbed to prove to all they are indeed fully developed women: and at last overnight the undergraduates and graduate students who act as if they own our town which they do.
>
> As I watch them, I realize that some are overloud and others profoundly silent, but all are aware of each other, seeking to discover, what's in, what's out, what costume shall I try this semester?
>
> I do not scorn this trying on masks or ridicule it. I remember my own efforts at sophistication by emulation. *My freshman year I spent hours with an* Esquire *magazine diagram and the mirror leaning how to tie a Windsor knot.*

Away from our parents and our hometown reputation, we confront ourselves. No one to blame but ourselves.

The students I pitied the most had not yet found their dreams but when they did in geology, sociology, hotel management, drama, or engineering class I could tell by the way they walked. Th~~ey~~IR POSTURE AND STRIDE revealed a new IDENTITY ~~confidence~~ and a new ~~energy~~ COMMITMENT.

And a new anxiety as well ~~Many have no dreams and they confront their purposelessness, but I found that those who had dreams confronted a special terror~~ when a professor like myself said, "You have the talent, but I don't know if you have the energy. If you do, your dream of being a writer will come true."

I remember the elation and the burden I felt when my *Freshman* English teacher, Mort Howell, submitted an editorial from the student paper at Tilton Junior College to the *Christian Science Monitor,* where it was published.

"You'll be a writer when you come home from the war." *NO EXCUSES NOW. IT WAS ENTIRELY UP TO ME TO STOP TALKING LIKE A WRITER AND WRITE. I DID A*nd ~~he was~~ *FOUND HIM* right. Three years at war, two more in college, four years in the City Room and I was writing three editorials a day *for the* Boston Herald *where I began to realize new dreams of books and poems might be possible.*

I had made, in a few short years *with the help of my teachers and then my editors,* my dream my reality, I had paid my own way to college and escaped my family's expectations. I was living a life they could not comprehend or approve of when they shook my hand—we did NOT hug—as I went off to college, a world they never knew.

YEARS LATER when I moved behind the desk and began to read and respond to my students individually in conference, I listened as they—hesitantly, apologetically—admitted their ambition to become writers. I learned to accept the fact that those with the greatest potential had the least confidence.

My task was not so much to instruct as encourage, to help them discover the value of their instinct. Together we

> *celebrated their first publications in student or local newspaper and magazines. And if I didn't teach too much but shared what I was learning with them, they passed from student, to friend, to published colleagues. We had EACH gone to college and made our dreams come true.*
>
> Now I watch the students flood my streets and wonder who will become a lawyer, scientist, politician, surgeon, entrepreneur, scholar, artist, actor, composer living the life *that had once been a dream.* ~~they chose at college when they were unsure the life they tried on would fit~~.

I will read it over realizing I have room if I see a spot when the reader needs a question answered, a fact documented, a definition inserted, a line or paragraph clarified. Now it is 667 words less 33 words cut which adds up to 634. I will submit it to my wife for editing, then my *Globe* editor who has a good eye and may suggest changes, and on deadline the copy desk will call seeking clarification or checking accuracy if it is necessary.

Now I imagine my editor wants me to cut it in half because it is going to be on a page with many other people's memories of going off to college. In this case I again look for what works best, then try to find large chunks that can be cut, and if that doesn't do it, go through it line by line, cutting a word here, a clause there, perhaps even a sentence.

The first cut I made was from the first word to "I remember the elation and the burden. . . ." Then I cut from "I had paid my own way . . ." to the end. It is only 133 words but if the editor is fitting many quotes on a page, he will be delighted with a short one. It seems to me to hold together and work:

> I remember the elation and the burden I felt when my Freshman English teacher, Mort Howell, submitted an editorial from the student paper at Tilton Junior College to the *Christian Science Monitor,* where it was published.
>
> "You'll be a writer when you come home from the war." No excuses now. It was entirely up to me to stop talking like a writer and write. I did and found him right. Three years at war, two more in college, four years in the City Room and I

> was writing three editorials a day for the *Boston Herald* where I began to realize new dreams of books and poems might be possible.
>
> I had made, in a few short years with the help of my teachers and then my editors, my dream my reality.

If indeed my editor wants more, I will add these paragraphs:

> Years later when I moved behind the desk and began to read and respond to my students individually in conference, I listened as they—hesitantly, apologetically—admitted their ambition to become writers. I learned to accept the fact that those with the greatest potential had the least confidence.
>
> My task was not so much to instruct as encourage, to help them discover the value of their instinct. Together we celebrated their first publications in student or local newspaper and magazines. And if I didn't teach too much but shared what I was learning with them, they passed from student, to friend, to published colleagues. We had each gone to college and made our dreams come true.

I enjoy the process of adding and cutting. It is always fascinating to see how a piece of writing changes with the addition or subtraction of just one word, one sentence, or one paragraph. Try it with a piece of your own writing to see how changing the length can make a subtle or dramatic difference in your draft.

Chapter 9
REWRITE BY EAR

The longer you stay a writer, the more voices you find in your own voice and the more voices you find in the world.

—Allan Gurganus

Each work of fiction has its own distinctive voice and the challenge for the writer—at times a challenge that evokes intense anxiety—is to discover and to refine the voice that is unique to that work.

—Joyce Carol Oates

The first line sets the tone, the melody. If I hear the tone, the melody, then I have the book.

—Elie Wiesel

I write by ear, hearing the words as I write them. I do not need to see them and can write a draft with the computer screen turned off. A draft is an exercise in word music as I not only hear the note, the word itself, but also the beat, the melody as words—the notes—and I hear how they relate to each other.

This process of musical composition with words is fun. It is the music of language that draws the writer to the writing desk and informs the writer of the meanings and feelings that lie within the subject; it is the music of language that attracts and holds the reader and causes the reader to trust and believe the writer; it is the music of language that provides emphasis and clarity; it is the music of language that makes the writer and the reader *hear* the printed word.

What Is Voice?

Voice is the magical heard quality in writing. Voice is what allows the reader's eyes to move over silent print and hear the writer speaking. Voice is the quality in writing, more than any other, that makes the reader read on, that makes the reader interested in what is being said and makes the reader trust the person who is saying it. We return to the columns, articles, poems, books we like because of the writer's individual voice. Voice is the music in language.

Many of the qualities writers call *voice* have been called *style* in the past, but writers today generally reject that term. *Style* implies something can be bought off the rack, something that can be easily imitated. *Tone* is another word used, but it seems limited to one aspect of writing. *Voice* is a more human term, and one with which we are familiar.

We all know—and make use of—the individual quality of voice. We recognize the voice of each member of our family from another room; we recognize the voices of our friends down the dormitory corridor or across the office. And we know that voice isn't just the sound of the voice, it is the way each person says things. We enjoy Anne's stories; Kevin's quick rejoinders; the fascinating details Chandra calls attention to; Jorge's quiet, straight-faced humor; Tori's mock anger.

Their voices reflect the way they see the world, how they think, how they feel, how they make us pay attention to the world they see. And we are used to using our own voices, plural intended, to tell others our concerns, our demands, our needs.

Voice also has a political element. Voice speaks out; voice demands to be heard. The person who has voice is empowered. A person whose voice can be heard in writing has an opportunity to influence the policies of a government, a school, an agency, a corporation, a society. Voices that demand listening may attract hearers who may add their voices to the cause. Information is power, and voice gives focus and significance to information.

Hearing Your Own Writing

When we write we should write out loud, hearing what we say as—or just before—we say it. Turn off the screen on your own computer. You should be able to write just as well—maybe better—as your ear edits what you say as you say it. I have just added a voice-activated program to my computer so I can dictate as I used to dictate drafts to my wife before I used a computer. I need to hear what I am saying as I write.

It is my voice that tells me, as much as any other element in writing, what I feel and what I think. It is relatively easy for the nonwriter to understand the connection between the emotions and voice but much harder to appreciate the connection between the intellect and voice.

Let me try to demonstrate how I use voice to discover how I feel and how I think.

I drove past the yard in front of my old elementary school, now turned into apartments for the elderly, and that started me thinking about the single word "playground." I started to write a number of versions to discover what I hear.

1. The playground that always comes first to memory is not the dirt field across the street from the Massachusetts Fields School in Wollaston, Massachusetts, that seemed huge when I was small, but the tar area just outside the school where we waited for the doors to open in the morning or after lunch and where we lined up after recess.
2. I see a large, chubby mother and a tiny, chubby boy holding her hand. No. I am the boy and then Mother is holding my hand. I can still feel her cruel grasp and my shame that Mother is taking me to school.
3. When I think of playground I remember a radio interview with Orson Welles, the great actor and dramatist. He said that once when he passed a playground filled with children out at recess he frantically rolled up the taxi windows. The driver said, "It's a happy sound," and Welles answered, "Not if you were a fat little boy."

4. When I type playground it comes out "prayground." I don't know if it is a slip of the typing fingers or of the mind but it is just the right word. It was there that I prayed to Jesus Christ before school in the morning, before recess and during recess, when returning to school after lunch, before and during afternoon recess, and in the afternoon before I could make my escape. Mother told me that if I believed in Jesus Christ and did not strike the first blow, the hand of the bully would be stayed. It was not. Then I blamed myself, later I blamed God, now I blame Mother.
5. If I was bad in elementary school, I was kept in from recess and I made sure I was bad. I got beaten up every recess. But my teachers caught on. I hid in the basement bathroom. They found me. They made me take recess, trying to make a little man of the pacifist who would not fight.
6. Violence in our schools today? I remember recess at the Massachusetts Field School where Mother and my teachers forced me to test my faith in Jesus Christ morning and afternoon. Then I thought I failed each test of faith when I was knocked to the ground and kicked. Now I think my teachers were the failures.
7. A grandson is being treated unfairly at school, and as my daughter describes how she defended him I am impressed by her wisdom, her caring, and I am surprised to feel another emotion, envy, and almost resentment for my grandson. My mother defended me. Teacher was always right. Her son was always wrong.
8. Tommy McDonald was half my size and twenty times as tough. He found out I would not hit back when punched and he would back me up against the great metal flagpole outside the Massachusetts Fields School and play rat-a-tat-tat with my skull against the cold, hard metal. But I had my revenge when, during World War II, he saw me in Piccadily Circus in London. He was in submarines and I, the boy he'd bullied for six long years, wore the wings of a paratrooper.

9. I wonder how much my life has been marked by the years when I was the victim of daily beatings on the playground of my elementary school. How much has it made me understand victims, have empathy, reach out to those who do not fit, give me the patience to help my wife with her Parkinson's; how must it have made me hit the guy across the line of scrimmage, squeeze the trigger in combat when the enemy head was in my sights, parade my strength in meetings, make cold decisions on promotion and tenure, remove life support from Father, Mother, and my daughter Lee?
10. I'm still pissed off at Tommy McDonald, the swaggering bully who beat up every recess the kid who would not strike back; at the teachers who forced me to march out to the bloody test on the playground and never tried to find out why I would not strike back; at a mother who, when I came home bloody or bruised or, yes, with blubbery tears, would force me to put my head on her knee and pray for a faith that would be so strong the bully's fist would be stayed.

For me, there is a different music in each beginning paragraph, but I am shocked at the darkness in them all. I have tried, time after time, to write in a light, humorous, nostalgic voice about the word "playground." But I fail. My voice tells me what I would like to deny: that for this boy the playground was never a place of pleasure, of delight, of athletic accomplishment, of innocent fun. It was always a place of male testing, a place I feared and where I learned to control and hide that fear.

This demonstrates the powerful instruction of voice. The music of my language tells me how important the subject is to me. Edna O'Brien, the Irish novelist, said,

> *An artist keeps going back to very wounded moments. Sometimes you're not aware of it, but they crop up of their own accord, because childhood and that absolute seepage of geography, language, death, and pain has gone into you. It's as organic as anything else. But if you write something about marriage or loss or childhood, fathers, mothers, the whole stew, it's never a catharsis. It glues you more to them. I get the food I am unable to get from human intercourse.*

Despite the sameness of mood in these examples of my voice, I hear similar but significantly different lines of music in each one that would lead me to the expression of different tones, different rhythms, different melodies, different feelings, and different thoughts. Each paragraph would lead to a different essay.

The magic of writing is that the words on the page will be heard by the reader. Individual writer speaks to individual reader. The heard quality of speech is put into writing by the writer. And what the reader will hear will depend on their childhood, their experiences in their home and school, on their playground.

Diagnosis: No Voice

"Upon due consideration, the committee decided, after a review of pertinent records and appropriate consideration of your fiscal demands, to deny you the Mortensen Scholarship. Such a decision should not be considered a rejection but simply an evaluative process subject to the resource demands of the university community." That is an example of a voiceless statement, an institutional voice used to avoid persona, and individual responsibility.

Lack of voice is the most common reason we stop reading, but we do not name it. Readers do not say, "We abhor the lack of voice here," and put down the article or book. They simply stop reading. Their minds float off the page. They realize they are not reading and turn to something else. They have heard no music where they do not realize there should be music. In the same way, readers who read on do not say, "We are being carried forward on the music of the writer's voice." They just read on, hearing and not knowing they are hearing a voice rising from the page.

As writers, however, we must become aware of the voice of what we write or aware of the lack of a voice. The signs of a draft without voice include the following:

- *No individual human being behind the page.* The page could have been written by anyone. The author is anonymous. The draft was not created by a living human animal but by a machine.

- *No intellectual challenge.* The page does not make intimate combat with the reader's mind. It does not stimulate, challenge, inform, surprise the reader, inspiring the mind-to-mind combat that marks good writing.
- *No emotional challenge.* The page does not engage the reader's emotions, encouraging the reader to feel as well as think.
- *No flow.* The reader is not carried forward by the energy of the voice that connects all the elements of writing into a powerful river of language that makes it hard for the reader to escape the page.
- *No magic.* In good writing, the sentence, the paragraph, the page, the entire draft is more than the orderly progression of correctly spelled words marching along in correct grammatical order. Good writing gives the words more meaning than they have while lying separate from each other in the dictionary. The magic of writing is that the voice rises from the spaces between the words as much as from the words themselves, carrying meaning to the reader.

Writers write with their ears, listening to the music rising from the page or from the computer screen as they write and rewrite.

Hearing the Writer's Voice

Once you are aware of the importance of voice, read good and bad writers to *hear* the music of their writing—and the marvelous diversity of human voices writing in every genre, for every purpose.

Enjoy the examples of voice I admire:

> Here is an account of a few years in the life of Quoyle, born in Brooklyn and raised in a shuffle of dreary upstate towns.

Hive-spangled, gut roaring with gas and cramp, he survived childhood; at the state university, hand clapped over his chin, he camouflaged torment with smiles and silence. Stumbled through his twenties and into his thirties learning to separate his feelings from his life, counting on nothing. He ate prodigiously, liked a ham knuckle, buttered spuds.

His jobs: distributor of vending machine candy, all-night clerk in a convenience store, a third-rate newspaper man. At thirty-six, bereft, brimming with grief and thwarted love, Quoyle steered away to Newfoundland, the rock that had generated his ancestors, a place he had never been nor thought to go.

E. Annie Proulx
The Shipping News

The Shipping News had been recommended to me and when I saw it in a bookstore I picked it up and read these first three paragraphs. I closed the book and bought it. This one I must read. What caught me was the writer's voice. It was individual, powerful, eccentric (another word for individual?) and entertaining. I wanted to hear this voice spin me a story.

In many U.S. school systems, there is a curriculum director whose job it is to puzzle out what a curriculum is. The etymology of the word is promising: it comes from the Latin word currere, "to run," and is closely related to the word curricle, a two-horse chariot used for short races. Presumably, curricles went around in circles just as curricula trends do in this country, the only difference being that curricle drivers knew they were always going over the same ground, and we often don't. The curriculum director, and those who specialize in this murky science in colleges of education, generally tries to keep the chariots moving in the same direction at roughly the same pace.

Yet the very order suggested by the word "curriculum"—that fixed track upon which the race occurs—seems antithetical to schooling that acknowledges the individual interests and abilities of students. Too often, decisions about what students do at what age are purely arbitrary, and claims by publishers that their work is developmentally sound are only promotional hype. The organization of instruction often shades into regimentation, an interminable forced march through exercises and work sheets. Any misstep, the teacher's manuals imply, might lead to serious problems—like those of the ducklings who didn't learn how to follow their mother at the right time and ended up following the zoo-keeper instead.

Thomas Newkirk
More Than Stories—The Range of Children's Writing

Here is a fine example of academic writing in which the author's scholarship is worn lightly and the ideas are presented with clarity, vigor, and grace. This is a seminal study on children's writing, yet there is a place for humor, and you sense the personality of the author from the voice you hear on the page.

There is a loneliness that can be rocked. Arms crossed, knees drawn up; holding, holding on, this motion, unlike a ship's, smooths and contains the rocker. It's an inside kind—wrapped tight like skin. Then there is a loneliness that roams. No rocking can hold it down. It is alive, on its own. A dry and spreading thing that makes the sound of one's own feet going seem to come from a far-off place.

Everybody knew what she was called, but nobody anywhere knew her name. Disremembered and unaccounted for, she cannot be lost because no one is looking for her, and even if they were, how can they call her if they don't know her name? Although she has claim, she is not claimed. In the place where long grass opens, the girl who waited to be loved and cry shame erupts into her separate parts, to make it easy for the chewing laughter to swallow her all away.

Toni Morrison
Beloved

These are two paragraphs from the last chapter of Nobel laureate Morrison's Pulitzer Prize-winning novel. She has the ability to go to the edge of where most of us write

and pass beyond it. Her voice has its own fullness, its own passion, its own richness. It is individual. It is her.

I became an escapee—one of the ones others talked about. I became the one who got away, who got glasses from the Lions Club, a job from Lyndon Johnson's War on Poverty, and finally went to college on a scholarship. There I met the people I always read about: girls whose fathers loved them—innocently; boys who drove cars they had not stolen; whole armies of the middle and upper classes I had not truly believed to be real; the children to whom I could not help but compare myself. I matched their innocence, their confidence, their capacity to trust, to love, to be generous against the bitterness, the rage, the pure and terrible hatred that consumed me. Like many others who had gone before me, I began to dream longingly of my own death.

Dorothy Allison
Trash

This is the opening of the introduction to novelist Dorothy Allison's first book of short stories. You cannot deny the authority, power, and toughness of this individual voice that writes with such emotion tempered with talent and craft. And notice the specifics that establish her authority.

Having proposed a biochemical explanation for sensitization, Kandel was ready to take on classical conditioning. By 1981, he and his colleagues had finally got Aplysia to demonstrate what they had claimed was a simple form of conditioning, although the interpretation of the experiment is still hotly disputed. In the earlier experiments the electrical shock to the tail was used to sensitize the snail, causing it to respond more strongly to the tapping on its siphon by withdrawing its gill. But as they played around with Aplysia, trying to uncover other reflexes to study, Kandel and his colleagues found that a tail shock alone could also cause the gill to withdraw. In the new experiments they discovered that if they repeatedly followed a touch of the siphon with a shock to the tail, they could get Aplysia to learn that the touch was a predictor for the shock. Here the electric shock was the unconditioned stimulus. Without any training, it caused the Aplysia to reflexively withdraw its gill. A light tap to the siphon was the conditioned stimulus. At first it caused only a slight gill withdrawal. But if the scientists paired the two stimuli, always following the tap by the shock, the snail would learn to vigorously withdraw the gill just at the tapping.

George Johnson
In the Palaces of Memory

Science writing has produced some of the best voices in our language. It is a particularly disciplined form of writing in which precision of diction and sequence of information must be followed while the author defines each term and makes clear the implication of what is being recorded, yet still manages to communicate the aesthetic importance of what is being reported. Johnson maintains an appropriate distance with his voice. I compare this voice to the whispery voice of the TV golf commentator. Johnson allows us to stand beside him, and as we observe the scientists at work he explains what they are doing and what is important about it.

Bao Yanshan's wife was in labour, about to give birth on her bed at home. Big Dog, the son of Baotown's troop leader, ran shouting down to the Lake to find Yanshan. He came sauntering up, hands behind his back, hoe tucked under one arm, thinking what a common occurrence this had become. The seventh belly, no problem, he was thinking—she's just like an old mother hen dropping another egg. To have it come three months early was just that much better; this time of year there was plenty to eat. But whether it was three months or three days, or three hours, it was not worth getting excited about.

Wang Anyi
Baotown

The author's voice comes through translation, and we hear her beginning her book about the remote village to which she was exiled during China's Cultural Revolution. In these few lines her voice takes us into the place

> ***far removed from my New Hampshire home, and also takes me into the mind of a person who is my contemporary, yet lives in a different time.***

Hearing Your Own Voice

Voice is often seen as a mystery, an element in writing that is sophisticated, difficult for the student to understand. But I have never had a student who did not come to the first class knowing—and using—many voices.

Before going to first grade, children know there are voices they use in playing they may not use in church, ways of speaking that are not appropriate in front of Grandmother, voices that will win permission from one parent and not another, voices that will make peers come over to play or run away home. We all speak before we have language, when we cry from the crib, with many voices, and it is all those voices that may eventually be turned into voices that will arise from our pages as we write.

Ethnic Influences

We are the product of our racial and ethnic heritage. There is such a thing as Jewish humor or black humor, which may not be Black humor. Sorry, that may be an example of Scottish humor. On my first visit to Scotland I looked up a relative and found an old man digging in a garden. "Are you Donald Bell?" I asked. "Guilty as charged," he answered. I had thought that was a family joke in America and found it was Scottish humor that emigrated to America. It was not a family but a typically Scottish retort. My voice—and yours—is a product of your heritage, all those elements that are passed down in your genes.

Regional Influences

Our voices are also the product of the speaking habits of the area where we are brought up. My speech is urban not country, street language not field language. I speak fast and say "Cuber" for Cuba, "pahk" for park and "Hahvud Squah" for Harvard Square; I speak Boston—perhaps the ugliest accent in America—not Boston Brahmin, the accent we used to describe as speaking with a hot potato in your mouth, of the lace curtain Irish of the Kennedy family, but Boston working class. Our ears pick up the patterns of speech around us and we make them our own.

Family Influences

Each family—yours and the Kennedys', for example—has its own way of speaking and we learn speech by imitation. No wonder, that for the rest of our lives, we hear the ghosts of those family members who are dead or live far away in our spoken and written voices.

Daily Influences

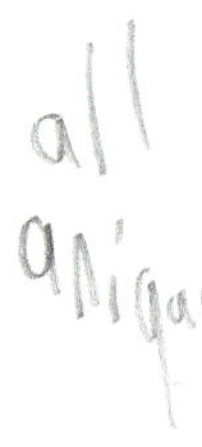

We all swim in a sea of language. We hear language from radio and television, from the people around us, and, by telephone, from those far away. We respond to language. We read e-mail and snail mail, home pages, fliers, brochures, newspapers, magazines, books. We respond with language. We send e-mail and snail mail; write papers and exams and memos; notes to others and ourselves.

Professional Influences

We are influenced by the language of our work place. When you take a job you have to learn the language of your craft, speaking nurse talk or police talk, marketing talk or lawyer talk, engineer talk or teacher talk. This professional language, full of the jargon of our craft, is often taken home and we speak the language of work at home where a more intimate language is spoken.

Your Language or Mine?

It is the responsibility of schools to teach the rules educated people follow most of the time when they speak, write, and read, successfully communicating with each other. But it should also be the responsibility of schools to teach the other times when the rules can be broken to achieve clarity. Language should not be taught as an absolute, a matter of clear right and wrong. The history of language is the history of change; the rules evolve.

This inevitably gets mixed up with status and etiquette. The educated person speaks differently than the uneducated one; the person in power uses language differently from the person out of power; the well-mannered person speaks differently from the uncouth, uncultured one.

I am uncomfortable with those ideas, but they have a truth. I do not come from a well-educated family. They did pay a great deal of attention to speaking properly, but my education isolated me from my background and my family. I recognize the need of people to learn the language of those who have power over them, but I also respect the languages and dialects of all the diverse cultures in our society. The grandmother who brought me up spoke Gaelic, but she would not teach a word of it to me. I was to be an American and to speak American. Sadly, I became monolingual and was cheated of the heritage of Gaelic literature, oral and written, with which I should have been familiar.

I am writing a textbook of revision and inevitably I seem to say, "Write like me," and that makes me uncomfortable. And yet, the world judges you, more than it should, by how you speak and write. If you want to be heard, to be empowered, you have to find your way to use our language, not your own, and eventually to enrich our language with your own.

The Importance of Voice

Voice is the most important element in writing. It is what attracts, holds, and persuades your readers.

Significance

Voice illuminates and emphasizes information. Voice makes what appears to be insignificant information significant, and an ineffective voice can make what is significant for readers appear to be insignificant.

Character

Voice is a matter of character. The great essayist E. B. White once said, "Style results more from what a person is than from what he knows." When we write we reveal how we think, how we feel, how we care, how we respond to the world.

Trust

An effective voice demonstrates it is an authority on the subject. It speaks with confidence in specific terms. It is sure enough to qualify, to admit problems, to allow weaknesses of argument; it does not shout and bang the desk but speaks quietly to the individual reader, for writing is a private act—one writer to one reader. The writer's voice endeavors to earn the trust of the reader.

Music

Language is music. Writing is heard as it is read. The effective voice is tuned to the message, the situation, and the reader. The music of the writer's voice, similar to the music accompanying a movie, supports and advances the meaning of the entire text.

Communication

The effective voice can be heard, respected, and understood by a reader. Writing is a public act performed in private and received in private. Both reader and writer are alone. The writer must anticipate the language of the reader so that the act of writing will be completed when the writer's message is absorbed by the reader.

The Expected Voice

Society has voices it expects from us according to the message we have to deliver and the place it will be delivered. The victorious locker-room voice is different from the losing voice; the funeral voice different from the party voice. When we read science fiction, a newspaper sports story, a war report in a magazine, an economics or composition textbook, we have expectations.

The effective writer knows what the reader expects and decides to write within or against those expectations. But if the writer works against the expectations—using a poem to report on a football game, a narrative as a corporation's annual report—the reader must be informed in some way that the writer is aware of going against expectations. The reader must be prepared, because the expectations of the reader are always strong.

The Formal Voice

In school and at work, we learn the traditions of the formal voice, the literary research paper, the lab report, the nursing notation, the business memo. These formal traditions are usually rigid for good reason. The doctor scanning the nurse's nighttime notations is not looking for an aesthetic experience or a philosophical essay on pain but clear, specific information to help modify treatment.

The Informal Voice

The informal voice also has its own traditions. When we write a thank-you note to Aunt Agatha, a humor column in a college newspaper, a note stuck on a door to tell a friend where we are eating, we also follow traditions. The style may be casual, but it is usually in a casual tradition. Jeans and sneakers may be just as traditional as tux and gown. We need to know the tradition, then try to vary it if the tradition interferes with the delivery of our message.

Genre Voices

Narrative, journalism, drama, poetry, biography, and autobiography all have their own traditions that you can discover by asking people in those fields to tell you the tradition, where it is published, or by reading in that form. There are many languages of lyric poetry or of jazz, folk, or rock lyrics, but each belongs to a tradition that can be defined and described.

The Voice of the Draft

Traditional education focuses on the traditional voice; untraditional education focuses on the personal voice. I think they both miss the target. We need to know how to use the conventions of traditional language, and we need to be able to hear the sound of our personal voice, but the focus should be on the voice of the individual draft. Voice, as we have said, is a matter of situation; what is appropriate for one message, in one genre, for one reader, may not be in another.

Listen to the Voice of the Draft

We need to train ourselves to listen to the voice that emerges from the draft, we need to hear how language is being used in this particular case. Of course, what we will hear will be a blend of personal and traditional voices woven together for this particular purpose. That should provide the focus: What is needed here? What is strong and right? What needs to be extended and developed?

We have to be able to work at the console of language, mixing the tracks we hear so they work together to produce a combined voice—the voice of the draft—that will communicate our meaning.

Choose a personal experience that has affected your life and take ten minutes to describe it in writing. If you work on a computer, turn the screen off; if not, try not to pay attention to how your draft looks. Speak the draft out loud, hear what you are saying as you are saying it, follow the beat, the rhythm, the tone, the melody of what you are saying. Stop after ten minutes and read your draft aloud to hear your voice rise from the page.

Case History of a Professional Writer

Donald M. Murray

I start the day with an informal breakfast club in which the members became obsessed with healthy food and exercise. It wasn't that they ate healthy food and exercised—sometimes they did, mostly they didn't—but they talked about it all the time. I passed through anger to guilt—I wasn't eating right or exercising—to boredom to wondering about the real old-timers—I'm only seventy-five—I know who pay no attention to diet or exercise and seem to keep going just fine into their eighties and nineties, even beyond.

A piece like this depends on voice so I test the voice in the lead. It only takes a few lines to hear the music of a draft. I play with leads in my head and then try some on the computer screen:

> I'm fed up with health food. I want to start the day with a plate of well-greased animal parts collected in a sausage that drips with flavor, two real eggs over easy, hash brown potatoes sparkling with droplets of fat, buttered toast and apricot jam. The health food of my childhood.

***

> When I was a skinny child the doctor told my family to fatten me up—mashed potato WITH gravy; bread with butter and jam; meat dripping with blood; thick soups; ice cream ON pie; snacks, seconds, thirds, more and more and more until I grew into the pear-shaped adult of their dreams. Now my friends peck at leaves, phony meat, deflavored eggs, and even drink healthy, unflavored water. They are skinny—and unhappy. They must be.

***

> I used to go out to breakfast with friends. Now I draw the curtains, turn off all the lights but a small one in the kitchen, and eat my bacon, eggs, toast and marmalade, and

> caffeinated coffee, quickly, furtively, hoping the diet police will not break down the kitchen door.
>
> ***
>
> I have 134 cholesterol and yet have had one heart attack, one triple bypass, one angioplasty. Before the heart attack I dieted and took 34 health pills a day—fish oil and stuff I don't want to know where it comes from. So much for health food.
>
> ***
>
> When I was a boy everyone was obsessed with bowel movements. Some of my friends even had to keep charts. My mother just made sure. When I had a stomachache, I had a laxative until my appendix blew up and I almost died.
>
> I was fifteen and I have been a health cynic ever since. Tell me it's good for me and I doubt it.
>
> ***
>
> When a friend of mine got cancer she felt betrayed. She had jogged, eaten organic, meditated. She couldn't get cancer, but she did.
>
> She recovered from her cancer quicker than from her anger. She had made a deal with God and paid attention to diet fashion. She didn't know that God makes no deals.
>
> ***
>
> I'm a grown-up. I survived the food fads of my childhood—fat is good—and I will survive the food fads of adulthood—fat is bad. Just don't make every meal a competition to see who can eat better.
>
> I don't care what you eat—garden burgers, raw carrots, kiwi, sprouts without dressing—just don't smear your smug on me.

I finally decided to lighten up when my writer friend Don Graves told me how he pretends he only has a rotary phone when automated messages try to make him choose touch-tone alternatives. I began to hear the voice of an old-timer who has made modern times adjust to him rather than the other way around. I listened and wrote the following column, which is an exercise in voice: my column voice and the created voice of Ephraim Graves.

> When I get confused about what the news says about how I should live my life, I drive out to the Piscataqua Pond and visit Ephraim Graves. He is 111 years old, cuts his own wood, grows his own vegetables, kills his own protein, and has never been to a doctor in his life.
>
> "Mr. Graves," I ask (he comes from a more formal era, I'd never call him Eph), "I've got dry knees."
>
> "Kinda like sandpaper in the joints in the morning, kinda grindy?"
>
> "Yep. You're right."
>
> "What you have is ungreased joints. Had the same thing when I was young, 'bout 71, maybe '2. Bad case of ungreased joints. I doubled my morning bacon to eight strips, two over-easy eggs, started to butter my pie. That made the difference."
>
> "Butter your pie?"
>
> " 'Course."
>
> "Pie at breakfast. That'll kill you."
>
> "Ain't yet."
>
> "Maybe because you exercise."
>
> "I don't believe in it."
>
> "But you cut your own wood."
>
> "Who would if I didn't, huh? That's a chore, not exercising. I see them running by here all the time. Gives them the jiggles. Jogging, they call it."
>
> "The jiggles?"
>
> "Running shakes up your organs, jiggles them. Kidneys, liver, intestine, stomach, heart, they're all jammed into the same area, run and they bang into each other. Get bruised. The jiggles, bad stuff."
>
> "I worry about forgetting names."
>
> "I revel in it. Can't remember the names of my first two wives. Good thing, only make me mad. Same as the kids. They tried to put me in a home. Forget them."
>
> "You don't let life get to you, do you? Just maintain a kind of transcendental peace."

"What kinda peace?"

"I mean you don't let things bother you."

"I let everything bother me. Angrifying yourself is good, keeps the blood circling."

"What angrifies you?"

"Mosquitoes. Stray dogs. Neighbors. Grown-up people that ride bicycles three abreast down the highway. Love to scatter them. Kids with baseball caps on backwards. Republicans. Democrats. People that wear metal in their nose, tongues, God knows where else. Clothes too large for 'em. Wear advertisements on their shirts. Salad bars. Don't eat raw vegetables. Cook 'em first. Broccoli. Idiots that buy designer water. Canned laughter on TV. Sushi. Taco. Pizza. Bagels. Eat American I say."

"All that makes you mad?"

"Right. I get up in the morning calm, peaceful like, then I turn on the TV. The world infuriates me. Dole. Clinton. Princess Di. The Red Sox. I feel the rage start to percolate. Know I'm alive. Angry. Mad."

"Doesn't that, well, cause stress?"

"Damn right. Need stress to keep alive. Gets the heart beating, stretches the arteries, magnifies the brain."

"I thought stress kills."

"Naw. Happiness. Content. They kill. First you're bored, then you're dead, you don't even know the difference. Get aggravated, that's the way to live. Look at those of us who have survived. We're crusty, grumpy, growly, cantankerous."

"Proud of it?"

"Damn right. None of them smiling little drawings for us. Smiles, they call 'em. Not for me."

"No 'have a good day'?"

"Never. Who's going to tell me how to live my day? I want a bad day, full of irritation. No more boring days for me. I want some Moxie in my life."

"What is a good, I mean a bad, day for you?"

"I like to start the day by hanging up on some telephone solicitor. 'Don't want whatever you're peddling.' Slam down the receiver. Feels great. Grand way to start the day. Better, the mail comes and I get overcharged on a bill. I love to argue about a bill. Got a trick for you."

"What is it?"

"When them dang machine voices on the phone tell you to punch 1 if you have a touch-tone phone, don't."

"But I have one. Should I lie?"

"It isn't lying when you're talking to an electronic robot. Stay on the line. They'll think you have a rotary phone. A human being comes on the phone. You can be nasty to a human being."

"Nasty?"

"That's what gets your dang-blamed computer bill corrected —good old rage—and it's what keeps you young."

"Being nasty?"

"Nothing like it. Elixir of youth. Stay stress-gravated and you'll stay around—and have fun. But never admit it."

"Never admit what?"

"Being old. Angry. Nasty. Mean. I love it. Heard a young fella say the other day, 'Watch out, here comes old Graves. He's the nastiest old man I've ever known.' Best day of my life."

"Keeps you young?"

"Who wants to be young? More fun being old—and mean."

The column got an enormous response and most who responded wanted to visit Ephraim. Of course, Ephraim only lives behind the screen on my monitor. I may go there to see him again, but the effectiveness of the column depends on voice—my voice tuned to an individual vision of our world.

I hope you can hear old Ephraim Graves speaking from the page, and I hope you can hear your own voice, tuned to an individual of your own, come aloud on your page.

Chapter 10
REWRITE WITH CLARITY

Just to write a good sentence—that's the postulate I go by. I guess I've always felt that if you could keep a kind of fidelity toward the individual sentence, that you could work toward the rest.

—RICHARD FORD

Language is where you live, it's a real place, more important than geography.

—JONATHAN RABAN

Punctuation for me is very important, even more important than names. It accounts for the rhythm of a story. A comma left out can mean an entirely different feeling, and one put in can mean disaster, if it doesn't belong there.

—EUDORA WELTY

I wake early, eager to get to my writing desk. It is time for the final edit. Having stood back and reconsidered the topic, focus, genre, structure, documentation, development, and voice it is time to return to the word. I will enjoy the satisfactions of craft. All the large questions have been answered and all that is left is line-by-line editing. Practicing this series of small acts of clarity, I attend to all the larger questions of accuracy, truth, and communication.

To show you the fun and satisfactions of craft I experience, I am going to take a paragraph of autobiography and go through it line by line:

~~*My wife wakes me. It is 3:03 AM*~~	**Is better as "My wife wakes me at 3:03 in the morning . . ."? Or "My wife taps me on the shoulder just as I am about to score a touchdown. It is 3:03 AM and she needs to go to the john."? Toilet? Bathroom? No. John. It is the term we use and the voice that piece has developed is not tragic. It reveals survival not hoplessness.** **Cut any word such as "the" that can be cut.**
and she needs help getting to the john. She has Parkinson's and ~~she~~ can't make it by herself. I pull the covers down, swing her feet over the edge of ~~her~~ our bed, take her hands and	**I have to put this in context for the reader.** **The specific details put the reader there beside us.** **The "our" bed is important. We still sleep together = we have a life and a marriage despite Parkinson's.**
haul her up. As she sits on the edge of the bed, I hand her ~~her~~ THE cane, and	**"her her" was what I wrote and we can speak it, making it clear by inflection, but we can't do this in writing. Make it "the" cane.**
taking her other ~~hand stark naked~~ we make our way to the bathroom stark naked, ~~laughing~~ what WOULD the ~~at what the neighbors say if the could look through the bedroom wall.~~ Neighbors say	**The"stark naked" more than the "laughing" shows that we are not to be pitied—show don't tell.** **By showing, the reader knows we are not to be pitied and if this happens to them, they may be able to maintain a life and a marriage.**

As you can see, I first clarify for myself and then for the reader, becoming the reader's advocate. I distance myself from my ego and try to read as a stranger. Years ago the poet John Ciardi said, "The last act of the writing must be to become one's own reader. It is, I suppose, a schizophrenic process. To begin passionately and to end critically, to begin hot and to end cold; and, more important, to try to be passion-hot and critic-cold at the same time."

If you watch a painter at work, you will see her step back from the canvas, look critically at what has been done, then return to do more. It is not a painful process for me to step back. In fact, I find it fun to detach myself from my work and read it as a stranger. I discover what I have done as well as what I have not done—and must do.

Yet many beginning writers find it difficult to stand back and take what they think is a final first draft and treat it like a beginning draft needing change, cutting, adding, moving around. To help you, I have developed a list of ways to distance yourself from a first draft that may seem finished.

Twenty Ways to Unfinal a Draft

When your draft suffers from premature completion, try one—or two or three—of these activities to make the draft alive again.

1. *Listen to the draft.* Learn to hear what the draft is saying. It may be wiser and more interesting than what you intended to write.
2. *Welcome the unexpected.* Whatever contradicts, challenges, qualifies, questions what you intended to write is evidence of thought and may be worth exploring in a new draft.
3. *Expand what works.* Push the edge. Take what is most successful, strongest, and well written, and develop it further, beyond where you think it can go.
4. *Tune the music of the draft.* Hear what the voice of the draft is saying. What does it emphasize; what makes

the voice angry, sad, worried, happy, confident, shy, combative? Follow the voice toward its meaning.

5. *Start closer to the end.* Introductions are not necessary in most drafts. Start as near the end as you can and fold in the information readers need when they need it.
6. *Cut the end.* It is too late to tell the reader what you have said, why you have said it, how important it is for the reader to know it.
7. *Cut or extend the length.* Play with the length. You may just be telling readers, not giving them the evidence they need. Realize that shorter is usually better than longer.
8. *Play with a new focus.* Move back or in close; narrow or expand the focus of the draft.
9. *Reconsider the audience.* Limit, extend, or switch the readers you are trying to reach.
10. *Put the draft in a new context.* Each draft has its own context, the place it fits into the world. It can be illuminating to see the draft make a new connection with the world.
11. *Make new connections.* Meaning is constructed as specific pieces of information connected to other information. Change the connections to discover new meanings.
12. *Reorder the draft.* Write backward, sideways, or start in the middle to see what a new logic reveals.
13. *Change the pace.* Each piece of writing moves at its own pace, slowing down to allow readers to comprehend, speeding up to keep them interested.
14. *Unbalance the proportions.* There is an internal relationship between the size and weight of each part of a draft. Play with a new relationship.
15. *Try a new genre.* The draft may work better in a new genre or it may be improved by crossing genre, using narrative to argue, a profile to tell a story.

16. *Add new evidence.* New documentation or new forms of documentation, anecdote instead of statistic, quotation instead of generality, may produce a better draft.
17. *Look for instructive failure.* The moment of failure as in a scientific experiment may be the moment of revelation. Syntax often breaks down at the point of discovery.
18. *Role-play a reader.* Imagine a specific reader and read through that person's eyes to see what is being said and what may be said.
19. *Use a test reader.* Tell a reader the kind of reading you need—a quick read for meaning or order, a line-by-line read for language—and consider the response.
20. *Observe the draft.* Study how the draft is evolving. The struggle within a draft may be between the form you are imposing and the form its meaning needs.

The Attitude of the Editing Writer

I used to hate to rewrite, but my attitude changed with the experience of editing. I learned to be comfortable operating surgically on my draft. I saw how it improved my drafts and began to enjoy it. Here are some attitudes I bring to editing.

Writing Is Editing

It is not an admission of failure when you have to edit. It is a normal part of the process of making meaning with language. Editing is not punishment, but opportunity.

Imagine the Reader

To get distance on my own copy I often become the reader. I think of a person I know whom I respect but who has no interest in the subject I am writing about. I may walk around my office like that person walks, imitating their gestures, even their speech patterns. Then I read my words through that person's eyes, line by line.

In this way I see my writing from a stranger's point of view. Not someone who is a lunkhead but an intelligent person I want to reach who does not share my assumptions about the subject.

My Ear Is a Better Editor Than My Eye

We spoke before we wrote, historically and individually. Writing is not quite speech written down, but it is speech transformed so that it may be heard. The voice lies silent within the page, ready to be turned on by a reader. Writing is an oral/aural act, and we do well to edit out loud, hearing the text as we revise and polish it.

The Draft Will Tell You What It Needs

I have learned to respect my draft. Writing is not an ignorant act. Something was happening when the draft was being written. Writers know the contradiction of art: There is usually reason in accident. Try to understand the draft on its own terms. Do not make it what you or the world expects, but what the draft itself commands.

Welcome Surprise

Many people fear surprise. They hunger for control, and so do I in many parts of my life. But I have trained myself to remember that it is the unexpected that instructs me, the accident, the failure. When I say what I do not expect to say, it is evidence I have been thinking. I have to stop and consider the surprise. It may not mean anything this time, but most times it will mean a great deal. It will point me to my meaning.

Language Is Alive and Changing

This writer sees language as ever-changing. I may not like all the changes—I growl at split infinitives and grump when people use *host* as a verb or *fun* as an adjective—but most of the time I delight in our changing language and work as a writer at the edge of tradition. That is where the writer is using language to say what has not quite been said before in a way that has not quite been heard before.

The writer's rule is not to judge what is right or wrong—correct or incorrect—but what works and what doesn't. No decision about language can be made in the abstract any more than a surgeon should decide to operate without first examining the patient. All editing decisions are context oriented; what may be correct in one place may not be in another. Writing's job is not to be correct but to communicate meaning.

Accept Limitations

I accept the limitations of my craft—the assigned length of the draft, the expected form and tone, the targeted reader, the deadline—then go beyond the acceptance to view the limitations as a creative challenge. The mural is different from the miniature, the song from the opera, the jazz combo from the big band. The limitations of any art contribute to its breakthroughs; it is not discipline or freedom alone that are at the center of craft but the tension between freedom and discipline.

Establish Achievable Standards

Student writers and professional writers, myself certainly included, tend to dream an impossible draft. That is a certain route to failure. We give up before beginning the draft, knowing we can't do it; we quit while drafting because we are not living up to an imaginary standard; we toss the final draft because it doesn't measure up to an unreasonable standard.

Interview Your Draft

The draft will tell you what is needed, if you know how to ask. The skillful writer is first a skillful reader who can read what is on the page and what is not on the page rather than what the writer hopes is on the page.

- *What is the one thing I wanted to say, the single, most important message I intended to deliver?*
  Writing is thinking, and the best writing usually produces a draft that surprises us. It says what we did not expect. The writer should not feel a sense of failure but satisfaction when this happens. Then the writer has to decide whether to force the writing back to its intention as the writing assignment may demand or follow the draft toward its evolving meaning.
- *What single message does the draft deliver?*
  It may help to underline that message if it is established in a single, clear sentence within the draft or to write it out in a sentence so it will be a North Star during the revision process.
- *To whom is the message being sent?*
  If the message has a specific reader, the writer must know the reader and anticipate that reader's response. If there is no specific reader, the writer should call to mind a specific person who is intelligent but does not know the subject or care about it. Then the writer should read the draft from that person's point of view. Of course, the writer is always the first reader, and effective writers learn to distance themselves from a draft and read it as a stranger would.
- *What form or genre will deliver the information the reader needs most effectively?*
  The most effective forms grow organically from what needs to be said. We have discussed how rhetorical forms result from the study of what has worked for writers in the past. The writer who is trying to discover meaning in material and communicate it has to look at the writing task, the material, and the prospective reader to see what form will deliver that meaning to that reader.

  The material shapes the form. It may be problem/solution, a narrative, an argument, an explanation, a case history, a report. With some writing assignments, a specific form is required and the writer has to adapt the form to the material.

- *Does everything in the draft support or advance that message?*
  In effective writing, one meaning dominates and everything supports that meaning, grows from that meaning, develops that meaning.
- *Where are the strongest places or what are the most effective elements in the draft?*
  Effective revision is usually more the product of developing and extending the strengths within the draft than correcting errors in the draft.
- *Where are the greatest failures in the draft?*
  Failure is instructive. Often the place where the syntax breaks down or the structure takes an illogical turn is the point where the writer is starting to say something important the writer does not yet know how to say. It may be a point of discovery, not failure.
- *Are the reader's questions answered when they will be asked?*
  It is helpful to write down the questions the reader will ask—not the ones you want them to ask, the ones they will ask—and then put them in the order the reader will ask them.
- *Is the draft written with information, not just language?*
  Remember that the reader is not hungry for your fancy words, your ability to turn a mean phrase, but for specific, accurate information.
- *Is each point supported by documented evidence?*
  Do not depend on the reader taking anything on trust.
- *Is the voice of the draft appropriate to the subject and the reader?*
  In revising, the writer must read the draft aloud and tune the music of the draft so it supports the meaning. The voice of the draft is what makes readers read and trust the writer.
- *Does the draft exist within the shared world of the writer and reader?*

Everything in the draft should be in context; it should ring true to the experience the writer and reader share.

- *Is there anything that can be cut?*
  E. B. White, the great essayist, quoted his teacher Will Strunk as saying, "Vigorous writing is concise. A sentence should contain no unnecessary words, a paragraph no unnecessary sentences, for the same reason that a drawing should have no unnecessary lines and a machine no unnecessary parts. This requires not that the writer make all his sentences short, or that he avoid all detail and treat his subjects only in outline, but that every word tell." I kept that quotation over my desk for decades until it was etched on the inside of my forehead.
- *Does the typography and visual layout of the draft support and make the message clear?*
  The reader is influenced by the professional appearance of the draft.
- *Are the portions of information adequate?*
  The reader is hungry for information and that hunger must be satisfied.
- *Will the reader keep reading?*
  The pace of the draft should be slow enough so the reader can absorb the information and its meaning, fast enough to keep the reader interested. The proportion between the parts of the draft often determines the pace. Is there anything— spelling, grammar, mechanics—that gets between the reader and the message?
- *What does a test reader say?*
  Be careful who you have read your draft. As I've said, my rule is to use someone who makes me want to write when I hear his or her response. That response may be a critical one, but a good reader motivates me to rush to fix the draft. The writer should also be aware that most readers have expectations and are uncomfortable when the draft does not say what they expect in the way they expect it. It helps to tell the test reader what kind of reading you want: Would you believe this? Would you keep reading? Are there any spelling or

punctuation errors you can see? What does the draft say to you? Where do I say too much or too little? What evidence do you need?

- *What do you expect the reader to do after finishing the draft?*
  We write to make the reader think, feel, and act. We should try to predict the response of the reader and revise to achieve the response we want.
- *If you were the reader, would you do it?*
  If you wouldn't feel, think, or act because of reading your draft, the reader won't, either.

Solutions to Common Editing Problems

As we edit our drafts, we begin to recognize some problems that occur over and over again. You may want to make a written as well as a mental list of some of those problems and their solutions. Here is mine.

How Do I Recognize Surprise?

Effective writing is built on recognizing and developing the strength of an early draft. The strength is usually what surprises the writer, but how does the writer recognize surprise? The surprise is often an instructive failure, but how does the writer see what is an instructive failure and what is true failure?

- I am saying what I have not said before.
- I am saying what I have said before in a new way.
- My voice contradicts my meaning and I listen to the voice.
- I contradict intent.
- The syntax breaks down: I am trying to say what I do not yet know how to say.
- The draft tries to use an unexpected genre.
- The flow of language takes a sudden turn.
- The writing comes easily.

- The voice reinforces the meaning.
- I discover I know what I did not know I knew.
- I am making unexpected and appropriate connections between specific information I did not think had a relationship.
- The specifics resonate.
- I am following the draft as it rushes toward its own meaning.
- The draft asks questions I—and the reader—must have answered.
- I receive novelist and critic Edmund Wilson's "shock of recognition": This is true.
- I try to change the structure or the order within the structure and can't.
- A test reader recognizes a strength I didn't.
- The draft poses a problem that would be interesting to solve.

How to Read to Edit

It is wise to do several quick readings of a draft, focusing on one form of exploration at a time, rather than trying to do them simultaneously.

Reading the Whole

The writer needs to step back from the word-by-word, phrase-by-phrase, sentence-by-sentence concentration essential to produce a draft and take an aerial view of the entire draft, not worrying—during this reading—about spelling, mechanics, typography, neatness. I have trained myself to become the detached reader—changing from the possessive, defensive writer of the draft to a stranger who is reading what actually appears on the page—in a matter of minutes, say after a mug of coffee. But if I cannot achieve the distance I need, that is, the reader's view of the draft, I imagine I am someone I know and respect who is not interested in the subject. That gives me the distance I need.

Reading the Parts

After reading the whole, I move a bit closer to see the parts of the whole, the sections that develop each part of the overall meaning. I read to find their relationship: Are they in the order the reader needs to come to the final meaning? Are they paced so the reader will continue to read—fast enough to keep the reader awake and interested, slow enough so that it is not a blur but gives the reader time to absorb the meaning of the draft? Do the proportions of the draft support the meaning—long enough but not too long? What is the relationship between the sections; do they interact in an effective way?

Reading the Line

Once the writer has the vision of the whole draft and sees how the sections fit the vision of the whole, the writer can read the draft closely, line by line. Each word, each phrase, each sentence, each paragraph is scanned to see how it fulfills the vision. The reading writer needs to keep moving in close but never to allow the eye to focus entirely on details. Reading line by line means seeing how the details support and develop the meaning that the entire draft is designed to communicate to a reader. Many people read too closely too early and get lost in the details of writing—word choice, spelling, grammar, punctuation—before they have solved the larger problems of meaning, development, organization, proportion.

Reading Out Loud

And all through this, I hear the voice of the draft. *Voice,* the writer's word for style, is thought of as a final, superficial concern, the living room pickup before a guest's arrival. But voice is not superficial; indeed, it may be the most important element in writing. It is the way, more times than not, that I discover meaning in reading my notes and early drafts. I find that meaning is often revealed through the music of the draft the same way that the meaning of a movie scene is revealed by the musical score. The voice of the draft is tuned to the meaning of what is being written.

How to Edit a Boring Draft so It Isn't

All of us face writing tasks that are boring. We have done it before, and before that: a report for the corporate record that may never be read, yet another term paper, a revision required when it is not necessary, a rejected proposal that is being submitted to yet another agency, a personal report that must follow a specific form, an essay exam at the end of an uninteresting course, and, worst of all, another version of a well-written piece of writing that you have done several times before. Once it was frightening and demanding, now it is far too familiar.

I know. Tomorrow I will write my 700th-and-something newspaper column, and this is the fifth edition of a textbook that I thought was fine each time I finished an edition. In a few months I will start the eighth edition of another textbook.

Edit in Many Short Bursts of Time

First I have to break down any task longer than a few pages into brief morning tasks. I produce more when I write less at a sitting but return frequently. I work in spurts—15, 20, 30, 45, 60, 90 minutes. More than that and my attention wavers; I become sloppy.

I must decide on specific tasks that can be fitted into an appropriate writing period. And the earlier in the day, the more I can accomplish in a shorter period of time. I also need to reward myself after I finish a task: one section and a cup of coffee, three pages and a walk around the yard, ten pages and I can read a few pages of a novel, a chapter and I can go to a bookstore. The breaks revive me and I can go back to the next task.

Once I am within the task, here are some of the ways I make boring writing interesting to me—and, I hope, the reader.

See the Extraordinary in the Ordinary

I take advantage of anything that will allow me to see the familiar subject in a new way. My closest friend was complaining about starting a book that is published annually. He had done it last year and the year before that. At first it was a challenge, now it is routine. He asked me, "Do you find writing a new edition of one of your books boring?"

I answered, "Yes, I suppose, but . . . well, I break the book down into specific daily tasks—what is new, what needs to be cut, what needs sharpening and brightening."

I knew I hadn't answered his question adequately, and I saw that as an opportunity to figure out what to do. If I figured it out in writing, I would have the draft of a section for this edition. It wouldn't be boring to write because I would be learning something I could apply to other writing tasks, and it wouldn't be boring for my readers, since they all face writing tasks that have become too familiar.

Look for Technical Challenges

The novelist Tom Williams once told me that the writer should have "a technical problem to solve in each draft to keep him interested." This problem should be a secret from the reader, it should never show, but it makes each new story or book—and each revision—fresh for the writer and, therefore, for the reader.

I have followed his wise counsel. The technical problem may be a small one but it challenges my craft as I work on a page, a section, a chapter. Here are some of the technical problems I have set for myself:

- Switching from first person to third or back.
- Retuning the voice of the draft or the narrator.
- Writing in the present tense or the past.

- Using shorter sentences or paragraphs. Using longer, more fully developed sentences and paragraphs. Writing in the active voice. Cutting to a specific length. Expanding to a specific length. Appealing to a different audience or an additional audience.
- Changing the documentation from anecdotal to statistical or reversing it, depending on academic citations or personal experience.
- Adding or cutting quotations.
- Using dialogue.
- Switching the genre from prose to poetry to essay to dramatic scene to memo to argument.
- Changing the point of view from which the subject is viewed.

This is all play but play with a purpose. I make the changes to see if they will reveal the subject with greater insight or clarity, if they will hold readers' interest and persuade them.

The subject, the form, the audience may be familiar, but when I consciously establish a technical problem, I become interested in solving the problem. It only takes me a line or two, perhaps a paragraph, when I am within the draft, not only discovering how to say it anew but also usually discovering that I have new things to say.

The changes I am making may seem small at first, but often the result surprises me. James Baldwin once said,

> *I remember standing on a street corner with the black painter Beauford Delaney down in the Village, waiting for the light to change, and he pointed down and said, "Look." I looked and all I saw was water. And he said, "Look again," which I did, and I saw oil on the water and the city reflected in the puddle. It was a great revelation to me. I can't explain it. He taught me how to see, and how to trust what I saw. Painters have often taught writers how to see. And once you've had that experience, you see differently. . . . It is true that the more one learns the less one knows. I'm still learning how to write. I don't know what technique is. All I know is that you have to make the reader see it.*

A new seeing does not mean a new view but a new way of looking at the familiar. I rarely see what can be done to make a familiar text new by looking at it from a distance. I have to put my pen or cursor to work, striking out, inserting, moving words, phrases, sentences, paragraphs around, and I find I am lost in the work. As the sculptor Alexander Calder said, "If you keep working, inspiration comes."

In the most apparently boring writing tasks, I discover a joy in craft. The making provides its own pleasure and its own importance. As Don DeLillo says, "Working at sentences and rhythms is probably the most satisfying thing I do as a writer. I think after a while a writer can begin to know himself through his language. He sees someone or something reflected back at him from these constructions." There are few tasks that appear to be as boring as fixing language that you feel doesn't need fixing; there are few tasks as exciting as following language that unexpectedly comes alive under your hand, making the familiar strange word by word, line by line.

Leave Well Enough Alone

And, of course, some things do not need to be changed: What needs to be said is said with clarity and grace. It is just as much an act of craft *not* to change as it is to change. The purpose of writing is not to show the writer at work but to discover meaning and communicate it directly to a reader who should not be aware of the writer but the writing.

The Craft of Editing

When I write and rewrite there is an unconscious element in what I do. I do not want to become so aware of how my feet are placed as I go downstairs that I will cross them and tumble down three flights, and it is that way when I write and rewrite. I often work instinctively. But as I pass through the revision process, the writing becomes self-conscious. I need to be aware of how I do what I do, of my reader, of tradition, of my purpose.

The Tools of Revision

Beginning writers have too much respect for their written drafts. They have been taught to respect—or fear, or stand in awe of, or admire without question—the printed text. The writing, especially if it is typed, appears finished.

The experienced writer likes nothing so much as despoiling a neatly printed text. The writer cuts and adds and moves around and puts back what was just cut and discards and redrafts.

Now I write on a computer where my best friend is the button marked DELETE. I draft and revise while always having a neat, readable text on my screen. But for decades before computers I revised, and my office still has the tools I used—and occasionally still use— to make my final draft look easy, natural, even spontaneous.

My tools are a wastebasket, large; scissors; glue, stapler, cellophane tape; a black, thick-line felt marker; an extra-fine black pen. I can discard, cut and paste, cross out and insert.

When I first learned how professional editors mark copy, I realized that each mark is a tool. Each reminds me of a way I may be able to make the draft clearer and more graceful. Here some of these tools:

Cross out	The ~~lazy~~ dog runs slowly.
Take out	The lazy dog runs slowly.
Put back in	The ~~lazy~~ dog runs slowly.
Transpose	The lazy dog slowly runs.
Insert	the lazy dog ^ ~~runs slowly.~~ saunters
Move	The lazy dog runs slowly.
Period	The lazy dog runs slowly
Capital	the lazy dog runs slowly.

Mark the draft so you can see the changes, and read the draft as it will appear after the changes are made to see if more changes are necessary. They usually are because the particular changes the meaning, and the meaning influences the particular.

A Student Case History

Roger LePage Jr.

It is the ultimate compliment when I work through a young writer's paper line by line. Many students want this attention, but there are reasons not to do it most of the time.

One, you can't do an effective job of line-by-line editing of your own draft—or anyone else's—unless the writer has something to say that is worth saying. As novelist and writing teacher Wallace Stegner said, "You can't sharpen a knife on a wheel of cheese." Two, I do not know the writer's subject, and my editing must be based on understanding what the student has written, and what the student has known but left out. Most writing is left out in the sense that good writing grows from abundant soil, and I am fearful I will take the piece of writing away from the student as I edit it, inevitably, to my vision of the student's world. For example, Roger LePage's fine piece here describes the Rollinsford, New Hampshire, dump. I live nearby but have never been to that dump. I do not have the specific details in my notebook or my memory from which effective writing could be constructed. I do not have Roger's vision of this world, and I do not have his way of using our language. There is a conflict here: I want Roger to see one professional writer at work on his prose, but I fear I will appropriate his prose and make it mine.

And when I do edit line by line, I am always fearful the student will take me too seriously. I tend to do this with only the best, most resistant students. The student who slavishly follows my editing will learn nothing; the student who questions what I have done and how I have done it may learn a great deal.

The Student's Original Draft

The Dump

Roger LePage Jr.

Summer days in Rollinsford, New Hampshire were very boring until we discovered the dump. As ten-year-olds we didn't have summer jobs—except, of course, finding amusement and adventure. We didn't even do that well until the time one of us, maybe me, maybe one of the others, steered his bike off of Main Street and led the pack onto the dirt dump road. The intriguing pillar of smoke that was perpetually rising above the trees from the dump may have drawn us in. Or it could have been the "NO TRESPASSING" sign and the locked gate—things like that always invited us into abandoned houses. Whatever the reason, we discovered the dump and were not bored for the rest of the summer.

That first day we didn't even make it into the actual dump. The dirt road leading in was about half a mile long, and about halfway down that we discovered a slimy little pond with lots of frogs and snakes around its fringe. We spent most of the day hunting them and trying to catch them. This didn't hold its appeal too long for me though. One of my friends, Jason, was very cruel and whenever he caught a frog he would first put it on the road and torment it with a stick, and then he would pick it up and squeeze it to death in his hand and throw the guts at whoever was within range. I was made target twice and decided it was time to go home.

But soon we made it past all the distractions along the road, which were many, including the rusting corpses of several kitchen appliances and one time there was the ass end of a deer, the stench of which was still strong for a quarter mile radius. But nothing could be compared to the adventures found in the dump itself. We began in the huge pile of discarded tires, immediately abandoning our bikes right in front of it and trying to race to the top. "King of Tire Mountain" lasted for weeks, producing many bruises and scuffles and many hurt feelings. Then we built forts within the inner depths of Tire Mountain—a much more peaceful game. When it was time to try to furnish our forts we began exploring the junk in the rest of the dump.

That was when we discovered the greatest thing possible in a ten-year-old boy's mind: dirty magazines. I'm not sure who discovered them first, but there was soon a huge uproar and race to see who could collect and hoard the most. We would bring them back to our forts and pile them up, going through each one with great enthusiasm. We would organize them according to their appeal to us: the ones with girls showing everything spread out and accessible were our favorites, the ones with boys and girls were second, the plain boob shots were last. We had another pile of "girls with girls" which we didn't know how to take but spent the most time looking at. We would move around in funny ways, always moving around to maximize that great new ache in our pants while looking at the magazines, and we all seemed to have the shakes.

***

I would also go to the dump on Saturday mornings with my dad. It was part of our Saturday morning errands: the dump, the barbers, the grocery store, then church. Most of the time he didn't even have anything to throw away. It was a Saturday morning meeting place for the true Rollinsford men—those who still called the town Salmon Falls, and a group to which my dad belongs because he was born and raised there. It was also a place of refuge from their wives: Friday night was poker night (I could always hear the door slam from my bedroom when my dad stumbled in just before daybreak,) and on Saturday morning the men were red-eyed and "in the dog house" as they put it.

But my dad would go to the dump mainly to pay his respects to the toothless old Greek who I've only heard referred to as The Greek, and who was a great drinking partner of my dad's father. The Greek worked there. He made sure you didn't put metals or combustibles in with the burnables and he took his job very seriously. He tended the fire and if you tried to interfere, his toothless smile would disappear and he would straightway banish you. Banishment from the dump is one of the lowest dishonors in our town.

You wouldn't think anyone would be overly enthusiastic about being friends with the man who tends the dump, but in towns like mine occupation is not nearly as socially relevant as age or drinking ability. There were other reasons why The Greek was respected: he did once have an occupation, but he retired and instead of sitting around all day, or bagging groceries in some supermarket, he opted to tend the dump. That choice was respectable and The Greek knew this and took his job very seriously. Also he was a great old drinker and fighter, actually legendary. His missing teeth were the proof. Everybody knew that "he got them knocked out" in a fight years back. The important thing was that "he got them knocked out," not "somebody knocked his teeth out" because the latter would imply The Greek was not in control at the time. And even though it was rumored that his wife, also something of a drinker and fighter herself, has his tooth marks on her knuckles, The Greek was still respected; he earned the right to be toothless. He brandished this honor too, by smiling all the time—but I never thought The Greek was such a happy man.

After my friends and I started spending so much time in the dump I began to look at the Saturday morning visits with my dad in a new way. I fancied myself a spy, watching our forts as inconspicuously as possible and always listening for clues to find out if anyone was on to us. I thought that sometimes The Greek would catch me looking at the tire pile and possibly know our secret, but I wasn't sure. I felt that it was just strange that he looked at me at all, because before my friends and I started playing at the dump The Greek never seemed to notice me. I thought then, that maybe I just never noticed him noticing me before because it wouldn't have mattered if he did. Whatever the case, I was wary.

***

Then one day we were playing at the dump, alternating between culling our dirty magazines and our next best discovery: combustibles. It was Jason, the sadistic frog squisher who discovered this one, I'm sure; he was fond of destruction in any form. On one of his devilish whims, he threw a paint can into the dump fire and silently waited for something to happen. The rest of us were busy going through junk and exploring and didn't even notice. The explosion sent us running for cover, yelling all of the profanities we knew (most of which we got out of our new magazine collection,) and nearly pissing our pants. When we realized what had taken place, the excitement of the whole thing brought us together giggling, wrestling and rolling around in the dirt. This was probably why we didn't hear the pick-up coming down the dump road.

When we did finally notice it, it had pulled up right beside us. We all jumped to our feet and stood there, not sure what to do. I recognized the green, rusty, beat-up old thing—it was The Greek's truck. He got out and stared at us with full-blown adult contempt, "What are you kids doing? You the ones been down here vandalizing?"

Even at ten I wondered how the hell anybody could vandalize a dump, but as I said, The Greek took his job very seriously.

"Aren't you Roger's boy? I knew I'd catch you down here," he stared at me with his exaggerated toothless frown and shook his head. His nose looked like a spoiled piece of fruit. "There's nothing but piss and vinegar running through your veins. I know. Knew your grandfather, same thing. Your dad too," he was still staring and shaking his head, the loose flaps of his jaw skin shook around violently. "I knew I'd catch you down here. How would you like me to tell your old man what you've been doing?"

No ten year old wants his parents to know what he does on summer afternoons; it's a child's first glimpse of independence and the privacy is treasured, locked away in the child's heart. When one comes along and tries to adulterate that treasure, as adults always do, the loss of the treasure is a far greater tragedy than any thought of impending punishment. I asked him meekly, "Please don't tell." The Greek looked at me and then at my companions. He turned and walked along the dirt towards Tire Mountain. I thought I was going to be sick. The Greek knew! He was on to us. First we would be banished from the dump, then from our homes and then we would be kicked out of the town altogether. Maybe even sent to prison or reform school.

"How would your mothers feel if they knew you were looking at those kinds of things?"

Oh God! I thought. It's one thing to lose your cherished summer freedom, or even to be locked away, but to have your mother think you're a pervert, to have her think you are one of those weirdos like fat old Slow Jimmy who smiles at you funny and always asks you to go for a walk. To have your mother know you look at dirty magazines! It was absolutely the worst thing imaginable.

The Greek paused and looked around. He looked at me hard. I'm sure he could see I was about to commit the unspeakable in front of my friends—that I was about to cry. He had done his job, and done it well. The Greek took his job very seriously. "Well, if I catch any of you kids here again, your parents will all get a call from me. And if I catch you here again LePage, I'll give you a beating myself."

So we pedaled the hell out of there, still shaken and guilty. We resolved never to return to the dump, and we didn't . . . at least for the rest of the week. But after all, as kids we also took our jobs very seriously.

A Professional's Editing

The Dump

Roger LePage Jr.

(very makes it less somehow)

(Too many flat statements—draw us in as you have below.)

~~Summer days in Rollinsford, New Hampshire were very boring until we discovered the dump. As ten-year olds we didn't have summer jobs—except, of course, finding amusement and adventure. We didn't even do that well until the time one of us, maybe me, maybe one of the others, steered his bike off of Main Street and led the pack onto the dirt dump road.~~

The intriguing pillar of smoke that was perpetually rising above the trees from the dump may have drawn us in. Or it could have been the "NO TRESPASSING" sign and the locked gate—things like that always invited us into abandoned houses. ~~Whatever the reason,~~ we ~~discovered~~ the dump ~~and were not bored for the rest of the summer.~~

That first day we didn't even make it into the actual dump. The dirt road leading in was about half a mile long, and about halfway down that we discovered a slimy little pond with ~~lots of~~ frogs and snakes around its fringe. We spent most of the day hunting ~~them and~~ trying to catch them. ~~This didn't hold its appeal too long for me though.~~ ~~One of my friends~~, Jason, ~~was very cruel and whenever he~~ caught a frog he would first put it on the road and torment it with a stick, ~~and~~ then he would pick it up and squeeze it to death in ~~his~~ hand and throw the guts at whoever was within range. I was ~~made~~ target twice and ~~decided it was time to go~~ home.

But ~~soon~~ we made it past ~~all the distractions along the road, which were many, including~~ the rusting corpses of several kitchen appliances and ~~one time there was~~ the ass end of a deer, ~~the stench of which was still strong~~ for a quarter mile ~~radius.~~ ~~But nothing could be compared to the adventures found in the dump itself. We began in the~~ huge pile of discarded tires, ~~immediately~~ abandoning our bikes ~~right in front of it~~ and ~~trying~~ to race to the top. "King of Tire Mountain" lasted for weeks, ~~producing many bruises and scuffles and many hurt feelings.~~ Then we built forts within the inner depths of Tire Mountain~~, a much more peaceful game.~~ When it was time to try to furnish our forts we ~~began~~ exploring the junk in the rest of the dump.

That was when we discovered ~~the greatest thing possible in a ten-year-old boy's mind:~~ dirty magazines. ~~I'm not sure who discovered them first, but there was soon a huge uproar and race to see who could collect and hoard the most.~~ We ~~would bring~~ them back to our forts and ~~pile them up, going through each one with great enthusiasm. We would~~ organize them ~~according to their appeal to us:~~ the ones with girls showing everything spread out ~~and accessible were our favorites~~, the ones with boys and girls ~~were~~ second, ~~the~~ plain boob shots were last. We had another pile of "girls with girls" which we didn't know how to take but spent the most time looking at. We ~~would~~ move around ~~in funny ways, always moving around~~ to maximize that ~~great~~ new ache in our pants while looking at the magazines, and we all seemed to have the shakes.

(watch out for would) ***

I ~~would~~ also ~~go~~ to the dump on Saturday mornings with my dad. ~~It was part of our Saturday morning errands~~: the dump, the barbers, the grocery store, then church. Most of the time he didn't even have anything to throw away. It was a Saturday morning meeting place for the ~~true~~ Rollinsford men ~~—those~~ who still called the town Salmon Falls, and ~~a group to which my dad belongs because he was~~ born and raised there. It was also a place of refuge from their wives: Friday night was poker night (I could always hear the door slam from my bedroom when my dad stumbled in just before daybreak,) and on Saturday morning the men were red-eyed and in the dog house as they put it.

~~But~~ my dad ~~would go~~ to the dump mainly to pay his respects to the toothless old Greek, ~~who I've only heard referred to as The Greek, and who was~~ a ~~great~~ drinking partner of my dad's father. The Greek ~~worked there. He~~ made sure you didn't put metals or combustibles in with the burnables and he took his job very seriously. He tended the fire and if you tried to interfere, his toothless smile would disappear and he would ~~straightway~~ banish you. Banishment from the dump is ~~one of~~ the ~~lowest~~ dishonors in our town.

~~You wouldn't think anyone would be overly enthusiastic about being friends with the man who tends the dump, but in towns like mine occupation is not nearly as socially relevant as age or drinking ability. There were other reasons why~~ The Greek was respected: ~~he did once have an occupation, but~~ he retired ~~and instead of~~ sitting around all day, or bagging groceries ~~in some~~ supermarket, ~~he opted to tend~~

the dump. ~~That choice was respectable and The Greek knew this and took his job very seriously. Also~~ he was a great old drinker and fighter, actually legendary. His missing teeth were ~~the proof. Everybody knew that "he got them~~ knocked out" in a fight years back. The important thing was that "he got them knocked out," not "somebody knocked his teeth out" because the latter would imply The Greek was not in control at the time. ~~And even though~~ it was rumored that his wife, also something of a drinker and fighter herself, has his tooth marks on her knuckles, ~~The Greek was still respected; he~~ earned the right to be toothless. He brandished this honor too, by smiling all the time—but I never thought The Greek was ~~such~~ a happy man.

After my friends and I started spending so much time in the dump I began to look at the Saturday morning visits with my dad in a new way. I fancied myself a spy, watching our forts as inconspicuously as possible and always listening for clues to find out if anyone was on to us. I thought that sometimes The Greek would catch me looking at the tire pile and possibly know our secret, but I wasn't sure. I felt that it was just strange that he looked at me at all, because before my friends and I started playing at the dump The Greek never seemed to notice me. I thought then, that maybe I just never noticed him noticing me before because it wouldn't have mattered if he did. Whatever the case, I was wary.

***

~~Then~~ one day we were playing at the dump, alternating between culling our dirty magazines and our next best discovery: combustibles. It was Jason, of course, who ~~the sadistic frog squisher who discovered this one, I'm sure; he was fond of destruction in any form. On one of his devilish whims, he~~ threw a paint can into the dump fire and ~~silently~~ waited for something to happen. The rest of us were busy going through junk and exploring and didn't even notice. The explosion sent us running for cover, yelling all of the profanities we knew, (most of which we got out of our new magazine collection) ~~and nearly pissing our pants.~~ When we realized what Jason had done ~~had taken place,~~ the excitement ~~of the~~

(next paragraph great—puts all this in a deeper context—a stage of growing and growing away from a parent)

~~whole thing~~ brought us together giggling, wrestling and rolling around in the dirt. ~~This was probably why~~ we didn't hear the pick-up coming down the dump road.

~~When we did finally notice it,~~ it ~~had~~ pulled up right beside us, and ~~We all~~ jumped to our feet, ~~and stood there,~~ not sure what to do. I recognized the green, rusty, beat-up old thing— (Plymouth, Ford, what?) it was The Greek's truck. He got out and stared at us with ~~full blown adult~~ contempt, ~~"What are you kids doing?~~ "You the ones been down here vandalizing?"

Even at ten I wondered how the hell anybody could vandalize a dump, but ~~as I said~~, The Greek took his job ~~very~~ seriously.

"Aren't you Roger's boy? I knew I'd catch you down here," he stared at me with his exaggerated toothless frown and shook his head. His nose looked like a spoiled piece of fruit. "There's nothing but piss and vinegar running through your veins. I know. Knew your grandfather, same thing. Your dad too." he was still staring and shaking his head, the loose flaps of his jaw skin shook around violently. "I knew I'd catch you down here. How would you like me to tell your old man what you've been doing?"

No ten year old wants his parents to know what he does on summer afternoons; ~~it's a child's first glimpse of independence and the privacy is treasured, locked away in the child's heart. When one comes along and tries to adulterate that treasure, as adults always do, the loss of the treasure is a far greater tragedy than any thought of impending punishment.~~ I asked him ~~meekly~~, "Please don't tell." The Greek looked at me and then at my companions. He turned and walked along the dirt towards Tire Mountain. ~~I thought I was going to be sick.~~ The Greek knew! He was on to us. First we would be banished from the dump, then from our homes and then we would be kicked out of the town altogether. Maybe even sent to prison or reform school.

"How would your mothers feel if they knew you were looking at those kinds of things?"

Oh God! I thought. ~~It's one thing to lose your cherished summer freedom, or even to be locked away, but to have your mother think you're a pervert~~, to have Mother ~~her~~ think you are

> ~~one of those weirdos~~ like fat old Slow Jimmy who smiles at you funny and always asks you to go for a walk. To have your mother know you look at dirty magazines! ~~It was absolutely the worst thing imaginable.~~
>
> The Greek paused and looked around. He looked at me hard. I'm sure he could see I was about to ~~commit the unspeakable in front of my friends—that I was about to~~ cry. ~~He had done his job, and done it well. The Greek took his job very seriously. "Well,~~ "If I catch any of you kids here again, your parents will all get a call from me. And if I catch you here again LePage, I'll give you a beating myself."
>
> ~~So we pedaled the hell out of there, still shaken and guilty.~~ We ~~resolved never to~~ didn't return to the dump, ~~and we didn't . . . at least~~ for ~~the rest of the~~ a week. ~~But after all, as kids we also took our jobs very seriously.~~

I find this a good rite-of-passage piece about an interesting and mysterious place that has depth and texture: children setting out in the world, beginning to have secret life apart from parents; a son's relationship to his father; the boy's tense relationship with Jason, the cruel leader of the boys; the narrative of their explorations of the world; The Greek, his history and status, and what it means. And the writing is good, full of potential as well as wordiness and the unevenness of language expected from a beginning writer.

I thought he was ready to learn from what one writer might do to his draft. Primarily, I was interested in cutting, in clearing away the underbrush and revealing the good writing hidden by it. I was aware of the danger that I would take over the piece and make his vision and his voice mine. I hoped he would be strong and wise enough to resist me.

In going over this for the book, I have not changed my editing, which was done quickly for purpose of instruction and in a spirit of play: "I wonder what would happen if I . . . ?" I have also realized how limited my editing was because I did not want to overwhelm the writer. I would edit myself more severely, and if I was editing the piece for publication I also would have caught all sorts of things I let go.

Go back and edit Roger LePage's piece yourself alone or with a partner. Try to edit so that you reveal his vision of the world and free his voice from the draft. Work slowly with pen in hand. When you are finished compare your editing with mine.

The Student's Reaction to Professional Editing

The good writing student will listen to what the readers of his drafts have to say—fellow writers, instructors, editors—but will resist when necessary. LePage reacted strongly to my line-by-line editing:

> ***I'll start off with the problem I had with the revised story, just to get it out of the way. The first thing I did when I received your edited version of my draft was to rewrite the story using all of your suggestions. Then I read it aloud over and over, and something just didn't sound right. I have no specific examples of the revisions that caused this, but some element seemed to be missing. I was down to the bare essentials of the story, the skeleton. The problem with this, as I see it, is all skeletons took alike. It's the flesh that gives the narration character.***
>
> ***I'll use Raymond Carver as an example. He is sometimes referred to as a "minimalist" (as I'm sure you know) because at first glance his stories appear to be whittled down to skeleton form. However, that is not completely the case. He adds the flesh to the narration where it is necessary and he does it in such a way that the narrator, whether first person or not, booms with personality. For example, in the excellent story "Cathedral," Carver describes a meal in this way: "We dug in. We ate everything there was to eat on the table. We ate like there was no tomorrow. We didn't talk. We ate. We scarfed. We grazed that table. We were into serious eating!" I don't know any editors, but I would guess that most would pull their hair out over a passage like this.***

There is unnecessary repetition and clichés. But what's great about it is we are allowed to understand the narrator: he is a regular guy with a good sense of humor and a natural joy for life. We understand this only because Carver knows how and when to break the rules, and he knows how his narrator is supposed to sound.

So I had to make the story sound right to me. When I talk about sound, I think I'm talking about voice, but I'm not sure. My idea of sound is this: when you're sitting at your writing desk and reading your work aloud and the person in the next room doesn't ask what you're reading from, but who you're talking to, then it's good. I think this is the most important element in a story, that it sounds right. The second would be that you have a good story to tell.

What the revisions did was help to make my story move. I'm learning slowly, mostly as I gain confidence and experience, that I don't need to reinforce every point I have shown through anecdote or image by stating it explicitly. Phrases such as "a much more peaceful game," not only slow the story down but insult the reader. Other phrases like, "the greatest thing possible in a ten-year-old boy's mind," cause a similar problem. For one thing, I might be alienating some readers who may not have been, at ten years old, so enthusiastic to see dirty magazines as I was. Further, even if all ten-year-olds do share this interest, there is no need for me to state it. I'm getting between the reader and the story. I am inserting an annoying little voice that whispers over the reader's ear and tells him how to feel and what to think, just in case my narrator is not doing his job.

The way I originally opened the story was also a sort of distraction in that it bored the reader, rather than engaging his interest. Instead of flatly stating that we were bored and the dump was exciting, it is much better to open with the same image that attracted us into the dump: the pillar of smoke. The reader will then pick

up on our journey right at the exact point where we began and join us in discovering the source of the smoke. The reader needs to "see" what we saw, the actual scene, not some filtered, transmuted secondhand account of it. The idea of voice is still pertinent here, though it's much more subtle, almost subliminal. It's the idea that the reader becomes subconsciously aware of the person, the personality, telling the story and will pass judgment on that personality just as on any other stranger. Whether the reader likes or dislikes this personality is irrelevant, what matters is that the reader trusts him. The only way I know to make the reader trust my narration is to tell the truth, pimples and all. If a Freudian were to get a hold of this piece and make conclusions about me or my upbringing, so be it. I had to tell it like it is.

I also had problems describing The Greek. Aside from the flat statement similar to those that opened the story, and aside from the annoying little voice that tried to dictate how the reader should feel about The Greek, I created a kind of refrain with, "The Greek took his job very seriously." The technique could work, I believe, but only if the story was centrally about this character. My story did not center on The Greek but around a group of ten-year-old boys and for this reason a refrain about The Greek is misleading.

Lastly, my concluding paragraph was originally too drawn out, and like the opening paragraph, too flat. The fact is, we were afraid, embarrassed and eager to flee, but all that should be obvious. Again, I don't need to state it. The only problem with the revised ending was that it didn't sound right. It was too abrupt. I had to find a medium point that kept the rhythm of the piece, sounded right, yet didn't give the reader the urge to skip over it.

My worry now is that in correcting old mistakes I have created new ones. I don't know if I'll ever in my life be able to say, "Okay, this is done."

That is an ideal example of a student response. He pays attention and learns but makes up his mind. It is, after all, his essay.

The Student's Revision

The Dump

Roger LePage Jr.

The pillar of smoke that perpetually rose above the trees into a puffy gray cloud over the Rollinsford, New Hampshire, dump may have drawn us in. Or it could have been the "NO TRESPASSING" sign and the locked gate—things like that always invited us into abandoned houses. As ten-year-olds out of school for the summer we only wanted to be where we shouldn't or where the possibility of adventure seemed fullest. The town dump was to become our spot.

The first day we didn't even make it into the actual dump. The dirt road leading in was about half a mile long, and about halfway down that we discovered a slimy little pond with lots of frogs and snakes around its fringe. We spent most of the day hunting, trying to catch them. But that eventually stopped being fun, at least for me, because when Jason caught a frog he would first put it on the road and torment it with a stick, then he would pick up the frog and squeeze it to death in one hand and throw the guts at whoever was in range. I was the target twice and took off for home.

But another day we made it past all the rusting corpses of stoves, refrigerators and washer machines and even past the ass end of a deer with a stench that seemed to linger around us for at least a quarter mile. When we got into the dump, we first came upon the huge pile of discarded tires and immediately ditched our bikes right in front of it and raced to the top. "King of Tire Mountain" lasted for weeks, and each day when we became too bruised and tired for that game, we built forts within the inner depths of the mountain. When it was time to try to furnish our forts we headed for the junk in the rest of the dump.

That was when we discovered dirty magazines. There was a huge race to see who could collect and hoard the most. We hurried them back to our forts and then organized them: the ones with girls showing everything spread out was the first pile, the ones with boys and girls was second, plain boob shots were last.

We had another pile of "girls with girls" which we didn't know how to take but spent the most time looking at. We lay down on our stomachs to look at them, maximizing that new ache in our pants, and we all seemed to have the shakes.

***

I also went to the dump on Saturday mornings with my dad: the dump, the barbers, the grocery store, then church. Most of the time he didn't even have anything to throw away. It was a Saturday morning meeting place for the Rollinsford men—those who still called the town Salmon Falls and were born and raised there. It was also a place of refuge from their wives: Friday night was poker night (I could always hear the door slam from my bedroom when my dad stumbled in just before daybreak), and on Saturday morning the men were red-eyed and "in the dog house" as they put it.

My dad went to the dump mainly to pay his respects to the toothless old Greek, a drinking partner of my dad's father. The Greek made sure that you didn't put metals or combustibles in with the burnables and he took his job seriously. He tended the fire and if you tried to interfere, his toothless smile would disappear and he would banish you. Banishment from the dump is the greatest dishonor in our town.

The Greek was respected because when he retired from the railroad he didn't sit around all day or bag groceries at the supermarket: he took over the dump. Also he was a legendary old drinker and fighter. His missing teeth were "knocked out" in a fight years back. The important thing was that "he got them knocked out," not "somebody knocked his teeth out," because the latter would imply that The Greek was not in control at the time. It was rumored that his wife, also something of a drinker and fighter herself, had his tooth marks on her knuckles. But he earned the right to be toothless. And he brandished this honor too, by smiling all the time—though I never thought for a minute The Greek was a happy man.

After my friends and I started spending so much time in the dump I began to look at the Saturday morning visits with my dad in a new way. I was no longer a mere tagalong, I had a need to be there of my own—a mission. I was not a child by my father's side, but a grown man, a spy watching our forts as inconspicuously as possible and always listening for clues to find out if anyone was on to us. I thought that sometimes The Greek would catch me looking at the tire pile and possibly know our secret, but I wasn't sure. I felt that it was just strange that he looked at me at all, because before my friends and I started playing at the dump The Greek never seemed to notice me. This, I decided, was because of my new identity: a man (even if he is a spy) automatically earns another's notice. But just in case, I remained wary.

***

One day when we were playing at the dump, alternating between culling our dirty magazines and exploring the junk piles, we came upon our next best discovery: combustibles. It was Jason, of course, who threw a paint can into the dump fire and waited for something to happen. The rest of us were too engrossed in the junk to notice. The explosion sent us running for cover, yelling all of the profanities we knew—most of which we got out of our new magazine collection. When we realized what Jason had done, the excitement heaved us together giggling, wrestling and rolling around in the dirt. We didn't hear the pickup coming down the dump road.

It pulled up right beside me and we jumped to our feet, not sure what to do. I recognized the green, rusty, beat up old "Ford"—it was The Greek's truck. He got out and stared at us with contempt. "You the ones been down here vandalizing?"

Even at ten I wondered how the hell anybody could vandalize a dump. The Greek did take his job seriously.

"Aren't you Roger's boy? I knew I'd catch you down here," he stared at me with his exaggerated toothless frown and shook his head. His nose looked like a spoiled piece of fruit. "There's nothing but piss and vinegar running through your veins. I know. Knew your grandfather, same thing. Your dad too." He was still staring and shaking his head, the loose flaps of his jaw skin shook around violently. "I knew I'd catch you down here. How would you like me to tell your old man what you've been doing?"

No ten-year-old wants his parents to know what he does on summer afternoons. I asked him, "Please don't tell."

The Greek looked at me and my companions. He turned and walked along the dirt towards Tire Mountain. The Greek knew! He was on to us. First we would be banished from the dump, then from our homes and then we would be kicked out of the town altogether. Maybe even sent to prison or reform school.

"How would your mothers feel if they knew you were looking at those things?"

Oh God! I thought. To have your mother think you're like fat old Slow Jimmy who smiles at you funny and always asks you to go for a walk. To have her know you look at dirty magazines!

The Greek paused and looked around. He looked at me hard. I'm sure he could see I was about to cry. "If I catch any of you kids here again, your parents will all get a call from me. And if I catch you here again, LePage, I'll give you a beating myself."

We scrambled for our bikes never to return again, and didn't—for the rest of the week anyway.

Chapter 11

THE CRAFT OF LETTING GO

For decades, I blew deadlines, refused to let go of manuscripts, and wasted countless hours and reams of paper over drafts that were never good enough. Now, at 52, I am trying to learn to tell myself "It's good enough," to hit the send button and move on to the next story. It's not easy. To a perfectionist, "good enough" sounds more like an epithet. But lowering my standards is the only way I can achieve my writing dreams of productivity and publication. My writing will probably never be perfect, but perhaps if I'm lucky it will be good enough.

—CHRISTOPHER SCANLAN

Fiction finished has to bear the responsibility of its own meaning, it is its own memory. It is now a thing apart from the writer; like a letter mailed, it is nearer by now to its reader.

—EUDORA WELTY

All art is knowing when to stop.

—TONI MORRISON

In the beginning of my long writing life I resisted rewriting. When an editor, teacher, agent, or fellow writer suggested it, I took it as a sign of failure. And what did they know anyway? I knew the subject and it was written my way as if I was the first person to write on the topic. It was spontaneous and would be ruined by revision. The more the manuscript needed revision, the more I resisted.

And then Bob Johnson, an editor of the *Saturday Evening Post,* a magazine then that was one of the best—and best paid—publications, sent me a memo on how much needed to be changed.

His memo was longer than the 500-word article. He followed up on it by coming up to Boston from Philadelphia to go over it line by line. At the end of his visit, he said he'd hire someone else to rewrite my article. I begged him to allow me to rewrite my own article. He gave me 48 hours. I got up at 3 A.M. the next morning and rewrote half the article, then went to work on a newspaper where first-draft writing was good enough. The next morning I did the same thing. The article was accepted and published and I was converted. The rewrite had even made the final draft appear more spontaneous than the first.

I had learned what my writing friend Ralph Fletcher had known:

> *Modeling clay is cold and hard when you first buy it. You've got to take it out of the cellophane, work it in your hands, warm it up, and soften it, before you can mold it into anything. The same holds true for writing. The initial idea or triggering event is usually cold and stiff. I became a much better writer when I gave myself permission to work the clay in all sorts of ways—stretch, add, delete, connect, even lie—if it helps the material come alive.*

Now I had the problem of letting go. I could always see things that needed fixing. More than that, I saw interesting possibilities of content and technique. It became my habit to revise every article I wrote 30 times—yes, 30 times—before I submitted it. I became addicted to the craft of taking out, putting in, moving around.

I was not the only revision addict. In a famous *Paris Review* interview Ernest Hemingway said, "I rewrote the ending to *Farewell to Arms,* the last page of it, thirty-nine times before I was satisfied." George Plimpton asked, "Was there some technical problem there? What was it that had you stumped?" Hemingway answered, "Getting the words right."

Some writers never stop getting the words right. They keep fiddling with manuscripts that never get published because they are never submitted. If I ever end up in a mental institution it may be because I am starting a book and cannot get beyond the decision to begin with "A" or "The"—or was it "The" or "A"? Close attention to the writer's craft is important, but it can easily become obsessive.

A beginning writer I knew kept revising the first few pages of his book day after day, week after week. I taped a cardboard box so it could not be opened, cut a slot in the top, and then gave it to him. At the end of each day he put the day's pages in the box so he could not go back to them until the next morning. He had to move on to write new pages. He wrote the book and it became very influential in its field.

I wanted to write books and could not revise a whole book 30 times—Hemingway was only dealing with the ending. If I wanted to write other books I had to learn the difficult craft of letting go.

Why Writers Don't Let Go

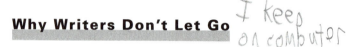

Most of us have good reasons for keeping our drafts stored in memory. There is a secret delight in examining them in the privacy of our computer room. Alone, we can bring up the draft, mark where more research will help, draft a new order, move a section up earlier or back later, repack a paragraph, connect two sentences or cut a long one in two, sharpen a phrase, activate a verb, pick a nicer typeface, run the spell check, zap the draft back into memory.

Fear of Exposure

We act as though sending a manuscript out and getting it published will reveal ourselves—and it will. What we write reveals how we think and feel. The information we collect and value, the way we order it into meaning, the music or voice we use to share it with a reader exposes both our brain and our heart.

But so does silence. If we do not speak we are heard as a person who is not involved, who neither thinks nor feels. Writing and publishing is nothing more than an act of living. When we think and care and share our thoughts and our feelings, we are participating in the remaking of the world, nothing less. We need to develop the courage to reveal ourselves and it does take courage. As a teacher I often found that those who had the most to say were most reluctant to say it.

Obsession with Correctness

The best students not only care about their subject matter, they care about their craft. These students want to write right. They have a fear of error and at school, home, and work they had been marked down or even ridiculed because they made a mistake in usage, mechanics, or spelling. Often the person who was most critical was wrong—"You have to start with a topic sentence" (Wrong); "You can't use a sentence fragment" (Wrong); "You can't use a contraction" (Wrong); "You can't start a sentence with *but* or *and*" (Wrong); "A paragraph must have five sentences" (Wrong)—but they sound as if they know what they are saying. And who wants to get yelled at? Better to not make yourself vulnerable.

It is good to clean up the final draft—run the spell check, make sure the punctuation only breaks tradition for good reason, print out a clean copy free of typographical errors—but the writer must realize that each publisher or editor or teacher has individual rules that contradict each other and cannot be anticipated. I do a weekly column, but I have different editors with different rules on the copydesk; I write books for different publishers who, in turn, hire different copyeditors. I must make my writing as clear as I can; I must break the traditions of writing only if it is necessary to make my evolving meaning clear. Then, I have to submit my drafts.

Continuing Discovery

It is easier for me to battle my obsession with error than to stop the process of discovery that goes on with each draft. I do not so much write to produce a problem-free draft as I write to explore my world. I come to the desk tired of the subject, ready—even eager—to let it go and start tinkering with a line or a paragraph, and I catch something in the draft in the corner of my eye that needs exploration. For example, I am describing my dysfunctional childhood and spot an idea new to me: I was more comfortable than many soldiers with the surrealistic confusion of combat because I was familiar with the surrealistic confusion of my home. I want to include that in what I am writing when I should put it aside. It is worth a new poem, an essay, a chapter in the novel I am writing.

Most of us become obsessive, compulsive, never-let-go rewriters because of the excitement and satisfaction of revision. We do not as often learn how little we know as how much we know. The act of revision ignites memory, connects information that we had never connected until we begin to rewrite. We could go on, revising this draft for a week, a month, a year, and some writers—or nonwriters—have gone on revising for a lifetime.

How to Let Go

We have to teach ourselves to let go, to deliver the term paper or the scientific paper or the memo or the critical essay or the story or the research paper or the poem or the grant proposal or the screenplay or the case history. The piece of writing that remains in the computer is wasted.

Deadlines

The most effective way to let go is to establish a deadline and meet it. I write my columns a week ahead, on Monday morning before lunch, and I love lunch. All my books are written to a final deadline broken down into monthly, weekly, daily deadlines. I will not go as far as the famous Victorian novelist Anthony Trollope who worked as postal inspector and wrote on the road between inspections or even when he was on vacation. He wrote,

> *As I journeyed across France and Marseilles, and made thence a terribly rough voyage to Alexandria, I wrote my allotted number of pages every day. On this occasion more than once I left my paper on the cabin table, rushing away to be sick in the privacy of my stateroom. It was February, and the weather was miserable; but still I did my work. It has . . . become my custom . . . to write with my watch before me, and to require from myself 250 words every quarter of an hour. I have found that the 250 words have been forthcoming as regularly as my watch went.*

Collaboration

Another reason to let go is to collaborate with a fellow writer, a classmate, a colleague, a teacher, an editor who can help you see what needs to be done and how it may be accomplished. This book, as many of my books have been, is a team effort with my editor, Laurie Runion. I have cultivated a community of writers to whom I can send a draft that does not yet seem right. Sometimes they even tell me revision is not necessary, but most times I learn what needs to be done, do it, then let the manuscript go.

Decreased Discovery

The most aesthetic reason is the most rare for me. That is when you see little possibility in the draft. There is no discovery, no learning, no excitement. If that happens, let it go. It deserves a life of its own.

When You Let Go

Writing is an act of communication. Of course, that communication early on is between writer and draft, but as the draft gets its own legs under itself, hears its own voice, it needs to go off on its own.

Readers Make the Draft Theirs

Letting drafts go is like letting children go. It is hard to, but they return—most of the time—as adults and friends. They have changed, and you can delight in their difference and their similarity. We do not own our children and we do not own our drafts. In a column, I wrote about the experience of meeting my readers:

> As long as I have written, I am still surprised by the intimate and individual relationship I have with each reader. We meet in the privacy of each other's minds and then, on occasion, we meet in the flesh and are suddenly strangers, not quite

the people we were when one of us wrote alone and the other read alone.

A short time ago I met many of my readers at one time as Minnie Mae and I sat in the *Globe* booth at the CVS Senior Expo in Boston. It was a wonderful and disconcerting experience. I have grown relatively comfortable with my neighbors who read the column, although often startled when they start talking. I have usually written the column they have read a week or more before, have written another column or two since, and am rehearsing the one I will write next. The reader, fresh from the column they have read, must wonder at my confusion as I try to pick up the thread of the private conversation the reader had with me when I was on the page.

I am often flattered but startled at what they have read in my piece. They have not read the column I wrote but an essay that has been written in their mind as their autobiography changes my text.

Write to communicate, we say in class and that was, in fact, the title of an elementary school writing program I wrote that has long been out of print. But what we communicate is not what we intend—at least not in fiction, poetry, or the personal essay.

I was disconcerted by that when I was first published, but I soon came to realize that was the magic of writing. Nothing I wrote was read as I expected. Readers with their own experiences, feelings, needs came to my published draft, and when things went well we shared in the creation of a draft that was neither mine nor theirs, but ours.

And then we meet in the supermarket, on the sidewalk or parking lot, at Ron's, The Bagelry or Pine Garden. We know each other so well. We have written a text that helps us battle the fear of aging, survive the death of a child, or makes us laugh at the fact that young people are behaving, God forbid, as we did when we were young.

But the column was written in the privacy of my office, often when my shoes—and sometimes a good deal more—were off, and then was read by a reader in nightclothes at the kitchen table, in bed, or even in what we call the reading room.

When we create this draft, we speak to each other, perhaps more intimately than we have spoken to those close to

> us or even to ourselves. Amazed at what we have said in private, we do not know what to say in public, and so readers praise us, telling us how wonderfully we write and we preen and shuffle in what may appear to be false modesty.
>
> It is not modesty at all. What makes me uncomfortable when I am praised for what I have written is that each of us has collaborated on these drafts.
>
> I write and it is only ink on paper. It comes alive when a reader smiles, nods, sheds a tear, seeing, feeling, thinking what I cannot know. The draft has become, as it should, the reader's draft.
>
> I write of my daughter and a reader sees a son long gone; I write of Minnie Mae and a reader sees Ralph with whom she shares the sometimes terrifying, sometimes hilarious experience of growing old; I write of infantry war in Europe and he sees naval warfare in the Pacific.
>
> And so when we meet away from the page and shake hands and a reader tells me he or she likes my column, I smile and mumble appreciation but want to say what I am saying now.
>
> It is our column. The magic is that each Tuesday I write the column I need to write—to stare down my ghosts, to accept, to relive, to mourn, to understand, to rage, to laugh, and then you, the reader, bring your life to my page.
>
> We write a column together, sharing a personal moment when we remember, think, feel together. It is not a column I have written, but what we have written in collaboration that is my wonder and my delight. Thank you for what we have written together at the kitchen table or in the reading room.

Let your writing go and you will be in touch with readers who will take your writing and make it their own. You will be playing a role in the human community, having your say.

Free to Write

When you let go of your draft you are free to write again, to do as my closest writing friend, Chip Scanlan, says, "To do the writing only you can do." We need to know what you have discovered you know by writing and rewriting and revising and editing and, at the end, by letting go.

INDEX